THE KESSACK LIFE

The Kessack Life

Novella Kessack

AuthorHouse™
1663 Liberty Drive
Bloomington, IN 47403
www.authorhouse.com
Phone: 1-800-839-8640

First published by AuthorHouse   02/23/2012

ISBN: 978-1-4685-5483-0 (sc)
ISBN: 978-1-4685-5484-7 (ebk)

Library of Congress Control Number: 2012903164

Printed in the United States of America

This book is dedicated to the memory of Novella Midkiff Kessack 1906-1971. I would also like to thank Jim and Beverly Kessack. If it were not for them this story would not have been told.

TABLE OF CONTENTS

Novella

Midkiff Family

Novella

Written May 1, 1971

I write this story of my life and dedicate it to my 12 children and many grandchildren. There is always an amount of human curiosity of our ancestry. That there may be no doubts in any of their minds I have blast off.

CHAPTER 1
NOVELLA

Born one cold winter night in a floorless shanty with a lean-to in a rural area of Knox County in Indiana, I put in my howling entry to Josephine Robinson Midkiff. Short, dark brown eyes black hair beautiful of Spanish gypsy ancestry, and William David Midkiff a Spanish American war vet of Russian and Pennsylvania Dutch Ancestry. Tall red hair and beard with sparkling blue eyes, who were already parents of three. Jesse Florence, Helen Grace and, Frank Midkiff. My Aunt Lulu on my father's side and Uncle John my father's brother and his wife Bertha were there to welcome me and help out. Uncle John held me up and remarked "What a dainty little Rosebud in this nest of thorns." Aunt Lulu gently took me from him and said nonsense let's call her Novella. My mother piping in said add Delores Midkiff, but my father always called me Rosebud. Shortly after my birth, we moved to a farm on the Wabash riverbank, between Gary and Vincennes Indiana. We had more of a home here. We had a horse and spring wagon, a cow and a pet hog named Moses. As kids go, we were more or less happy but my mother wasn't. My father often had to go to Vincennes for supplies'. This took most part of one day—a night—and a day back. Either it took that long or my father liked it that way. He was a heavy drinker, and my two uncles Jessy and David own a saloon in Vincennes and it was probably a pleasant way to spend a night in town. However as the old saying goes when the cat is away the mice will play. There was an insurance agent' that visited my mother on these occasions. On one of these occasions, we were left alone and my mother' was whisked away by her sneaky lover. My father came home and found us alone-done the best he could but my aunt Lulu advised him to take us to the Knox County Children's Home in Vincennes, which he did. Telling them our mother had left us and he was not able to care for us. I heard much later in life that he and his brothers held up a train that my mother and her love were on and took them off. They beat up the lover boy and I hope they gave him a punch for me; anyway, she consented to go back to my father if he would live in town. At this point, he was willing to do most anything to get his wife and family back. Well they got relocated and came to the home to reclaim their family. In the mean time my sister Helen Grace' had been adopted by a banker and his wife in Illinois, and I had been handed out on a trial bases to a minister Hugh C. Elliott and wife Ellen. They did however get Florence and Frank. Shortly after the Elliott's took me in their home, I came down with bad measles and malaria. They reported me dead to the Children's Home and took off to California with me, calling me Lucille Elliott. I was by this time two years nine months old. There were so many children seriously ill at the time the home accepted their report and that was that. I was small for my age and they had not been married long enough to have a child that old so they set my age back a year. In appearance, they resembled my parents but were more refined. I really did not get along with her at all, but did fairly well with him. They were very—very strict and devoutly religious in the Nazarene Church. There was something however, that bothered me. I did not actually remember my babyhood but something just didn't jibe, they got to calling me the frown girl. I' was not allowed the companionship of other children, always alone or with adults. I was taught to pray, say please and thank you-etc. My childhood passed as childhood will. I remember a great many episodes like the time we went from Texas to Mexico in a stagecoach. Stayed in a hotel overnight. We had a front bedroom over the saloon down stairs. A great commotion got up out of bed twice, a man with a hand organ and a dancing bear had made the scene. A bunch of dogs attacked the bear, drunks and dancing girls poured out of the saloon to watch the commotion. I also remember living in Kellogg Idaho and going on a trip down into silver mine. As I grew older, I had imaginary playmates, which I called by name and talked to because I was lonely. I remember two women watching me one saying to the other "that child is an odd one". The other one shrugging her shoulder saying, "what can you expect the way they shelter her". When I started school, I was really sharp on grades because I had been taught at home, but I did not know how to communicate with other children. By the time, I was in fourth grade we lived in Grandview Washington. By this time, I had learned how to be friends with other kids. I had one girlfriend that they seemed to approve of. Her father was the next preacher in the church; she lived across the street from us. One summer day when we were sitting under an apple tree in our yard sewing for our dolls, my girl friend Evilena asked me don't you get lonesome being the only one in the family? She did not realize what a sore spot she had hit. I did not intend to let her know so I thinking I was telling her the whopper of the day replied, "Oh no I will let you in on a big secret if you promise not to tell". She promised and I told her, these are not my real parents. I have a mother, two sisters and a brother and I meet them secretly. Some day when the right time comes I am going away with them. Well I felt pretty cool, because I could see she was real impressed. Quite shortly, she went home but she did not keep her promise, she told her family. They decided it was their Christian duty to talk to my father about it. So, he was sent for and presented with my story. Evilena told me later they thought at first it was true because he turned absolutely white, but denied the whole bit. He came home called me into the parlor and asked me why I had lied. I didn't seem to know. Since I didn't have an answer, he sure as hell had a punishment. I was strapped thoroughly and denied the privilege of Evilena's company for three months. Well I won't write about my thoughts at that time because I am sure they would set these pages on fire and I do want to finish my story. Well about this time, my curiosity about boys was getting to me. There were two next door, about my age and they had a baby brother about two. Well the oldest one was a real smart aleck, I didn't like him. He made fun of me but the other one was more reserve he used to watch his baby brother while his mother done other peoples laundry. I just had to know what a boy looked like so I got Vince and his baby brother in our barn and said "let's play Hide and seek", he agreed. I said you be it, I'll hide. I took the baby and hid in the back seat of my father's car. I took the baby's diaper off and had a good look, well I was quite amazed. I had to put the diaper back on before I got caught, the baby set up a howl not liking his privacy invaded. I said I don't want to play anymore and sat under a tree alone with my thoughts until a wagon came along loaded with watermelons going from the farm to the freight train to be shipped. I ran out and swiped one, we done it all the time and put it in the irrigation ditch to cool. After my episode with the baby I avoided Vince, we use to be friendly but it is nothing I can explain and he probably thought I was nuts. The next thing that stands out in my mind was the sun eclipse it was a total and Vince's mother came out of her back door carrying the baby and praying, she thought it was the end of the world and after all the things I had been up to I wasn't too sure myself. The great influenza epidemic hit that year and I had it at Christmas time. The church members brought many beautiful gifts to the house and put them on the front porch for me. I didn't usually get much, Ellen Elliott didn't believe in spending money needlessly. Consequently, I always wore second hand and made over clothes. I wasn't as well off as the song Second Hand Rose. I really looked tacky at times. The world war ended that year, I can still remember the people shouting and celebrating the day the news came. My father bought a Maxwell touring car and we were quite the dudes. About the first ride we took in it we drove past the peacock farm and he ran over one of them. I wanted the pretty feather from the tail but they wouldn't let me have them. We lived many interesting places after that but I will skip to where he built a house in Seattle on Evanston Avenue near Woodland Park. We moved in and I got started to school in the seventh grade. Father took to taking trips, different places and holding evangelistic meetings rather than just preaching in the parish. She {Ellen Elliott} shut up the main part of the house, we lived in the kitchen and each had our own bedroom. She must have been very lonely, didn't seem to have any friends. She loved to walk so every afternoon after school we would walk to Woodland Park. I think the animals got to know us. On Sundays, we went to the Nazarene Church. I had one girl friend that I really liked, her name was Martha Heinz, she played violin in the school orchestra of which I was very jealous. Once in a great while I was allowed to go to her house for one hour. This I enjoyed she had four little brothers that I adored. I told her I had a big brother that I didn't see very often and that I played the harp. She told the teachers at school and three of them got me cornered in the hall and asked some pointed questions that I couldn't answer. They knew I was lying. At the time the flapper style was swinging. I had long hair that I could sit on. I was compelled to wear in a braid and I hated it. They wouldn't let me cut it. A woman's hair was her crowning glory and they absolutely didn't follow fashion. Well I knew it was useless to argue so I cut off that braid one night. Sneaked out of the house and burned it, sneaked back in and set up a screaming fit. She came running in and I told her two men had climbed up a ladder came in my window and cut off my hair. Well she was pretty shook up, the neighbor lady, told her she should call up the police and damn if she didn't. Well two detectives came and questioned her and me, well I sure hadn't figured on all that shit but I was equal to the occasion and gave them a groovy story. They asked me how they got in, I said on a ladder through the window. What did they look like, I didn't know, they were taller than me, and had red hankies tied around their faces and big hats on. One of them had a gun he held on me while the other one took his scissors and snipped. O.K. what did the gun look like, never having seen a gun I had to think fast. Only thing I could think of was a big long gun with a bayonet on the end. They went downstairs to the front door entry and was talking to her. I feeling pretty uneasy about this time. I was standing back trying to decide rather to slit my throat or run away when old preacher Elliott walks in. I ran to him threw my arms around him sobbing Papa—Papa, something terrible has happened to me and they won't believe a word I say. Oh yes a reporter showed up than, Papa said no pictures. Well I don't know how they settled things, I guess I am lucky they weren't in a psychiatrist phase like they are now or I would have landed in the cookie jar pronto. They punished me by not letting me having my hair trimmed neatly, but wearing it all jagged as it turned out, being cut in a braid. The girls at school took care of that in the restroom at recess. I read a lot these days, as I was quite lonely. Teenagers found me just a little queer. I was really glad when we moved east of the mountains to Trinidad or Crescent Bar down on the Columbia

River. At least they didn't know me here and I could start out fresh. We went to a two roomed school, one had the first four grades the other had upper four grades. The teachers lived in a cottage on the school ground. At this time, I had grown and developed. I thought a lot about sex and what it must be like. I had a girl friend next door named Laura Davies. She was the oldest of seven children. She really wasn't much to look at. She knew at a shot how dumb I was so she laid it on thick how wonderfully wise she was. Papa and I went to work that summer for a peach framer, his daughter Flossie would be my teacher the following fall. She taught me how to wrap and pack the peaches. In the cool of the morning, Papa and I would pick the peaches, in the afternoon her and I would pack them. She was easy to talk too. I probably opened up to her more than I had to anyone in my life; she seemed to understand my lonely feelings, my curiosity about life. Before school started, I fell head over heels in love with Dell Green, he was twenty, had a model T Ford. After school started, he would pick me up at noon and we would go for rides in the country. He didn't dare come near my home. I wasn't supposed to even think, of boys. I was to dedicate my life to becoming a missionary. They put my summer earnings in a bank. I wanted to buy clothes, which I really needed, but no it was to go for an education. They knew what was best for me. Well the tighter they got the more sympathy I got out of Flossie. In the early fall it was still hot enough to go swimming in the Columbia River. The best spot was right behind our house. I was allowed to swim with the kids but I couldn't wear a swimming suit. It was immodest; I had to wear a shirt and old pair of bib overalls. One of the girl's, sixteen-year-old Marge finding this out put her swimming suit on, a tight red one piece on and was she stacked. She put her clothes on over it. She would drive her convertible right up by our front porch where Papa sat in his rocker studying his sermons. Then she would stand up in full view and start peeling off her clothes, dramatically giving her luscious curves every advantage. He would sit there a bit then close his bible and go in the house. She knew he would peek through the curtains until she was standing poised in the revealing suit. Good thing bikinis weren't in style, she would probably peeled to the nude. Come Halloween the teachers threw a big costume party for the kids and I wasn't allowed to go. Well I was burned but it really got to Flossie, she got me a mother's helper job in Ephrata for the County Agriculture agent's wife. I left home with the clothes I had on my back, although Flossie helped me get some. I received room and board and five dollars a week. I was also allowed to go out with Dell on Saturday nights, and if they were not having company on Sundays he could come for dinner. Well I was really somebody now. I began to take a little interest on how I looked. I was really seventeen because you see they had set my age back a year. Dell took me to my first movie, it was a silent one. Fatty Arbuckle and Charlie Chaplin were in it. After being there a month, Dell brought me a letter from Papa saying if I would come out Sunday afternoon after church I could have my money and clothes and they had something of importance to tell me. I decided to go, more for the eighty-five dollars then anything. Well they gave me my belongings, which were pitifully few, they were in a suitcase then he handed me a paper and quote "you are our adopted daughter, this is your real name and the address of the children's home where we got you". We feel somewhere we failed you and if you have loving relatives you might want to contact them. Well you could have knocked me over with a feather. Dell sat down with his mouth open; really, I was at a loss for words. She began to cry, she said I wanted to tell you a great many times. I said well I am glad I now know the truth and I won't hold any hard feelings and I will let you know from time to time what I'm doing. He being the religious man he was said let's have a word of prayer. Dell and I went and told his mother Mrs. Green and Flossie, then Mr. and Mrs. Chase the people I worked for. He helped me write a letter to the children's home and they both told me not to get exhilarated sometimes people find out things they are better off not knowing. A tumbling sea could not have dampened me at that point. Time dragged as I waited for my answer. When it finally arrived, I was so shook up I just stood there holding it; I was too emotional to open it. Mrs. Chase said do you want me to open it. This brought me too. I opened it and read, "You have a living mother who has remarried a married sister and a brother all living in Terra Haute Indiana, a sister who was adopted and you will have to have her adopted parents' permission to write her. We have written them all and given them your where abouts and address. I don't recall that I felt anything, I was numb. The next week letters began to arrive. They had tried in vain in many ways to find Helen but had thought I was dead. Letters and pictures were rapidly exchanged. Dell still came, but somehow my feelings toward him had cooled somewhat. He felt left out. He wanted us to be engaged. More to shut him up then anything I agreed. Well naturally, we wanted to get together, but that cost money. The story got in the Terra Haute newspaper. A fund for my trip home was started and a lawyer appointed to handle it. Soon $350.00 was sent, I bought a ticket home. They had a going away party for me. To get the train to Chicago where I would change to get to Terra Haute I had to be driven to a railroad crossing out in the middle of nowhere at 3 in the morning. Dell wanted to do it but no Mr. Chase had the sheriff do it, and that big fat slob put his arm around me and kept trying to get me all shook up. I was scared stupid. I guess he figured me with a 20 year old boyfriend knew the score, but he was wrong.

I was an innocent virgin, he finally gave up. I got on the train and away I went. I ran into problems like in the dining car, I didn't know I was supposed to tip the waiter. A big fat businessman seen my predicament. He came and sat down beside me and started giving me advice. Well I called the porter and told him the guy was bothering me and a black boy told him to get to the other end of the car and leave me alone. Then the porter came and told me about tipping. Well I made it. When I got off the train half the town of Terra Haute was there. My family, the lawyer, reporters, cameras, I felt like a celebrity. We went to Florence's apartment and had supper. Her married name was O'Toole. Her husband was sitting in a chair, he winked at me and said hello little sister gotta a kiss for me? Well I was embarrassed, didn't have sense enough to know him and my stepfather Everett Potter were drunk on white mule. Well how could I? I never seen anyone drunk before. My little nieces Helen and Alberta took to me right off. I wanted to be more friendly with my brother Frank but didn't know how and his stony-faced wife didn't help any. My mother finally said, "Well Novella has had a long trip, we better go home" which was next door. The place was three big rooms, bare floors only plain necessary furniture and an old heater. I was use to rugs, and pictures. I shivered, she put her arm around me and said poor baby you sleep with me tonight, so Everett was banished to the single bed meant for me. As I climbed into bed with her and she tried to talk endearing to me, I felt very strange, I shut my eyes all I could see was my adopted mother sitting, sobbing in her chair like the last time I had seen her. Troubled I said I was tired and pretended to be asleep, but my thoughts were confused far into the night. Morning came as mornings do and I was about to become acquainted with a new way of life. Everett was a short dark man who looked like he never took a bath. I was amazed to find my mothers and sisters cupboards both bare. Fuel for the day was brought at the front the door from a man with a horse and wagon. Twenty—five cents for a bushel of coal—ten cents for a bundle of sticks. Food was bought for each meal if you had the money. I had $250.00 left in my purse, I gave it to my mother she snatched it and later told me I should not have given it to her in front of Everett. She did not explain why. I didn't like him; he was always following me around with his beady eyes. Nobody seemed to have anything to do all day. I played with my sisters three children. Helen was four so chubby they called her teddy. Alberta 2 and Jr. the baby boy who later died with spinal meningitis. Teddy became my shadow, Alberta was a mischief, she got out the front door one day on a very busy street, we searched and called for four hours. She was found hiding under an apple box. Another time we were downtown shopping in a dime store, Alberta seeing a doll she wanted picked it up and refused to part with it. Florence chased her half way around the store and Alberta threw the doll and hit a clerk on the head with it. Well, we got out of that store in a hurry with a few choice words following us. Teddy and I were given a dime each night and sent to the neighborhood movies. I have never been quite sure why we were gotten rid of but a couple times we came home to find strange men with my mother. One afternoon I went to town with my mother, she bought a pair of shoes for Florence's baby for fifty cents at a sale. It turned out the shoes were too small. Florence and I went back the next afternoon to change them; the clerk said they couldn't exchange sale goods. She argued, he said he would get the manager. On a table of shoes, we both saw it at the same time a purse. She picked it up we fled out the store door and down the street. We heard the clerk and a woman yelling behind us, we dove in a doorway, ran through a hallway and out into an alley. Looked in the purse there was two hundred eighty five dollars cash in it. She took the cash threw the purse in a garbage can and away we went. She gave me a twenty-dollar bill to buy some clothes with. My mother was mad and said" I should have half". So we all moved to Vincennes. Everett went ahead and said he had a house ready. Well the house a one-room shack with no floor, on Spring Garden Ave beside the Wabash River. Mother was furious, next day she went up the street two blocks and got a two-room house with floors. It had a heater in it with a flat top, we cooked on it. A faucet outside the door and an outdoor privy, it was clean. One day she took me across town to meet my Aunt Liz and Cousin Lloyd. He was almost seven feet tall, the Harold Lloyd type. Big glasses with brown rims. He and I hit it off, smack from then on it was Novella and Lloyd period. He was a world war vet and had been shell shocked, he got money somewhere from the government. I suppose he was married but his wife had left him. No children, he had a race bug and we flipped around Indiana in it like we owned the state. Picnic's—shows, life was Ho, Ho, Ho. About this time, Helen wrote from Mt Carmel Illinois. She was a schoolteacher, living with her adopted parents and wished me to come and visit, please reply they would send my ticket. Well I accepted. They were very nice to me. My sister and I got along swell. They found out I could sew and gave me many things to make for Florence's kids. Lloyd wrote to me daily. I was supposed to stay three weeks, at the end of the second week I became lonesome for Lloyd and announced I was leaving. They left rolls of money sitting around the house to see if I would take it. It must have been hard on Helen, they said she had never accepted the story of my death and always said someday she would find me. Well I wasn't expected home either, so no one was there, I went in. Finally, Everett came, I asked him where mother was, he said she went to visit Frank and wouldn't be home for two days. I'm going to say right here, if any of you are parents or if you ever become parents tell your young daughter about QX!^#(! so they can protect themselves. I learn that night in a brutal no good way that made me sick, and as the expression goes, "guess who is coming to dinner". Well o.k. guess who else came home early and unexpected? You guessed right MOTHER and if you ever seen a screaming hysterical mess I bet it couldn't equal that one in the middle. In the middle of it, I stepped out the door and ran barefoot half dressed through the night to Lloyd's house. I cried banging on the door, let me in. Lloyd let me in. Aunt Liz got up; they put a robe on me and got my story out of me. Lloyd got his service gun and was going to go get Everett, but Liz stopped him. She said we will all calm down, go to bed and decide in the morning what to do. Well come morning I told Liz well I'm not going back there to live. She said well it wouldn't look right me staying in the same house with Lloyd. Everett had a sister named Midge, she lived alone and worked in a poultry house and agreed I could stay there. She personally went and got my things. I went to work with her picking chickens. WOW what a job. You got five chickens tied on a stick with blood cups hanging on their heads, their bodies still kicking and warm. You got four cents a chicken for getting the feathers off. You stood in dry flying feathers up to your knees and chicken lice crawling all over you. You worked ten hours a day, if you were lucky you might get an egg if one of the chickens was good to you. There were about twenty women working there, some of them young like me only they were happy. They would talk all day about being out with their boyfriends the night before, screwing on the riverbanks. Crawling under fences didn't seem to bother them any. For lunch, we went to a house one block down and one of the girl's husbands had boiled white beans, corn pone and black coffee for twenty-five cents. For supper you got whatever you could buy on the way home. After three weeks of earning around eight dollars a week, my mother stuck her head in Midges front door and said there you are. The cops are going to get you. I don't know what I was, I was scared of but I ran anyway to the bridge over the Wabash River and jumped in. Next, I knew somebody was pulling me out, people, cops; they took me back to Midges. A doctor that was there said I seemed to be o.k. A Miss Hannah came in a big black car and hauled me off to the Children Home. I asked her why? She said I was not yet of age and since I had left Elliott's I would have to stay in the home until they decided what to do about me. Well we had our meals; we ate six at a table. We were allowed all we wanted but whatever we put on our plate, we had to eat. Most of the kids went to school but one other girl and I didn't, so all afternoon we were allowed to walk around the grounds. After the third day, I figured this isn't for me. So I told the girl to hide her eyes and count to one hundred while I hid. Well did I blast off. I went to Midges she had company from Indianapolis, a young couple with children. They said you can come stay with us and baby sit for a place to sleep and find a job to feed and clothe yourself. So away, I went to the big city. Well they lived near the big Indianapolis racetrack. I got a job six hours a day, washing dishes in a small restaurant right across the street from the tracks. For 1 meal and eight dollars a week. Well I slept in a double bed with three kids under four. The parents went out dancing and drinking almost every night, their name was Kidwell he was a tall red head and said he used to go with my sister Florence before she married O'Toole. In fact, him and Florence had won a dance contest. Well every chance he got he was making passes at me, which I tried to ignore. I did like his wife and I had no other place to stay, but that ain't all. The cook at the restaurant decided I was there for his convenience every time business was slack he would be out there trying to kiss me. Maybe by this time some of you might be seeing the light when I yell about men, my gosh they got one-track minds. I looked through the little window one morning and seen Miss Hannah come in the front door. I grabbed my coat and purse and went out the back and caught a streetcar to downtown Indianapolis. Well here, I was about $3.00 cash in my purse just a cotton dress on in a strange city. We didn't have social security numbers then fortunately or unions either. I spotted an eating-place with a sign, Under New Management. I went in; the lady says, "Well who are you"? I said I am Aryl Gray, my husband deserted me and I need a job. She said, "Well I rent rooms too, if you want to clean rooms make beds, help in the kitchen, and wait tables you can have a room all you want to eat and what tips you can get". Well how lucky can you get? I bought another dress and a pair of underpants, so I could change and we were in business. I never was lazy, so she got her money's worth. I averaged a dollar a day in tips. The sole began to flap on my shoe I knew I would have to do something about that. A man that always wears a suit and always ate there said, what size shoe do you wear? I like the dumb—dumb I was, told him. That night when I went to bed there was a package on in the bed, a nice pair of slippers and a note. "Here is your present, when do I get mine"? Hell has no fury to what I felt, I was mad. I went with the shoes and a note to the lady I worked for. She read the note, looked at me, and said, "You sure are a dumb kid aren't you? How did you think you was going to get your tips"? Well I can honestly say at that moment I wished I were back in Papa Elliott's parlor listening to a word of prayer. Well the lady decided she was not going to send me down the prim rose path to hell, so she put a cot in her room and had me sleep there and told me I better contact my folks if I had any and get the hell out of there. I wrote a letter to Papa that night, he wrote back Special Delivery and told me to go to Reverend so and so and stay there until he could send me a ticket home. Well I talked to the ladies married son into taking me to Reverend so and so and the preacher wasn't about to swallow the story, but another preacher that knew me was due the next day. So they decided to let me stay the night and if the preacher identified me ok. Well that part turned out ok but the Reverend so and so had a seventeen-year-old daughter and a sixteen-year-old son. The daughter had her intentions very firmly fixed on a young man that came to church by the name of Ellis Mitchell, well the sixteen-year-old son flipped for me like the walls of Jericho fell on him. If you never had a sixteen-year-old boy flip for you, I guess you wouldn't understand what it is like. You don't want to hurt the kid; you don't want to give in. I decided I'll just have to pay attention to someone else. Well Ellis was the only one available and we hit it off real well, but then the daughter was mad. Well I spent two hectic weeks. Those two kids drove everybody crazy. Finally my tickets and ten dollars to eat on came. Ellis offered to take me to the train; I think Reverend so and so was glad to see me go. Ellis was sweet he bought me a magazine and candy bar, got me settled, and left, waving as the train pulled out. My emotions were pretty mixed as I rode along headed now for Arlington Washington. Believe it or not, I felt like I was going home. A whole lot wiser I'll clue you. A Travelers aide kept Papa informed as to when I would arrive. He was there to meet me. When I walked into the house and seen the familiar rugs, pictures, furniture, the dam broke I cried like my heart would break but I was really happy. After getting adjusted, I begin to think of work. A chicken farmer named Patrick that belonged to Papas church and lived two miles out of town said, his wife and him could keep me busy for the summer. For my dinner and $3.00 a day. I arose every morning and hiked the two miles and done whatever was to be done. Cleaned eggs, picked berries, harvested mangle, housework, whatever there was. She was a heavenly cook. I enjoyed the work and paid back Papa for my ticket. When fall came and there wasn't going to be any work, he told me of a lady that lived at Bryant that kept boarders that needed help and he helped us get together so I went to work for Mrs. Jacobson, she had about fifteen men. The Italian section gang and some bridge builders from the logging camp. My duties were to set the tables wait on them, clean them off, wash dishes, sweep and mop floors, make beds and iron. For these services, I received room and board and ten dollars a week. It was up early and to bed late. I made a bargain with the man upstairs the day I went up there, "Oh Lord if you can scare me up a good man I am ready to get married and settle down". I came to work at one, by five the boarders were marching in. I was standing in the kitchen by the sink when he walked in. Our eyes locked and so did our hearts. From that moment on it was Jim Kessack and I. We needed no introduction nothing. I knew him three months before I knew the guy he called Sandy, who was his brother Alec. They were Scotch, born and raised in Scotland. Their parents lived in Kent Washington on a farm. The past was forgot, there was only today and our future. I trusted him implicitly. Sex just came naturally, nothing dirty or sneaky to it, just accepted between us. Even when I realized I was pregnant, I wasn't upset. I was taken to meet Jim's parents at Christmas, we stayed a week. Grandma had asked for a new corset for Christmas, Alec bought it and handed it to me and said give it to her and I hadn't even met the woman. Grandpa talked so broken I couldn't understand him. Also met the sister Aggie Brown and her husband Eddie. I never seen so much eating and drinking in my life. At breakfast, it was tea, scones, and boiled eggs. Everyone had an eggcup. I had never seen one before, so I broke my boiled egg and put it in my dish. I was embarrassed to look around the table and see everybody daintily eating eggs out of these little cups. Well in Feb, I told Jim I was pregnant, he told me to quit my job and pack my things. He took me to Everett and rented an apartment under the name of Stewart, he said we would get married as soon as the camp shut down. He paid the rent filled the cupboards with groceries gave me $5.00 for spending money. He came every weekend, he got so he brought Alec too. After two months I was really showing, my parents did not know where I was. Jim was staying in camp now. One Sunday night I didn't feel so good, he stayed over till Monday. By noon I was hemorrhaging, he went and got a Doctor. I was ordered to Everett General Hospital. The landlady wanting to be helpful climbed in the car and went too. I was rushed to the emergency room; someone asked Jim what our name was he said Kessack. Someone else asked the landlady and she said Stewart. Somebody asked me what my name was I said Midkiff. Well they all got together and had a merry mix-up. I lost the baby but was all right to leave the next day. Jim had all our things loaded in the car when he picked me up at the hospital. We went to Seattle courthouse and were married by Judge Johnson. I was hungry; afterwards we stopped in a little restaurant and had oxtail soup. Jim said we will go on out to Kent to see the folks and tomorrow we will go to Bryant and find a house to rent. Well we had a flat tire between Seattle and Kent. When we got to the ranch, grandma said, "How nice I just fixed a young turkey". Today is our wedding anniversary, {April 28} and the Browns and Colman's, the neighbors are coming over." So Jim" told them we were married, they dined and played cards and drank wine to well in the night. I was really tired. When grandma finally showed me to the room we would sleep in she said "won't you feel funny sleeping with a man"? I thought to myself darling if you only knew, but just smiled and let it pass. Well I guess it would be nice about this time to say we lived happily ever after, but that is just in fairy tales. We said our good-byes and left for Bryant, his job and our new home. Jim rented an old farmhouse up on a hill one mile from anyone. A bachelor had been living there until he died. It had either early Goodwill or late Salvation Army furniture and a wood stove with a water reservoir on the back for hot water. We bought groceries on the way home so were tired enough to sleep that night. He had to leave at five thirty in the morning to go to work and did not get home until six at night. I had to get my water across the road from a pitcher pump in a pasture, it was hard work lugging it up the hill and I only had one bucket. Being used to being alone I got along with myself fairly well. Jim made the remark, we really didn't need any children I was all he needed. He was ten years older than I. Guess he wasn't really considering my feeling because I wanted a family. It wasn't long until Alec was living with us, to put it Jims way "why should poor Sandy live in a camp when his brother had a home." I thought to myself maybe poor Sandy could get a home of his own, but outwardly accepted it. One night Jim was late coming home and I was worried by this time. I realized I was pregnant again and had not told him. When he did come he had half a beef over his shoulder for me to can, hadn't asked me if I knew how or would just let some jerk fill him with home brew and tell him it was the thing to do. Nobody had heard of a freezer or refrigerator at this time. We spent half the night borrowing knives, buying jars and a boiler so I could spend the next two days canning meat. I done a good job of it too, if I might say. His next thought of genius was to make home brew, so Saturday we went to Arlington, bought a five-gallon crock, bottle capper, bottles and the ingredients for home brew. The smell of the stuff brewing got to me and he found out my little secret. Well his reaction was to get a bottle of bootleg whiskey and get mighty drunk. As time went on, I began to realize my prince charming was a stinker, but I loved him anyway. Everything revolved around Sandy, what we ate, what we done, I began to feel like a servant to Jim and his brother Sandy. When spring came I was heavy with child, I had forty dollars in a bank account from working days of my own. I withdrew it and made baby clothes. I was very excited over the coming event. One day a salesman knocked on my door and was selling sewing machines, I was completely sold on it. It was forty-five dollars, on time payments of five dollars a month. I wanted it, the salesman knew it. He said I will leave it on a five-day trial; I will come back at night when your husband is home. I never dreamed Jim wouldn't buy it, but he was furious. I sewed like mad those five days. I burned food, neglected the house ignored Sandy, kicked the cat, and sulked, all to no avail. When the salesman came, him and his sewing machine went sailing down that hill with the greatest of ease. The next Saturday Jim took me to Marysville and bought me a second hand machine for three dollars, my first real experience with a Scotchman with a bank account. I made up my mind I would never ask him for another thing never dreaming he would give me eleven more children. Agnes was born at home 1st of March at midnight and has been kicking up her heals every since, more to that story later. The camp shut down in May. So as they usually done when camps shut down, they decided to go to granddads, me, baby and all. Well grandma had a house full of visiting relatives from Portland and did not appreciate this at all and really let me know it. I was miserable, little Aggie cried continuously. I told Jim you will have to get me my own place, which turned out to be a one-room shack at Panther Lake with a heater to cook on and heat my wash water and such. He spent his days and half his nights at the ranch as he called it. Granddad raised berries, eggs and milk. He went to town in a horse and buggy. Grandma got the bright idea of Jim buying a car for him, Jim told me one night. I said ok Mr. Kessack you buy me a stove to cook on and then go buy your father a car. Well Jim did not buy either one. He and Alec leased a five-acre berry ranch between Sumner and Auburn. Of course, it was Jim's money that finances the deal, anyway there was a new house five rooms, the kitchen and front rooms were finished but the bedrooms and up stairs were not. Jim and granddad went to Seattle and bought second hand furniture for the house and we moved in, at least I had I had more room and a stove to cook on. A water faucet just outside the back door. I felt really pretty pampered. They worked endless hours getting the berry vines in shape and the bunkhouse where the pickers could live. It consisted of three rooms a sleeping room with cots for women, the same for men and a community room for cooking, eating, whatever else. The Adam and Eve rooms of course were outdoors accommodations. Neither men working our savings went fast. Jim and Alex accepted small jobs when ever and where ever they could. Their brother in-law Bob Brown got them a job wheeling cement in wheelbarrows on a building that was going up in Auburn. When they got paid for that job, Jim said we will have grandma and granddad, and the Browns out for Sunday dinner. I was three months pregnant again by now. Jim said it was ok as long as I had a boy then we would quit. I agreed, but secretly had made up my mind I wanted four, two girls and two boys. That way each would have a brother and sister. I also decided to make the best of my marriage so I could have this family, which to me was rather important. I suppose to make up for my childhood disappointments. Well getting back to Sunday dinner he bought a ten-pound pork roast, I browned and seasoned it. He had built me a cooler on the back porch that consisted of an apple box with a shelf in the middle and a screen door on it with a wooden latch. Putting the roast on my one and only platter I put it in the cooler and stayed up half the night scrubbing the wood floors, had no rugs or linoleum, and sewing flour sacks together to make a white tablecloth. I arose early Sunday morning to get Agnes fed and settled. I went to get the pork roast to put it in the oven, the cooler door was open, the platter on the porch broke and the roast had done a disappearance act. Well I woke Jim up, he cussed and swore and raged, I said well fine but what are you going to feed your company? Agnes hearing the commotion had to help her daddy out by yelling her head off too. He went up the road to a farm and bought two live chickens, so I had to kill, clean, and cook two chickens, by the time the company got there. Of course, it took Jim and Sandy both to go get them in the model A we had. They had dinner, played cards and drank home brew all day. Then I had to fix supper before they would go home. Alex took them home so he could use the car to go see Jane Little afterwards. Jim laid down and went to sleep. Took me until midnight to clean up the mess. Things went along until picking time; they hired two college boys, a woman and her sixteen-year-old daughter and her seventeen-year-old husband, and local help. I picked with the pickers and done my house work too. The sixteen-year-old girl started flirting with the college boys and her husband got mad. Jim and Alex flirted with the local girls that came to pick and I was just plain miserable. I canned berries all summer and made jams. After the berry crop, one day I canned forty quarts of prunes, baked bread, cleaned house, I was just finishing up, when the water broke. I called Jim, he helped me to the bed and put Aggie in her crib and went two miles for the doctor. Old Doc Hughes said it's just a rip, she will be all right for another week and he had to hurry and go to a Doctors convention in Seattle. Alex left with a neighbor to go to some doings and wouldn't be home until morning. Well I started having pains but didn't say anything until two in the morning. They got pretty bad and Jim decided to go for Doc again, he wasn't out of the yard with the car until Peggy was born, there was no way to let him know. I pinched the cord laid back and pleaded with God to let her be all right. Old Doc wasn't back, but the lady that was going to help out was. She came back with Jim and cut the cord, cleaned and dressed little Margaret Jean all seven pounds of her. After berry crops were harvested there was no money coming in, but the rent had to be paid. Six months went by without it being paid. The Landlady a retired schoolteacher from Alaska came out and said pay up or else. Jim and Alex went to work in a logging camp. I was given five dollars a week for the two babies and myself to survive on. Jim and Alex would come home late Friday nights; Alex would drop Jim and their dirty work clothes for the week off and go to Kent with the car. I was supposed to wash both sets of logging clothes. Long johns and all, and have them dried and ironed, ready by Sunday night. I washed over a washboard and nature was my dryer. Quite often on Sunday, I was called on to entertain granddad, grandma and the Browns all day, and keep a smiling attitude and keep a weekend husband happy. I was really feeling cheated by Monday morning. One such weekend I was given three hundred fifty dollars and told to mail it on Monday to the landlady. Instead I cleaned up the house and Tuesday morning took my two babies and rode the electric train to Tacoma, rented a two room apartment. Wednesday morning I took the girls to the Day nursery and told them I was looking for work. I looked up my old girl friend Martha Heiny from Seattle school days and had a good time. Next day I really did not know what to do with myself, so just wandered around town. The third day I was just plain tuckered out and bored. I was just wandering around when who did I run into but Jim. He said the Lady across the street had seen me take off with the kids and a suitcase and called him up at the camp. He wanted to know what the score was, so I told him. He said well lets go home and talk it over, so we picked up the kids and went home. I told him, things were just not balanced up right. We were either a family or not. What we decided to do was, store our furniture in granddads barn, and go to Wenatchee valley and work in the orchards. We obtained a job—thinning apples for a farmer; we lived in a tent, the kids just played around. Pay day the farmer paid me twenty cents an hour more than Jim because I was experienced. This hurt his ego and we quit. We went to Wenatchee and rented a two-room house. He got a job working on a new highway they were putting in. That job lasted six weeks. Then we rented a large old house with two cabins behind it. We divided the house into apartments and rented them-also one cabin. We lived in the other cabin. He got a job where they were building a new storage bank. We lived off the profits of the rents and he banked his checks. In the fall, the apartments were beginning to be empty and the building was finished, the last day he worked, he wrenched his back and went to the doctors. We moved to Renton and lived a year on our savings and compensation from the state for his injury, which did not default his activities in bed because I was expecting again. We soon moved to a three-room house on Benson highway near Kent. Work was beginning to be hard to get. It was the start of the big depression. Jim got odd jobs, lived here and there, painting houses, fixing fences, digging gardens, cutting wood, anything to pay our fifteen dollar a month rent and put food on the table. He painted a house and put a new roof on a house for two elderly sisters that had never married. They gave him apples and some discarded clothing for me to make over for the kids. I was really quite happy at this time. I arose one morning at five thirty and got old wood stove going for breakfast. I had a bad pain, I got Jim up and told him he better stay home that day. The pains got pretty bad; he took the girls over to grandmas and got Doctor McGregor by seven thirty I presented Jim with his first son. Donald Duncan, twelve pounds of him. Jim gave him his first bath and was beside himself with pride and joy.

James and Novella Kessack Wedding Picture

Alex (Sandy), Agnes Brown, Jim, Grandma and Grandpa Kessack

CHAPTER 2

JOURNAL

1937

The first two pages of Novella's journal are missing so; I'm starting on page three in the middle of a sentence. Henry wasn't' home, but Lucile was, she was baking bread and washing diapers. Mrs. Clark was there visiting. The baby is fat and cute. Next, we went to Kent, took hamburger and buns, and went up to granddad Kessack's to see granddad, grandma, and Uncle Alex. Grandma was baking scones, granddad and uncle and little Jimmie were making wood from the nice maple tree that use to stand in the pasture. When we left and came back to Auburn, I found out, I had left my bag behind me. We went to Cugini's Grocery store and bought $17.43 worth of groceries. We then bought a P.D. paper and drove out to Curly's place, and bought meat, catsup and cookies. Then we came scooting home to rest of the family. Agnes Florence age 10, Jimmie Jr. age 6, Billy Joe age 4, George Frank or Buzz as we call him age 1-1/2, and of course Margaret Jean and Donald were back too. Everything was O.K; Skippy the dog was all right too.

<hr/>

Sunday Feb 7, 1937

Well Diary this has been one of those hectic days that turn you upside down. We woke up with the kids yelling for us to get up, that George was coming, the baby yelling, and the clock stopped. Well G. came in and stayed for 2 hours. He finally decided he wasn't being asked for breakfast and went home. We than had corn flakes, boiled eggs and toast. All morning the kids made valentines. I made a 10 qt crock full of brown Irish stew and baked meatballs. The house has {unable to read the next five lines.} Sure, hate to give up and go to sleep. It snowed 2" inches since 5 o'clock but it has stopped now. Daddy Jim is reading a book; the children are beginning to settle down. I am very tired so guess I will lay out school clothes for Agnes, Peggy, and Donnie. Make their lunches and go to bed. George came back over again this evening and drank some of our homemade beer. I let him smell the aroma of that nice brown stew, but he didn't get any to eat, oh no not a bite. Well diary I'm quitting now, so good-bye, until tomorrow, which will be another day.

Monday Feb. 8, 1937

Well I managed to hear the 6 O'clock alarm ring this morning, and got up and sent the three little ones to school in 3" inches of snow. I told them that if they were early for the bus to keep on walking, thinking of course they would go as far as Quinn's and wait with Buster. What was my surprise to find out, they hiked as far as the charcoal kilns and Rinky's picked them up, such is the tricks of kids, you never know what to expect next. They all took 3 cents to the Flood Relief Fund. Donald's teacher Miss Adams is acting teacher at present. I washed a large washing, baked bread and ginger cake. Every spare minute I get I'm making valentines. Daddy Jim helped me with the washing. Snookies has a rash but I don't think it is going to be serious. There was no mail today, but I wasn't expecting any, but I'm expecting the package from Montgomery Ward's tomorrow. The girls both were practicing their music tonight, Agnes the violin and Margaret Jean the cornet trumpet. Daddy is reading—Margaret is trying to study, but Donnie and Jimmie Jr. are making so much disturbance that no one can sit in comfort. Well I guess that is all the news today so nightie night.

Tuesday Feb. 9, 1937

The children were sent to school to early this morning, I must be more careful about this as they must have been cold. I was mending clothes on the sewing machine today. Buzz been rather fussy. Our package did not come today. I went to Quinn's today for eggs, and visited for a while with Opal and Jackie. Eggs are only 20 cents a dozen now. I rode home with Chester in the truck. I followed fresh deer tracks over. {Sentence ended here.} Agnes brought home a very bad report card today, I do wish she would try to do better. Buzz is waking up crying already, worst luck, he cried most of the night last night, I wish he would sleep tonight. Well I gave him a warm egg and we shall see what effect that will have on the young man. It is very warm and thawing tonight. That is all for today, I will be with you tomorrow. Mamma Kessack

Wednesday Feb.10, 1937

Well diary I've made up all the papers, colors, pencils, glue-etc, for in the house making Valentines. It is a thing one can't stop once they start. I baked bread and washed today. Jim and the little kids went to Auburn today. Our package is not here yet. Chet was over this morning and had a glass of beer. Donald brought home a gold star on his numbers paper today. Agnes and Margaret Jean practiced music tonight and done arithmetic. Donnie done numbers too. Snookies was giggling today, he sure is one cute baby. Buzz did not wear a diaper all day and only wet his pants once, hooray for Buzz. Mr. Atkinson gave Donnie 3 suckers and gave Virgil and Buster each one. They drew names for valentines at school. Donnie got Iva Myrtles, Agnes, Georgia Lee and Margaret Jean, drew Joan Mc Keo. It is pouring rain tonight the is barrel full. The children are all asleep, Daddy is reading Ivan Ho, I guess this is all, so I will get my book and finish reading the Calling of Dan Mathews, we will have coffee and go to bed. Ta-Ta, till another day.

Thursday Feb.11, 1937

Dear diary, I am not going to write much tonight, I am too cold and tired. We waited in the car with five small kids for the mailman to come with our package for 3 hours. It is evening now, the package came. I have been writing names on valentines for 2-1/2 hours. I am all in; I am going to fine Snookies and go to bed. So that's all except it is raining. Mamma Kessack

Friday Feb. 12, 1937

Well diary baby Snooks set up a howl at 5 O'clock this morning. I thought the poor child was in agony, but when I picked him up, he only laughed at me. Jimmie Jr. visited school today. Donald forgot to take his valentines and Agnes forgot her coat. I baked bread today and washed. Daddy Jim helped me. I iron tonight after supper. It was a lovely day today, and Buzz, much to his enjoyment got to play outdoors. Joe fell off the sideboard today and got a very bad bump on his head. Donnie's teacher Miss Wordang came back today. It is 9 o'clock—the kids are all asleep. Daddy Jim is reading a story that comes with the Sunday P.I. I am going to find Snookies then we will go to bed. I'm very sleepy. Mamma Kessack It is freezing tonight.

Feb. 13, 1937

Today we went to Auburn, Margaret Jean, Donald and Snookies went too. We went to Limburgers Grocery and bought crackers and soap. Daddy Jim got Margie and Donnie and I an ice cream cone. We then went to the post office to mail a card to Mrs. Kirkman to tell her to call for shoes for repair. We then went to Fergusons Café to eat. After we ate, Margie wanted to know if she had to wash the dishes, she was very shocked at us just walking out and leaving them there. We then went to the Auction Sale. We bought 3 boxes jello for 10 cents, 2 lbs salt for 10 cents 1 large bottle vanilla for 15 cents, 1 baby blanket 15 cents, 1 pair ice skates 10 cents, 1 man's leather jacket 50 cents, 1 highchair for 20 cents. After the sale, we went to Cujini's Grocery and bought $3.65 worth of groceries, then Daddy Jim went to Kloutzes Market to buy meat while Margie and Donnie went to the dime store to spend their pennies. Daddy also bought a Sunday P.I. We then came as far as Quinn's and bought 3 dozen eggs @ 20 cents a dozen. Then we came home and found everything O.K. had lunch. Now the kids are all in bed and Daddy and I are reading. It is snowing tonight and very cold. Mamma Kessack

Sunday Feb 14, 1937

Well I baked bread today. George was over this morning but as prospects for dinner didn't seem so good, he did not stay long. Little Buzz is very ill, sick stomach. His ruptured is down and can't get it back in place. I think I will fix up Snookies for night and call it a day. It is freezing but looks like more snow. Mamma Kessack

Feb 15, 1937

Dear diary, Little Buzz was very ill all night, vomited every hour, he was so much worse that Daddy Jim and Jimmie Jr. took him to Seattle Harborview Hospital, they admitted him right away, I don't know for a few days whether they will operate on him or not. It rained and blew all day and was very cold, I washed clothes. Chester came over about 10 for pig scraps, and brought a letter from Helen Grace full of valentines for the kids. Donnie took his valentine to school today and delivered them. Miss Evans the girl's teacher burned her hand. Agnes found her lost coat, Thanks be. Henry Coddle came up about 5 o'clock to find out what to feed their baby. They are going to put him on the bottle as he is driving them crazy as is. Daddy and Jimmie came home about 6 o'clock very—very tired. I do hope little Buzz will be all right. I am going to try and get some sewing done tomorrow. I have a boil on my chin and does it hurt. Daddy brought home ½ case of milk tonight and 3 pair shoes, 1 pair for Agnes,1 for Donnie and 1 for Joe. The children are all asleep and Daddy is reading the paper so this is all for today. Mamma Kessack

Tuesday Feb. 16, 1937

I did not hear the alarm this morning, and almost over slept. It has poured rain and hail all day, with a bad wind. I baked bread and washed Snookies clothes. I have been making Margaret Jean a new dress, a skirt and blouse. The skirt is box pleated and made of scarlet corded piqué, the blouse is made princess style of Nile green Canton crepe. I am planning on having it done by Thursday for her trip to Auburn. It has been very—very lonely without our little Buzz home today. The girl's teacher Miss. Evans was too ill to come to school today. Mrs. Adams took her place. Donnie and Jimmie went to Quinn's for 2 dozen eggs this evening, after Donnie came from school. I dug four tulip bulbs and two daffodil bulbs from the garden today, and put them in pots in the house. Daddy is reading the children are asleep and I almost am, so will go to bed. Mamma Kessack.

Wednesday Feb. 17, 1937

When we woke up this morning, the wind was howling and the rain pouring and blowing, so I did not send the little folks to school. I baked bread today. At 3 o'clock, we went to Auburn and called Harborview long distance to find out how Buzz was. They said he was just fine, and are not planning on operating. He will not be home for a few days. We went to Cugini's and bought bologna, rutabagas and a sack of potatoes. The store man gave Sissy a balloon. We then went to the dime store and bought a comb, a pad, and a music notebook, and some dye. We then went to Sumner to the Post Office and got the dipper we sent to Montgomery Ward's for. It was done up in a great big bundle with excelson. I finished Peggy Jeans dress it looks real nice. It snowed this afternoon. The kids are all asleep so I guess that is all for this day. Mamma Kessack

Thursday Feb 18, 1937

There was about 2" inches snow when we got up this morning. Donnie was sick at the stomach, so I kept him at home. The girls went to school, it being music day. Peggy wore her new dress. They went to Pacific City to play for their school. Snookies has not been very well today. I have been making Buzz some new clothes. In the afternoon, I went to Quinn's for eggs. I bought 3 dozen, they are 20 cents a dozen. She gave me six pair of stockings for the baby. Jackie was 2 years old yesterday. It is very cold tonight. Daddy is playing tunes on a saw. Well I guess we better go to bed or freeze. I don't know which. I hope Snookies sleeps well tonight. Mamma Kessack

In the heart of a seed buried deep, so deep a dear little plant lay fast asleep. Wake said the sunshine and creep to the light. Wake said the voice of raindrops bright. The little plant heard and it rose to see what the wonderful outside world might be.

Friday Feb 19, 1937

The three children went to school today. I baked bread and washed. Daddy made a seat for the front room. Our visiting Lady Mrs. Kirkman was out today and left cod liver oil, and ordered towels and mattress for us, and left us slips for dental work for the school kids and a physical exam for Peggy. Agnes played her first basket ball game today and her team won. She sure is thrilled. I finished Buzzy's new coat. The kids are acting crazy tonight and won't go to sleep. It is always that way when a person is extra tired. We made a crib quilt of wool and flannel today for Buzz. We sure miss that little kid and hope to have him home soon. My daffodil bulb is 3" inches high. That is all for today. Except I made black cap jelly and chocolate fudge. It is freezing tonight. Mamma Kessack

P.S. Daddy is going to take a bath.

Saturday Feb 20, 1937

Today was auction sale day. Daddy Jim and I went and took Snookies, Agnes and Jimmie Jr. I took down old electric curler, a potato masher, a salad fork, a crock, a food chopper, a washboard and a box. After the commission was paid, I had

47 cents. We bought 10 forks for 20 cents, 7 dishes and a teapot for 10 cents and a bunch of tools at a bargain price. 100 lbs potatoes @ $1.75. We bought $3.67 worth of groceries at Cujini's, meat at Kloutzes and buns at the bakery. We called up Harborview to see how Buzz was; they said O.K. but did not mention bringing him home. The wind is howling and cold tonight. I guess that is all for today. Mamma Kessack

I know the blue modest violets
gleaming with dew at noon
I know the place where you come from
and the way that you are born. When God cut
holes in heaven, the holes the stars look through
He let the scraps fall down to earth
the little scraps are you.

Sunday Feb 21, 1937

We got up at 8:30 this morning. George came in almost at once but did not stay long. I made 4 dozen raised doughnuts today and sent 18 big fat ones over to Edwards. The children were cranky today. I am glad they are all asleep. They make me nervous and tired. It has rained all day long. I done a big ironing and mended things as I went along. I made Buzz a red hat, and myself an underskirt. Well that is all for today. Thus another Sunday goes. Mamma Kessack

I do miss Buzz so much.

Monday Feb 22, 1937

A very lovely day it was today. I baked bread, done a large washing and scrubbed four rooms. I made a new nightgown for Buzz and started a new dress for Snookies. I sponged bathed Agnes, Margaret and Donnie. I am tired tonight and my foot hurts me. I also made 1 dozen cup cakes today. Agnes and Sissy went to Quinn's for 3 dozen eggs. The kids have played outdoors all day. We do miss little Buzz so very-very much. I guess that is all. Today was George Washington's birthday and there was no school, and that is why the kids were all home. School tomorrow. So for another day. Mamma Kessack

Oh moon in the night I have seen you sailing
and shinning so round and low
You are nothing now but a bow
You moon have done something wrong in heaven
that God has hidden your face
I hope if you have, you will soon be forgiven.
And shine again in your place. Jean Ingelaw

Tuesday Feb 23, 1937

Today was a beautiful, spring day that makes you feel just happy to be alive. I baked bread and cookies and washed. I finished Snookies new dress and made Sissy a blazer and Agnes an apron and ironed a few pieces. Snookies has been fussy today, I think he is cutting teeth. I walked to the mailbox this afternoon, but did not get any mail. Peggy Jean was sent home from school—broken out with a rash. I do not know what it is. I put her to bed and gave her aspirin and Casoria. Daddy

Jim cleaned up the yard today. I am wondering how little Buzz is tonight. Donnie and Agnes were doing arithmetic tonight. The kids played outdoors all day. Three frogs were croaking tonight so spring must be coming soon. All for today. Mamma Kessack

Spring, spring so bright and gay
Spring chased old winter away
Spring spring! Is here today. Beautiful spring has
come to stay.
Just a little ditty. I use to write so many verses that
I wanted to see if I still could, maybe a little
practice would help matters out.

Wednesday Feb 24, 1937

Another beautiful spring day. Agnes and Donnie went to school. Margaret Jean stayed home. I have been sewing today. Made myself two new aprons, and one clothes pin apron, and Sissy two new pair of bloomers. I walked to town and called Harborview Hospital long distance to find out how Buzz is. They said he is doing just fine and that's all they told us. Margaret Jean, Jimmie Jr., Joe and Sissy had pennies to spend. I went into Cugini's and bought two boxes of grape nut flakes. I went to the variety store and bought 60 cents worth of stuff. We came home; Daddy has been working on the car. Chester was over at supper time, he had some wood and paid Daddy up. I guess that is all. Mamma Kessack

The little birds fly over, and oh, how sweet they sing. To tell the happy children, that once again tis spring.

Thursday Feb 25, 1937

Agnes and Donnie went to school today. Daddy worked on the car this morning and I bottled beer. After lunch, Daddy and I went for a long hike; while we were gone, Mrs. Kellogg from Derringer and a minister came to our house. We met them on their way out. They want the children to come to Sunday school. I am in favor of it, but I don't know whether Daddy Jim will take them or not. Joe was sick this morning. He seems to be better this evening. It has been rainy and cold today. My bulbs are 6" inches high. I made a new dress for Agnes and new bloomers for Sissy. Margaret Jean and Donnie went to Quinn's for 3 dozen eggs. On their way home, they found a spear tied on a long pole. I am very sleepy tonight. So will call it a closed day. Mamma Kessack

Friday Feb. 26, 1937

There was a warm spring rain today. I baked bread and ginger cake and made fudge. Daddy Jim and I washed clothes and hiked to the mailbox. Joe woke up feeling sick this morning, he told Daddy he could get all better for a nickel. Agnes and Donald went to school today. I made a shirt for Jimmie Jr. and one for Joe. Sissy and Jimmie had a bath tonight. Daddy and I will too. The rest will bathe tomorrow. Daddy is reading. I have started a book entitled The Other Brown; this will be all for today. Mamma Kessack

Sat Feb 27 & Sun Feb 28 1937

I am writing this on Sun. night, as I didn't get a chance last night. We started to Auburn yesterday afternoon with Joe, Sissy and Snookies. Leaving Agnes who had a bad cold and headache, Peggy and Donnie at home. We got as far as the mailbox and found a message that Buzz was ready to come home. We came back, got his clothes and Jimmie Jr., went to Seattle, and got him. We stopped at Sears Roebucks and got a new battery for the car, costing $2.56 we then came by Renton and bought three pairs of shoes. Then came past Granddad Kessack's and gave them $10.00 wood money, got my bag I had left there, then stopped in Kent and bought groceries and came home. Today we took the children to Derringer Sunday school. I baked 56 cookies and made jello.

Sleep, little pigeon, and fold your wings
little blue pigeon with velvet eyes
Sleep to the singing of mother bird swinging.
Swinging—the nest where her little one lies.

In through the window a moon beam comes
Little gold moon beam with misty wings
All silently creeping, it asks is he sleeping?
Sleeping and dreaming while mother sings.

Sleep little pigeon and fold your wings
little blue pigeon with mournful eyes
Am I not singing? See I am swinging
Swinging the nest where my darling lies

For Aggies birthday tomorrow. Buzz is very weak and thin, and won't eat. Mamma Kessack

Monday March 1, 1937

Oh such a commotion underground,
when March called Ho! There—Ho! Such spreading
of rootlets far and wide
such whisperings to and fro

Today was Aggies birthday she was 11 years old. She had a party at school. Jimmie Jr. went to visit school. I baked bread and washed. Buzz is feeling some better and eating his food. Daddy sent for new brake lining today. Agnes has a terrible cold, I will Dr. up. My right leg hurts me terribly bad tonight. All the kids are cutting paper; I do wish they would realize that I get so tired I can't see straight. Well that is all except it poured rain all day long. Mamma Kessack

Tuesday March 2, 1937

We were very tired today as Buzz cried almost all night, he has also been quite cranky all day; he just wants to be held all day. The kids are all crazy tonight and won't go to sleep and as they have managed to get Snookies awake, I guess my evening is fairly well shot. Our check came today, which is one good thing. George left a cow here today and told us to milk her, which is another good thing. Daddy cut ½-cord wood today. It rained most of the day. Margaret started playing basketball today and I will have to make a pair of shorts for her. I guess that is all the days' doings. Mamma Kessack

Wed. March 3, 1937

Dear Diary, I hope to the goodness sake we never see another day as long as we live as trying and tiring as this one. We took all the kids to Kent, and took Donnie to the dentist. The generator in the car burned out. We went up East Hill to Granddads as Daddy wanted to see Alex about something. We then drove around by Browns to ask for Bobbie, as he is very sick. We next came back to Auburn to take Margaret Jean and Daddy Jim to Dr. Hughes. We had to wait 1 ½ hour. Buzz was cranky, Joe and Sissy was sick, Agnes had a headache and Donnie acted like a monkey all day. The kids fought in the car like wild Indians. It was just simply awful. Two dressed up Ladies were standing on the sidewalk shaking their heads in dismay at such a carload of kids, well anyway their nice kids. {So damn the old hens anyway} Dr. finally came. Margaret is 7 ½ lbs underweight, he gave her some tonic and treatments for her sore leg. He started today giving Daddy Jim serum treatments for arthritis. Well after that we went shopping at the variety store. I spent $1.65. At Cugini's we spent $6.63 thus goes the money. Well finally, we did start home; we left Margaret and Donnie at Quinn's to bring home 3 dozen eggs. We finally got home and got some supper cooking. Joe is very sick so is Agnes. Buzz is asleep but I don't know for how long. Well anyway, I suppose we will live through it all someway. Mamma Kessack

Thursday March 4, 1937

Buzz cried quite a lot last night, he coughs so much. Joe, Sissy, and Agnes were sick all night. Peggy and Donnie went to school. Daddy and I done an enormous washing today. It was a lovely spring day, the kids played outside all day. Joe fainted this morning, I can't quite figure out what is wrong with them. We put Snookies little bed out in the sun today and he slept outside all day. The frogs are all croaking tonight. That is all. Mamma Kessack

Saturday March 5, 1937

Daddy Jim went to Auburn today, he is going to put a new generator in the car. He also has a $13.00 grocery order. It was a beautiful day; I washed and made Jimmie Jr. a pair of pants out of an old wool dress. Tonight Alex stopped in on his way home from Buckley.

Sunday March 7, 1937

We got up at 8 o'clock rushed around and got the children to Sunday school on time. They love to go. While waiting for them, we drove around and seen Mrs. Dairds new house, it sure is a beauty. It was a wonderful day. Buzz has been out all day long. Daddy worked on the car all afternoon. Donnie does not act like he felt very well tonight, I sure hope he isn't going to be sick, but I am afraid he is. The girls all wore half sox today. Agnes is letting her hair grow long. I will have to start their Easter dresses this week. That is all. Mamma Kessack

Monday March 8, 1937

Agnes and Margaret went to school this morning. Daddy Jim cut wood and I baked bread. This afternoon we went to Kent. Donald went to Dentist Rugg and had three teeth filled, he was a very good boy. We seen Bob Brown, we mailed a wedding present and card to Helen Grace. We stopped in Auburn and mailed an order of $7.91 to Montgomery Ward CO., then we went over to Lucille's to see the baby. Then we started home. We met Myers on the way, they stopped us and asked if we would get their commodities tomorrow, of course we told them yes. We came home and had supper. I guess that is all for today, which was another swell spring day. Mamma Kessack

Tuesday March 9, 1937

Got up early this morning, the three school kids fought each other all morning. At noon, we went to Pacific City and got our commodities, this month we received 6 dozen eggs, 18 large cans meat and 16 lbs diced prunes. It rained all morning. In the afternoon I baked a large cake and done a big washing. The sun shined all afternoon. Well I don't feel good tonight and I am very tired. Donnie and Jimmie will not go to sleep and are acting so crazy, I don't know what to do with them. Buzz is sure feeling good now, sleeping and eating like a little boy should. Guess that is all. Mamma Kessack

Wednesday March 10, 1937

A beautiful day, I washed clothes, Daddy Jim cut wood. The kids played outside all day. We had waffles for supper. Jim just loves them. I told him I would make a bunch of them for him to eat like crackers when he and Sissy went to Grandmas, he said oh goody—goody. Sissy said, we will tell Grandma they are not very good and she will let us eat them all. I have pleurisy in my right lung tonight so bad I can hardly use my right arm. Daddy is reading a book. It looks like a big rainstorm is coming up so we brought in the clothes off the line. Buzz had lots of fun today. Snookies is looking swell. All the kids are O.K. Mamma Kessack

Thursday March 11, 1937

Today has been so busy, but everyone has been happy. Agnes was admitted to the school orchestra today. Daddy Jim cut wood; I helped him fell a tree. I baked beans, washed and ironed today. Our package came from Montgomery Ward today. Daddy did not want Joe and Sissy to follow him to the mailbox, so he told them there was a big red bull with blood in his eyes down by Edwards. Well they came running to the house all out of breath screaming, there is a big enormous blood in the eye down by the well with a bull in it. Well it is 9 o'clock and we have a long trip to make tomorrow so will call it a day. Mamma Kessack

Friday March 12, 1937

Today has been one of those days that you think back on and wonder how you ever stood it. Sissy and Buzz were both sick all night and neither slept until four in the morning. We had to leave here at 7:30 as Buzz had an appointment in surgery clinic at 9 o'clock in Harborview. We left Sissy and Joe at Granddad Kessack and sent Jimmie to school with the kids. We got into Harborview at 5 minutes to nine. I walked the floor with Buzz until 11:30, waiting for the Dr. to keep the 9 o'clock clinic and then he referred Buzz to another clinic at 12:30. Well I took him to the car and gave him warm milk and cookies. Then we got him into the clinic and they ordered a new kind of truss for him. And, are going to give him some kind of new rupture treatment. Finally, we got away from the hospital. Snookies stayed in the car all day and never cried. We went to a restaurant and had fried salmon dinner. Then drove to Renton and went to the Goodwill store. We bought two white shirts for Daddy for 45 cents—1 blue shirt for Donnie for 10 cents 1 pair shoes for Peggy for 10 cents 1 pair for Snookies, and a bathrobe for myself, and a hairbrush for us all. We then came past Granddads and picked up Joe and Sissy. Sissy was sick all day. We then came to Auburn and bought groceries at Cugini's and Vicks Vapor Rub and Casoria for Sissy. Then we came home. Aggie had hot fire mashed potatoes ready for us. Sissy is very—very sick tonight. I have a dreadful headache. The kids brought home report cards. Donnie is very good, Peggy's is good, Aggies very poor. An—awful—howling wind is blowing tonight. March winds I guess, but I wish it wouldn't blow so hard it is too scary. I guess, that is all and we are still alive. Mamma Kessack

Saturday March 13, 1937

The girls went visiting today; they left home in time to get to Gales at 10 o'clock. They came home at four. I was very busy baking bread and other work. Daddy Jim cut wood, the boys piled brush and bundle it. Sissy was so very—very sick, she broke out with measles. Chester came over in the evening and stayed 2 hours. Mamma Kessack

Sunday March 14, 1937

Daddy Jim had to go help Chester scale timber today, he left at 9 o'clock so the kids did not get to go Sunday school. It was a lovely day, the kids played outside all day. Alex came up about four o'clock with 4 lbs of nice fresh pork chops. We made a very nice supper. Daddy Jim did not get home until almost 7 o'clock, so he and Alex visited till about 10. I ironed all evening. Then we had coffee and lunch. Mamma Kessack

Monday March 15, 1937

A very lovely day. Agnes and Margaret Jean went to school. Sissy feels a lot better. Daddy Jim does not feel good, and Snookies has a terrible cold. Donnie went to the dentist at Kent, he had one tooth filled and 2 pulled, and he was a very-very good boy. We bought 100 lbs of carrots, 50 lbs potatoes, 10 lbs onions, 3 yeast cakes and 4 lbs mutton stew, 2lbs shortening. I guess that is all for today. Mamma Kessack

Tuesday March 16, 1937

Daddy Jim was building fences for Jack Zeddler today. I baked bread and washed and washed and washed, but still did not get the washing done. Mrs. Zeddler gave Daddy 2 lbs liver soup meat tonight. After supper Daddy Jim went down to Dr. Hughes to get a shot in the arm for arthritis. Buzz and I went too. We had an ice cream cone. My right arm is very sore, I don't know why. I weighed Buzz, he weighs 25 lbs now. I guess that is all, I gave Jim and Don a dose of Casoria as neither seems to feel just right. Mamma Kessack

Sissy has a bad cough.

March 17, 1937

The girls wore green hair bows today; Daddy Jim had a green bow on his cap. It blew and rained today. The girls went swimming in the tank. Daddy Jim was working up at Zeddler's today, he does not feel good. Has a terrible headache. Donnie and Agnes has sore throats, Sissy has a terrible cough. All for today. Mamma Kessack

Thursday March 18, 1937

The sun shone today, but a cold wind is blowing. It froze last night. The girls mailed an order to Montgomery Ward's for new half sox's and pink hair bows for Easter. Daddy worked at Zeddlers today, he still has an awful headache. Little Sissy has coughed all day, it almost sounds like whooping cough. Donnie's sore throat is bad tonight. Virgil Adams is sick. Chester was over this evening and had a glass of beer. All for today except, I washed and ironed and baked a cake which was a complete flop. Mamma Kessack

Friday March 19, 1937

Snookies is 5 months old today and sweet as roses. Sissy and Joe are sick, Donnie is sick, Agnes and Jimmie are coming down sick, and Buzz has an earache and Snookies a cold, amongst them they keep me busy. I washed today. Daddy worked at Zeddlers again today. Guess that is all for today, my head aches and I am tired.

Saturday March 20, 1937

Last night Sissy and Buzz cried all night. Sissy has a terrible cough and Buzz has the earache. This morning Joe vomited. It looked like it would be a nice day all day, but it turned cold, and hailed and rained. Alex came down and helped Daddy Jim do some repair work on our car. Daddy went to Auburn in the afternoon and bought a nice bunch of groceries and bought us 2qts ice cream. I done a big washing today and a messy one. Donnie had too much laxative and messed the bed. The girls received their ribbons from Montgomery Ward's today. I received a letter and picture from Helen Grace. She is planning on getting married Easter Sunday. Daddy is reading the P.I. and I think I will too, if the kids continue to sleep as they are now doing. Mamma Kessack

Sunday March 21, 1937

The wind blew and howled all night and little Sissy coughed, choked and cried all night. We got up at 7:30 had breakfast and took the kids to Sunday school. They received a St. Patrick treat of candies. Margaret Jean is not feeling well, Donnie has a terrible cough and Sissy is no better. Buzz seems to feel all right, but is so wide-awake I don't think he will ever go to sleep. The kids lit a fire at the bottom of the swamp. I just happened to see the smoke or the whole place would have gone up in blazes. There is still news in the P.I. so I guess this is all because I would like to read a while now. Mamma Kessack

Monday March 22, 1937

It rained and poured all day and was very cold. Donnie and Peggy were sick today and Agnes had to go to school alone. Joe is not feeling well and is very cranky indeed. I done some mending and sewing and baked hot cross buns. Daddy Jim built a play-yard for Buzz today with a picket fence around it. Tonight he helped Chester butcher a calf. Chester gave him the liver. We are putting mustard plaster on Donnie and Joe and Buzz tonight, they all have terrible coughs. Miss Nordang wrote a note objecting to Donnie's absence, but" I will not send them to school sick". Agnes brought home the orchestra picture, it sure is swell. The sky was red tonight, we may have a decent day tomorrow, here is hoping so anyway. We fixed a straw tick for Donnie and Jim Jr. to sleep on. Daddy also repaired the bedsprings. Guess that is all for today. Daddy just went over to the mailbox to see if there is any mail for today. He is not back yet. Mamma Kessack—Just wallpaper per catalog for mail.

Tuesday March 23, 1937

There was a white frost last night. Agnes and Donnie went to school today. Daddy Jim is working at Zeddlers. Mrs. Zeddler sent me a bundle of clothes all very good and useful. Buzz has been cranky today. I finished my new pink dress. Daddy does not feel good tonight. Sissy is feeling better. Joe and Donnie has terrible night coughs. I did not get my washing done today, worst luck. I don't expect Buzz to sleep tonight; he has an earache and cough. Guess that is all for today. Mamma Kessack

No mail today.

Wednesday March 24, 1937

Everything went smoothly today, until night. I put little Buzz to bed he drank his bottle and then cried. The other kids went to bed and still he cried. I took him up and his rupture came down. We took him to Auburn with the intentions of having Dr. Hughes putting it up, but he could not be found. We got Dr. Allen, finally he tried but could not get it up, he said take him to Harborview, so we did. They had not got it up when we came home. As far as they knew last night, they are going to operate. Mamma Kessack

Thursday March 25, 1937

I washed and ironed today and fixed dresses for the girls for Easter. Donnie is not feeling well. The other children are all O.K. Daddy Jim worked at Zeddlers. It looks like rain tonight but I hope it don't because I have a large washing out on the line. I wonder how Buzz is tonight. We miss him so very—very much. Mamma Kessack

Friday March 26, 1937

I washed today, and ironed the girls Easter dresses and pressed Daddy Jim's suit. The visiting Lady, Mrs. Kirkman was here and left a physical examination sheet for Daddy to take to Harborview. We went to the Sunday school Easter pageant this evening. We called up Harborview from Cole's service station. They said Buzz was resting better and his cold was much better. They had not decided definitely whether they would operate or not. The car is acting up something frightful. Don't know whether we will get Sat. trip to town or not. Mamma Kessack

Saturday March 27, 1937

I was very disappointed today. The car would not start so no trip to town. Daddy Jim hitch hiked and Cujini's two daughters Jenny and Evelyn brought him home with groceries. I washed. The girls helped me today. They also made pretty little Easter baskets. Mamma Kessack

Sunday March 28, 1937

Daddy Jim fixed the car this morning and we took the children to Sunday school. Then we went over to see Mr. & Mrs. Jim Murray, we hadn't seen them for about 9 years. We came home and had baked ham dinner. Bradford's came up. Then the children hunted for Easter eggs. Mabel brought up some clothes for me to make over for the kids. My sister Helen Grace who is 34 got married today in Mt Carmel Ill. Daddy and I went for a walk this evening after supper. Agnes, done up the work so nicely. Peggy put the kids to bed. Now we are going to read and go to sleep. Mamma Kessack

Monday March29, 1937

Daddy Jim worked on the car all day. I washed clothes. Agnes and Margaret Jean cleaned out cupboards and the cooler. At noon, they went to the mailbox. There was a notice that Buzz had been operated on this morning. Afternoon the girls popped corn for themselves and the little kids. After supper Daddy, Snookies and I went to Auburn to phone and see how

Buzz was. The nurse said his condition is good. We went over to Bradford's, and visited a while and get a sanitary couch they said we could have. And then came home, put Snooks to bed, had a lunch and went to bed too. Mamma Kessack

Tuesday March 30, 1937

It rained today and rained and rained and rained. In the afternoon, I went over to Quinn's for eggs and visited with Opal for about 2 hours, we had a pleasant time. I came home and baked a cake, cooked supper and now we are going to bed. We all miss little Buzz so much; I wonder how he is tonight. The girls, played house today and were dressing up in old clothes and having a good time. Guess that is all for today. Mamma Kessack—I have a severe pain in my left side and my abdomen, it hurts so bad I am very—very cranky. Sorry but it hurts.

Wednesday March 31, 1937

Daddy Jim and the boys hauled in wood with the car and trailer. I washed clothes. The girls were making puppets. In the evening, we went to Auburn and phoned up to see how Buzz is. He had no temperature and his condition is good, so the Nurse said. We bought a sack of potatoes some smelt and steak. Donnie was with us. He bought two ice cream cones for himself and me. I bought a writing tablet and birthday card. The card is for Mamma Elliott. I am going to write a letter to Helen Grace, so to bed. Mamma Kessack

April 1937

The April rain falls softly on earth so brown and bare—and suddenly the soft green grass is shining everywhere. For April is a seamstress. With needles of bright rain, she stitches earth a new spring dress. To make her gay again. And in the sunny moments, between the sudden showers, she buttons it from neck to hem, with dandelion flowers. Marion Doyle

April 1, 1937—Thursday

Daddy got wood and repaired the road today. I washed. After dinner, JoJo Daddy, and I went to the mailbox. We received the commodity notice and a note from Mabel asking us to her house next time we are in town as she has some things for us. Chester came over in the afternoon with the sad news that Mr. Adams died last night. We all feel very—very bad about it. We all took a bath tonight as we are going to Seattle. The wind is blowing hard tonight. We miss Buzz so much. Mamma Kessack

April 2nd Friday

We arose at five and got on our way at seven to Seattle. We left Agnes, Jimmie Jr., Joe and Sissy at Granddad Kessack in Kent. We took Margaret Jean, Donnie and Snookies with us. It was raining and very—very cold. It took us until three o'clock to finish our business and still we have to go back next Friday.

Buzz is getting along fine. We came back finally, all in and very—very tired. Mamma Kessack

Sat. April 3, 1937

We laid in bed late and it was such a rush to get away. We went to Mr. Adams funeral in the Presbyterian Church in Auburn. Then we went to Bradford's and got some clothes and magazines she had for us. Rinky's were there. We stopped in at Roy's place and had a glass of muscatel. It sure warmed me up, and sent me sailing. Then we went to Cugini's and got $9.65 of groceries. Then we got two cards of sympathy to Mrs. Adams & Virgil. Then we came home, and so to bed. Mamma Kessack.

April 4, 1937

It has rained and blown all day, and has been very cold. I have been ill all day. Got by with as little work as possible. I do hope the weather will clear up soon. The children go to school tomorrow. My left side pains me to an almost unbearable condition. Guess that is all for today. The children are singing themselves to sleep. Daddy Jim is reading, so to bed. Mamma Kessack

Monday April 5, 1937

Today was rainy and cold. Agnes, Margaret, Donnie went back to school today. At noon Daddy, the little kids and I went to Pacific City to get our commodities. We received 18 cans meat, 13 cans milk & 18 lbs prunes. Then we came home and washed clothes. And, so to bed. Mamma Kessack

Tuesday April 6, 1937

Today we washed clothes and cooked spinach all day. In the late afternoon, Mrs. Foster, Georgia Lee's mother and Mrs. Jackson from Sumner came up. They wanted the children to come to Sumner Sunday school, and have offered to come and get them with a car every Sunday. We have decided to let them go there in place of Derringer, it will be much more convenient for us and then Margaret & Georgia can be together. The boys Donnie and Jim acted up a fright while the visitors were here; I never was so embarrassed in all my life. Daddy has been feeling badly all day, and tonight he is quite ill. Mr. Atkinson our bus driver is ill. He gave Mr. Adams a blood transfusion before he died and contracted blood poisoning from him. Agnes sprained her ankle today at school. It is very swollen tonight. Mamma Kessack

Wednesday April 7, Thurs 8th

These two days have been hectic to the limit. Daddy Jim has been sick. Baby Snooks does not feel good and I feel terrible. No sleep nights—just sweat and cough. Rain—rain all day. Dr. Hughes was up to Daddy in the afternoon and left medicine. Uncle Alex was in, in the evening. The camps are out on strike, which means no work for him. I do wish I knew how darling little Buzz is. I do miss him so. Mamma Kessack

Friday April 9, 1937

Daddy has been sick all day and I certainly am a long ways from feeling good. Snookies has a very bad cough. I have an infection in the pointer finger on my left hand. It has been raining and cold all day. I done some washing, but got by with as little work as possible. Mamma Kessack

Saturday April 10, 1937

After a sleepless night, we arose to a cold windy, rainy day. Daddy was sick all night and also today. Alex came up from Kent with the very good intentions of hauling in and buzzing wood. He and Chester hauled in one load and here came a schoolteacher, looking for a job. He no sooner introduced himself, than six, more teachers came. Chet and Alex took them into the cow barn if you can imagine such a thing, one at a time and interviewed them. The rest, waiting their turn in the yard with the cows, dogs, and kids hounding around them, and the wind flapping their clothes. In the afternoon, Alex went to Auburn and got our weekly supplies and some medicine from Dr. Hughes for Daddy. He also phoned up about Buzz, he is ready to come home. We have a P.I. to read. Uncle is going to sleep here tonight. In the mean time, he and Chet are going to the Briar Patch the dance. Guess that is all. Mamma Kessack

Sunday April 11, 1937

The children started to the Sunday school at Sumner today. Alex and Grandma went to Seattle and brought little wee Buzz home. Daddy Jim is very sick. I done an enormous washing today. Little Buzz seem to know us all, but I had a little trouble getting him to sleep. But on the whole, we went through a trying day rather smoothly. Mamma Kessack

Who is this weeper with twinkling eye? This smiler, with the long drawn sigh? A spirit of beauty walks the hill, a spirit of love the plains, the shadows are bright and the sunshine fills the air with diamond rain. April Showers Bring May Flowers

Monday April 12, 1937

A pouring rain was what we awoke to this morning. The children went to school. Granddad and Alex came up and brought a hand washing machine. Alex tried to get the Buzz saw to going but it wouldn't budge. So no wood was cut today. Daddy Jim is surely in a bad shape, his cough is terrible. Little Buzz was so good and contented today. He seems so happy. I am so glad to have him home. He ate well and played in his little bed, and took a nap. There is a high wind tonight and rain, rain, rain. Earl Quinn was over in the evening to tell us our neighbor Mr. Rinkey died. We contributed 25 cents to the flower fund. He died from gangrene rupture. That is all for now. Mamma Kessack

Tuesday April 13, 1937

Well Diary, today has been very gloomy. Daddy was very sick last night, all night. This morning I made up my mind to get attention for him as my care was not doing him any good at all. I sent for Dr. Hughes by Chester. I watched for him all day, he did not come, but sent an officer from Auburn Police Station up with a lovely big car to take Daddy to Harborview Hospital. It made Daddy very, very angry at me. I worried for 2 days over him now, and love him so dearly that I want him to get better. But there was absolute hatred in his eyes before he left. He thought I didn't want him here, which is very untrue. It makes it very hard to stand, but I guess life is that way. Those you love best hurt you the worst. I am going to write a letter, I don't suppose he will appreciate it any, but he will get it anyway. Mamma Kessack

Wednesday April 14, 1937

Today has been long, stormy, gloomy and very, very lonely. Life is just empty without Daddy Jim. It stormed all day. I made a new pair of pants for Donnie, and done my regular work. Donnie brought home a card of thanks from Adams. The children took pennies to school for flowers for Mr. Rinkey. Guess that is all except I have a sty starting on my right eyelid, which is very painful. I mailed a letter to Daddy Jim, and hope and pray he is getting better soon, to return to us. I know he is very angry with me and is no doubt very disappointed in his married life, but oh, I do love him so much. Mamma Kessack

Thursday April 15, 1937

I cannot recall just what happened today so I will skip to Fri April 16, 1937. About 10:30, Uncle Alex and our nephew Eddie Brown came up. They buzzed up all the wood and Chester Edwards helped them. In the afternoon Uncle and I and Buzz went to Auburn and phoned in to see how Daddy Jim was. They said his condition is satisfactory. In the afternoon, Mrs. Kirkman the visiting Lady came up and told me that starting with May, we would get $98.00, clothing and rent, and I would get some teeth. Sure sounds good to me. She also wants me to find a different place to live; I am in favor of that too. I wrote a long letter to Daddy. I miss Daddy so much, I am so lonely. I bought Peggy Jean some dress up patent leather slippers, paid $1.49 for them. Agnes, Peggy, Donnie and Jim went to the musical program tonight. Peggy Jean is to spend the weekend with Georgia Lee. Chester E. baked a big coffee cake and brought over for supper. Mamma Kessack

Little stars that twinkle in the heavens blue. I have often wondered if you ever knew, how there rose one like you, leading wise old men from the east through Judah down to Bethlehem.

Letter from Daddy Jim

Dear Lucy,

Please send me my Razor and brush, wrap them up in heavy paper some new blades that Alex off to. The barber don't come to this part of the place so I hear. I was awfully sick last night but Doctor said I will get well with right care. I get so dizzy

I go flying off to nowhere at anytime. They give me five pills at 10 and 3 at noon and 5 at 4 they are all white but different sizes. They finely got my bowels to move last night the first time since I came to the hospital the nurse are all very kind and we get all we can eat, but it is not much frozen beets juice and cabbage spinach and rice a la tomato. But one good thing I get Big cup of coffee every morning hope everyone is well—love and kisses to all How is Buzz and Snukkys.

Dear Lucy,

I had an awful night of it cough—cough all night. I have double pneumonia. They have stopped putting me in the tank now. I was 24 hours steady, Thurs through Friday. Say they have a great rig here we could of used on sissie and she would not of known the diff, it is a high steel frame at the top of bed with blankets fixed. It's slit in the middle by pulling the corners over the pole and stick a inhaler under the tent it sure is a good thing. I am not feeling so good to day honey my head is kind of sore too much coughing last night. How is the kiddies give them my love. Some one left me the P.I. Saturday night I don't know who. Never mind about my razor I can borrow one. Mail only leaves here once every 3 days, as it has to be fumigated up stairs. We are on two. S. and every one on this floor has pneumonia. Another just got rid of it or they have sent him down a dark alley. How are you for split wood? Tell Chet to split some. There is money enough in that pocket book for that $8 from Zeddlers and $4 from wood that is $12 you have over the regular. How is Buzz and Snukkys give them my love and the rest of them too. I am a little weaker than when I came in, nothing to eat and tons, tons, of pills. Have you seen Alex again? If you need anything don't bother him, Caughiene is willing to take the stuff out and anything else you want. Well here's hoping I get over it. Love and kisses to all. Your loving Father Jim. Write Soon xxxxxx

Thursday April 29, 1937

Another cold bleak day. You really would think it was Jan, rather than April. This afternoon we went to Auburn and got Donnie's cords and Sissies anklets, some groceries and gas. We came home; I cooked supper washed diapers, baby blankets and ironed. The kids made May baskets after supper. The kids won't go to sleep tonight. Daddy isn't feeling at all well. I've got tonsillitis and am as cranky as a bear with a sore paw. I've a letter to write so will close. Mamma Kessack

Fri April 30, 1937—Sat May 1—Sun 2—Mon 3—
Tues 4—Wed 5

Friday I washed—scrubbed and ironed—Mrs. Kirkman came up in the afternoon. Saturday check came for $99—We went to the sale then had Hamburgers coffee and pie at Roy's Place. Then bought groceries at Cugini's and came home. Sunday the children went to Sunday school all except Joe who was not feeling well. Georgia lee Foster came home with Margaret Jean and stayed all night. Sunday night Agnes took sick. Mon. morning she was worse, sick with high fever. Daddy Jim went to Seattle to Hospital clinic they think he has T.B. he got my clothing from the supply house. Tuesday Aggie was worse at 7 o'clock in the evening she had a sever hemorrhage. Chester E. stayed with the kids and Daddy and I rushed her into Harborview.

Today I scrubbed, and disinfected and fumigated the sleeping rooms. In the afternoon, we went to Quinn's and bought 3 chickens, 3 dozen eggs, and 2 quarts milk. I have a terrible sore throat, sore ears and burning eyes. Mamma Kessack

Hark how the black bird whistles
Hark how the song sparrow trills
what are they calling
with snowflakes falling
And April, cold on the hills? Up—up the black birds
say Tulips and Lily and sweet daffodilly
Awake
For the coming of May
The voice of one who goes
before to make
The paths of June more
beautiful is thine
Sweet May

Thurs. Fri. Sat.

The last few days have been very busy ones. Thurs. afternoon we went to Auburn looked for vacant houses but found none. Called in about Agnes they said she was about the same. Fri. Donnie came home from school with a nice cookbook he made for me and a Mother's Day card. Margaret Jean brought me a card and a diamond cake Mrs. Foster made and sent me. Alex was down to visit us and brought ice cream. Today is Sat. we went to Auburn to the sale and bought groceries. Agnes is still very ill. I bathed all the kids tonight. Daddy is feeling a little better. The weather is rainy. Mamma Kessack

Sunday May 9, 1937

Today was Mothers Day. The kids went to Sunday school. Granddad, grandma and Alex were up for dinner. Grandma brought a nice cake and a gallon of milk. Alex called up about Agnes, they say she is much better. Grandma bought Agnes a brown crepe jumper dress with an eggshell blouse. We had a nice dinner. Creamed hen and Haddock, radishes—celery—green onions—and asparagus. Mince meat pie and whipped cream and cake. A nice day but rainy. Daddy and I put the kids to bed and went in the car to Quinn's for milk. Then came home and washed dishes and swept the floors. Daddy played some music on the violin and now we are in bed reading books. Mamma Kessack

Monday May 10, 1937

It rained today, and rained and poured. We went to Pacific City for commodities we, received—12 cans grapefruit juice—14 cans milk 20 lbs prunes. We hunted all over Pacific City and Algona for vacant houses and found none. Jimmie went to school with Donnie today. Tonight we got a notice that Agnes is ready to come home. Baby Alexander is ill today, has a high fever, he also has two new teeth. Mamma Kessack

Tuesday May 11, 1937

We done up the work this morning and about 10:30 left for Seattle. We left Joe and Sissy at grandma Kessack's and went by way of the Renton Highline and looked for empty houses but there were none. We went to Harborview and got Agnes then went to the Goodwill headquarters and bought three pair of shoes and a wash boiler. I seen Mrs. Hetzler then we came home. Mamma Kessack

Wed. May 12, 1937

We washed today and washed and washed. It was very hot today. We put little Snookies out in the sun and he got all sunburned. After supper, we took the car and went to Quinn's for eggs and milk. Agnes is very thin and weak. She had a good time reading and drawing today. The kids are full of meanness tonight and will not go to sleep its 9 o'clock and Buzz is howling his head off. He has had three bottles since supper and still won't go to sleep. I'm tired and cranky and a howling kid sure is pleasant. Mamma Kessack

Thurs. May 13, 1937

Today was just an ordinary day. Buzz had to be changed from head to foot 3 times this morning, because he rolled himself in fresh cow mess. I washed clothes and ironed. That's all I guess, except Mrs. Kellogg sent Agnes a lovely bouquet of peonies and wreath. Mamma Kessack

Friday May 14, 1937

Today was a pretty sun shiny day. Everybody was happy, the work went smoothly. Margaret Jean went to Pierce County track meet came in second in two 50-yard dashes and one 75-yard dash. Daddy was helping Chester work on a tractor today. No, mail no visitors so to bed. Mamma Kessack

Sat. May 15, 1937

We slept late today. Daddy, Agnes the two babies and I went to Auburn about 11:00. We went shopping, and ate hamburgers. We then went to the sale. I had a nice visit with Mrs. Smith from Kent. Then we came home. Everybody had a bath so to bed. Mamma Kessack

Sunday May 16, 1937

Today was inclined to be windy, cold and rainy. Daddy was helping Chester fix the tractor today. The children went to Sunday school. In the afternoon granddad, grandma, Alex, Aggie Brown, Eddie and Bobbie Jr. came up in Eddie's car and stayed for supper. They found a house in Kent, they thought we might like to rent. Alex is of an idea he would like to buy it. Don't know how it will all turn out. We are all invited to Browns Friday for supper and Auction sale at night. Boy, sure hope we go, it all sounds like fun. Mamma Kessack

Mon. May 17, 1937

We got up at 6 o'clock. Daddy went to Seattle to have an x-ray of his lungs. I washed and washed and scrubbed. Margaret Jean and I went to Quinn's for milk and eggs. That is all the news of the day. Mamma Kessack

Tues. May 18, 1937

Today was happy, yes. Washed and cleaned house that is the front room, the kitchen was a cyclone when about 4 o'clock here comes a car. I reached for the broom to get the kitchen swept and could not find it. I would have done anything to get that broom, but no broom could I find. The company was Mrs. Foster, Nancy, little David, Mrs. Bradley the girls Sunday school teacher and her two little children. They brought Agnes flowers fresh fruit and vegetables and some fancy canned goods, a bundle of clothing. We had such a lovely visit but all too short. I traded 24 quarts black berries with them for other fruit and canned peas. They will be up next Wed with my stuff. Well wish they could come more often. Daddy disc and plowed the future garden today. Tonight Daddy, Joe, Buzz and Snookies went to Auburn got some fresh bread, doughnuts and ice cream. Ten we went to Pacific City and bought steak at Jenkins store. Then we drove back to Bakers shop, Daddy had beer and I had strawberry pop. We brought home some pancake flour and then stopped at Quinn's and got the milk and came home. Daddy and I had coffee, steak and doughnuts.

So, to bed. I expect a busy day tomorrow so may not write again until Sat or Sunday. Mamma Kessack

Tuesday May 24, 1937

Haven't written in a long time. Last Friday we bathed and cleaned up ourselves and kids and went to Aunty Browns at Kent for supper, we left the big kids with Eddie, took the three little ones and went to an auction sale. Alex and grandma came down later. Daddy bought a 9x12 rug for 60 cents. It was about 10:30 when we got back to Browns. Kids were all tired and cranky. We came home and all piled into bed. Saturday Daddy worked with Chester all day and I washed. About 4 o'clock, we went to Auburn and bought groceries. Sunday was uneventful the children went to Sunday school. Chester and Daddy butchered Edwards pig. Monday Jimmie Jr. went to school, the rest of us went to Seattle, as Daddy had to go to clinic at Harborview. After he was through there, we went to John Hetzlers place and got some magazines. Today we papered part of our parlor. The visiting Lady Mrs. Kirkman came out, no clothing this month she said. Later Mrs. Murray from Auburn and a young Lady came out and wanted us to go fishing, but I had a big washing to do. Guess this is all the important things for now. Mamma Kessack

May 26-27—Wed & Thurs.

Wed., a usual day of washing and working. Thurs., about the same. Tomorrow is shopping day and Sat. the school picnic at Point Defiance, I am planning on going with the six oldest children, and Daddy says he will stay home with the two babies. Snookies played on the rug on the floor today for the first time. Mamma Kessack

Ring out, wild bells to the wild sky
the flying clouds, the frosty light
the year is dying in the night
Ring out wild bells, and let him die.
Ring out the old, ring in the new—
Ring happy bells across the snow
The year is going, let him go
Ring out the false, ring in the true

September

The goldenrod is yellow
The corn is turning brown
The trees in apple orchards
with fruit are bending down
The gentians bluest fringes
are curling in the sun
In dusty pods the milkweeds
Its hidden silk has spun
The sedges flaunt their harvest
In every meadow nook
and asters by the brook side
make asters in the brook
From dewy lanes at morning
the grapes sweet odor rise
at noon the roads all flutter

with yellow butterflies.
On woodlands ruddy with autumn
the amber sunshine lies. I know the lands are lit
with all the autumn blaze of goldenrod
and every where the purple asters nod.

Elliotts and James Kessack

Kessack Family

CHAPTER 3

MRS. KESSACK

Dates May through July 1946
Box 28, RT 3 Kent Washington.

May 8, 1946

It is a breezy spring day and I decided it would be an excellent time to start a written record of the family's daily comings and goings. We are at the time of this record a family of eleven. Father Jim age 47—Mother Novella age 37—Jim Jr. age 15—Joe age 13—Novella Jr.—more often called Sissy age—12 George called Buzz age—11 Alex called Sugar age—9 Sylvia called Patsy age 7—Geraldine called Yang Yang age 6—Gwendolyn called Gwenny age 5—Kathryn the baby age 2 ½ called Dee Dee. We live on 4 acres at the north end of Strawberry lane. We hope we own it. The question of ownership hanging in balance as the quick claim Deed we had on the place has mysteriously disappeared. We have a Jersey cow named Red a Bull named Bo—Bo. Six hens and a baby chick. A dog named Brownie 2 cats Junior and Scotty. We have ½ acre in garden. There are three older children belonging to the family. There is Aggie, she is married and has a boy 3, named Butchie, she is separated from her husband Bud Beall so Butchie boards with our neighbors Bill Rogers. Aggie is in Arizona, Bud is in Kent. Then there is Margaret age 18, she is married and lives in Cleveland Ohio. Her name is Mrs. A Hudock, she has a daughter age 3 months named Peggy Ann. When Margaret is mention we call her Peggy. Then there is the oldest boy Don he is 16, he is in the A.T.S. a branch of the marines so he is only home when his boat is in port at Seattle. Today the seven oldest are in school. Jim, Joe, Sissy, Buzz, Sugar, Patsy, Yang-Yang. Daddy Jim went to Auburn today to report for unemployed insurance as he is at present not working. On the way home, he will stop into see about getting new papers on the property so we will feel more safe in regards to our home. I am washing and doing the house work. Gwenny and Dee Dee are playing. I will write more tonight after the kids are in bed, as there will be more news at that time. So for now a cup of coffee and so to work. Well it is nine O'clock and as I said, there is more to tell. About the title, they said as long as the place is recorded in the county bldg in Seattle it was all O.K. Dad bought home doughnuts, bread, and meat at noon. Donnie got his discharge from A.T.S. and came home. He had to either quit or go to Hawaii for 1-1/2 years, so he stayed home. All the kids are in bed except Jim and Joe. Jim isn't home yet from Browns farm where he works after school. Joe is at the Green River boys club at Kent. Donnie and Jim Dad, are talking about buying a boat and going Halibut fishing. Now Jim and Joe are home so we will call it a day. Mom Kessack. P.S. I should have told also that Sissy found a 17 jewel Ladies Bulova

May 10, 1946.

We went to Kent this morning and bought spuds, apples, and sugar. Sugar played hooky today. Dad and Don worked in the garden today. It was very—very warm today, everyone was more or less droopy. No special news today maybe more tomorrow. Mom Kessack.

May 11, 1946 Weather hot.

Well this is Sat, and a busy hot one too. Don and Jim got up this morning and went to work at Murrays 5 and 10. The other kids have all gone to Kent to the school May Parade. Patsy and Yang are in it. This morning a Mrs. Dolan her 2 girls Barbra and Betty came up and claimed to own the watch, but 3 other also claim to own it. Sissy told them she lost it when playing in the canyon, they hunted for a long time but didn't find it. At noon two boys from the ship Donnie was on came and claimed Donnie owed them $9.00 for a knife. Well I just gave them the knife. Hope I done right. Well I'm hungry and very much work to do so I will eat and work. Will write more tonight. My garden looks very promising. Well the day is almost done. Don and Jim earned $6.00 each today. Jim gave me $2.00, Don gave Dad gas money. Don, Jim and Joe went to a show tonight. I'm going to iron awhile and then go to bed. Dad bought a pretty cake that says Mother on it for tomorrow is Mothers Day. Agnes sent a pretty card. Sylvia made one at school. Buzz made a little wooden cart for my windowsill. Dad cut my hair today real short, it feels cool but I look so silly. I will finish now. Mom Kessack.

Sunday May 12, 1946—Weather Cool.

We arose about 8:30 ate breakfast. Joe gave me $4.00—$2.00 he gives me every week to buy eggs with. The other $2.00 was for Mothers Day. I washed the dishes and we went to Martins corner and bought some groceries. Don, Jim and Dad went fishing. Sissy—Buzz—Sugar—Patsy—Yang and Gwenny went to the show, so Kathy and I are home alone this afternoon. I have some pennies to put in Kathy's book. All the pennies in the family are put in a bank for Kathy, she has $18.00 in the FIRST National Bank. That was all saved in pennies. We bought a $18.00 bond for her last birthday. It is much cooler today. I've done the washing, now I will wash the lunch dishes, swept the floors, then mend and iron clothes. If there is more news later in the day I will write it tonight. Alec and Olga that is Jim's brother and wife were here a little while in the afternoon. Dad and I went to the show this evening, Jimmy and Joe went to Auburn roller-skating with Red Roberts. We had hamburgers and coffee at Joe's Place on our way home. Sissy done the dishes and put the kids to bed. So another day. Good Night,-Mom.

May 13, 1946—Weather very cool almost cold.

Got up at five o'clock and sent Don to work, sat and sewed until time for the schoolchildren to get up. Dad went to Auburn this morning, was home for lunch. I washed and ironed. Don, Dad and I went shopping. At 4:30 bought $20.00 of food. John Strovey was up this afternoon. Dad has to work at Epperson's tomorrow. Everyone is in bed now, so I am going to bed too. Mom Kessack.

May 14, 1946 Tuesday. Weather cool.

Well today started out cool and collected enough. Sent, Don off at 5:30. The rest left for school at 8:00 and Dad went to Epperson's. Sugar came home early because the plumbing at Thomas School is all hay wired. About 3:30, The Kent Taxi came up, and out jumped Agnes. Now it's 10 o'clock at night and her and Don are out chasing around. I feel that now our troubles begin. Patsy does not feel so well, the back of her neck is stiff and sore and one leg hurts. I received a letter from Peggy today she says the baby has curls and sits in the corner of the davenport and plays. She says she is very happy with Andy and the baby. I planted a tree in the front yard today. I finished a piece of fancy work today, a dresser scarf with fringe on the ends and Mexican motifs embroidered on. Well I am very—very tired. I do wish Don was in bed, I would like to see him stick to his job and get somewhere this summer, but he certainly won't if he gets to chasing around nights. It has been cool and rain all day. Well this is all the news for today. I close hoping Don comes in very soon. We had brown beef stew for supper, bread and jelly. Mom Kessack.

May 15, 1946 Wed. Warm

Well another has come and gone. Dad worked at Epperson's, Don at Browns. Sugar played hooky again. A letter came from Peggy, she says she is very happy with her baby and husband. Mrs. McCullough brought 4 doz. eggs, she delivers them every Wed. Mr. Feroe a neighbor came down and borrowed a 50 ft cable. The school nurse was here today about Patsy's appointment next Wed. to Red Cross Clinic. No other special news, it's been a rather dragged out droopy day. Mom Kessack P.S. Chuck Groves was here with Agnes tonight, he is from Kent, 6' 2" tall and very handsome. Don is out again tonight. Joe is over to Rogers. So to bed.

May 16, 1946 Thursday Weather hot

Don and Aggie worked at Browns today. Dad worked at Epperson's. All the school children went to school. I washed and scrubbed today. The four little girls—Buzz and Sugar, all had a shower after supper. Gwenny, Kathy and I went to the mailbox at noon. Brownie went with us, he chased all the kids along the way. Junior caught a snake and dragged it into the kitchen. Joe went to boys club tonight. Don is out with Bud. Agnes went to bed early, she has been hoeing beans all day. No special news. We had pork and beans, peas and carrots, new potatoes, radishes and onion, canned peaches for supper. Bread and jam, coffee. I'm sleepy and tired. Goodnight. Mom Kessack

May 17, 1946 Friday Hot

Dad worked at Epperson's and is very tired tonight. Don and Jim worked at Browns. Aggie chased around with Lee Stark all day. Buzz got to go to the State Capital Olympia today with his teacher and principle. We planted more cabbage tonight. Joe burned his hand with lighter fluid tonight. He brought me a pair of rayon stocking tonight, I sure am glad I need them for best. A collie dog followed Joe home tonight. The Roger boys and Purdy boys are over visiting this evening. So to bed. Mom Kessack

May 18, 1946 Sat. Hot

This has been the kind of day-that leaves a person emotionally up set. Jim and Don left at 6 o'clock this morning for work. Joe Agnes and Dad left at eight. I washed—swept and made the beds, and kids lunch all by 11:30. I walked to town and had to turn around and walk right back up the hill because Pop wouldn't give me any money, I really don't like to be shoved around that way. Tonight Agnes gave me $1.00, Jim gave me $2.00, Don gave me $20.00, fifteen to bank for him, and $5.00 for the house. Tonight Agnes is out with Lee stark. Don is out with Buddy Beall, Joe and Jim are out with Buddy Rogers. Buzz went to the show with Gary Cornell's. The rest of the kids are in bed. Dad is laying down reading. I am going to sew and then to bed. Don bought Dad a plaid shirt today. Mom Kessack

May 19, 1946 Sunday Hot

Arose about 8, found out Donnie had stayed out all night with Buddy Beall, and that Buddy Rogers had stayed all night with Jimmy. Well, Bud brought Don home about 10, and Dave Morgan was with them. Arvin a neighbor girl came down and kept them all amused. Alex and Olga came from Carbonado with Grandma and Granddad and they sold their place. Then

Dad and I went back to Carbonado with them, and had supper. Sissy kept house for me. I washed in the morning. Well no other special news. I might say a word here, about the food situation. World War 2 is just nicely over. This country is attempting to help feed the world. It makes food very scarce and hard to get. I have quite a time keeping this large family fed. Well that's all now. Mom Kessack

Agnes brought Butchie over and Dad cut his hair. The rest of the day Agnes and Butch spent at Kent with Chuck Groves.

May 20, 1946 Mon. Cooler but warm

Monday is always sort of a hectic day, cleaning up after Sunday and it is also shopping day, and the little kids are always tired after Sun. Agnes started working at Blessings Café today. Her hours are 4 to 10, her wages 75 cents an hour and meals. She was home until 3:30 so I went to Kent and started Don a bank account, $20.00 savings account. I bought the groceries and walked home, and I am very tired so I'm going to bed. Goodnight. Mom P.S. Joan Brown, Joan Armstrong and Donna Shoud was up looking for the kids tonight. The Kent fire whistle just blew.

May 21, 1946 Tuesday Hot

This morning my neighbor Mrs. Feroe came down for a visit. About 10, Agnes went over and got Butchie, he stayed for lunch and then Aggie took him back to Rogers. I went to

North Road to the mailbox, I received a pretty Mothers Day picture and a card and a small picture of Peggy and her cute little baby. We couldn't get any bread anywhere today. Don planted 36 apricot trees tonight, sure hope they grow. I am tired tonight. I'm going to bed after I write Peggy a letter. Don and Joe are still out. I baked two raisin pies today and we had lamb stew. Goodnight Mom

May 22, 1946 Wed Weather quite cool.

Agnes, Sylvia and I took the 8 O'clock bus to Seattle this morning. We took Sylvia to Red Cross Clinic. Then we went to Rhodes dime store and ate sandwiches and coffee. Then to J.C. Penney's and bought shoes for Agnes and Kathy. Then to Newberry's and bought shoes for Gwenny and rubber balls. Then we walked through Kress's and went to Greens where we bought five pair girl's anklets. Then to Security Market and had doughnuts and coffee. Then to bus depot and to Kent. I done a little grocery shopping, Agnes went to the bank. Then to Joe Blessings and had hot beef sandwiches. Agnes stayed down to work, Sylvia and I walked home. Donnie's check came today. $36.30, he signed it so I can take it to the bank. I will bank $20.00 making him $40.00. I will pay the light bill $7.00—get a sack of feed at $4.00, buy 3 dozen tomato plants at $1.20, bring .75 cents home for the Sat. afternoon show money. Buy food with the rest. Well I done some mending tonight. Sissy kept house very nice today. I am glad we bought her a red purse, she was a good girl. I washed after I came home and cooked supper. We had meatballs in mushroom sauce, boiled new potatoes cream style corn, radishes, green onions and carrot straws, bread and jelly, coffee, milk. The news of the day is railroad strikes and scarcity of bread. Goodnight—I'm tired. Mom Kessack

May 23, 1946 Cooler

Agnes went to work 6 o'clock, came home tired, went out anyway. Jimmy hurt his hand at school and couldn't go to work. Joe is on the schoolboy patrol so got to go to a big picnic at play land today. We were all at supper, at the same time tonight for the first time in a long—long time. All here but Peggy, 13 of us. Mrs. Fox and her granddaughter Kay were over this afternoon to play and visit. Otherwise, it's been quite an ordinary day, wash, eat, etc. So, another 24 hours into oblivion and history. Mom Kessack

May 24, 1946 Friday—Hot

Today Dad and Agnes went to work. Jim and Sugar stayed home and worked in the garden. I went to town and cleared up a lot of messy little jobs, like paying lights, buying feed, and tomato plants, string for the peas and beans, buying the feed, sending for barber license and title to the property. Tonight Chuck came up to see Aggie. Everybody sat around the kitchen and told spooky stories. Joe had to work late tonight and isn't in yet everyone else is asleep. I bought Gwenny a little blue dress today. It is cooler tonight and looks like rain. So to bed I go. Goodnight Mom

May 25, 1946

A busy day as usual. Jim and Don worked at Browns. Aggie at Joe Blessings, Joe at Murrays, Dad at Epperson's. Sissy, Buzz and Sugar went to the show in the afternoon to see Red Ryder and Phocaea. At night, Don went out with Bud, Jim with George Rogers, Joe with Buddy Rogers, Aggie with Chuck. I washed some and scrubbed. No bread or meat to be bought today. They are shipping so much out you can't buy anything. Mom

May 26, 1946 Sunday—Rain a gloomy day.

I washed. We went to Martins corner to get bread and meat, we got neither. Aggie, Jim, Joe, and Don are all out today. Dad is—, Sissy has gone to a birthday party. I'm going to iron, clean up the little kids and when Sissy comes home, Pop and I will go to the show at Kent. If nothing unusual happens this is all I will write today, of course if an unusual occurrence comes up I will be sure to tell you. I kept tract of expenses this week and I find it is costing us $42.00 a week for groceries that is $6.00 a day for an average of 12 people. That is fifty cents a day a person. It does not include milk because we have Red the cow. Well dishes and ironing are waiting for me. Mom P.S. Well leave it to the kids, they are always good for a post-script. Buzz and Sugar walked to the party with Sissy. She was lagging along not thinking she had a present enough for her friend's birthday, they seen a sign on a window Puppies to give away. So they went in and got one and gave it to Donna for a present so the day ends successfully I hope. Jim and Joe are still out. Dad and I went to the show, we seen Bob Hope—Bing Crosby and

Dorothy Lamour in the Road to Utopia. We ate cube steak dinner at Joe Blessings afterwards. It's raining. Mom P.S. The two dinners cost $1.34, the show $1.00 we sure are getting extravagant in our old age. Another week begins tomorrow, the last week of school, the last week of May 1946 and the 1st day of June 1946 on Sat. What more could one little week want?

May 26, 1946 Monday Cold and wet.

Well Monday comes around, Sissy had a sore throat, Sugar didn't have a lunch, Patsy didn't feel good so those three stayed home from school. Everyone was more or less cranky today. And on top of that, it was shopping day. That always gets Pop Kessack up in the air. And to top it off there wasn't an egg for his breakfast and no bread for a lunch, so you can bet your boots by the time he paid $20.00 for groceries, and had to wait for his supper to cook, because the groceries had to be brought home before I could cook them. WOW—Bing, Bang, then finally he got supper and laid down to read his paper. When neighbors Osborne came over yelling the kids had wrecked his electric fence, boy we really got our ears sizzled then. Any way we lived through it all. In the morning I shampooed Sylvia's, Gwenny's and Dee Dee's hair and put em all up in curls. On my way home from town I stopped in to see Mrs. McCullough. She gave me a bouquet of pansies, some aster plants and brought me the rest of the way home. So you see there was a little sunshine this blue, dark Monday. Goodnight Mom

May 28, 1946 Tuesday Rain

Well Sylvia and I took a trip into Seattle this morning to the Orthopedic Hospital to see about her kidney condition. We got soaking wet. We had to walk home from Kent too. Don and Bud were up tonight a while. Gwenny got to dress up in her best clothes today and go to Thomas School picnic with Sugar, they took jello and cookies. They sure had a good time. Gwenny sure looks nice in curls, and a blue dress. I'm tired and cold tonight, its 9 O'clock and everyone else is asleep so Goodnight. Mom

May 29, 1946 Wed. Cool

Today Agnes did not go to work. Just left, without telling them so they could get someone else. Mrs. McCullough came with the eggs today. She brought me a bouquet of roses. We visited a while together. Agnes was home until 2 o'clock, then she went to town. Dad said when he came home from work she was in Dave's Tavern. She came up about seven in a car with a guy named Bonzo, they went to the Brown Derby. She came home about two in the morning. Don didn't come home at all. The iceman came today. No other news except this is the last full day of school this year. Mom

May 30, 1946 Memorial Day—Hot

Dad didn't have to work today. Just Jimmy Jr., he went down to Farmer Browns. Agnes laid around in a house coat all day, just got up for meals. Chuck came up about four. Sissy told him to ask Agnes, where she was the night before and did they scrap. Well anyway, they left here together and I haven't seen her since. Dad worked on the garden all day, it looks real good now. I washed and ironed. A very busy day, but a quiet happy one. Don didn't come home today and wasn't working either. Joe was out late last night chasing around. Well that is all. Mom P.S. Sugars sick all day, stomach and headache. I gave him aspirin and soda and put him to bed.

May 31, 1946 Friday-Cool and rainy

Well today school ends for this season. Dad went to work. The children went to school at 10, and came home at one. Gwenny and Kathy went too. Everybody passed. Jim finished grade school. Sissy enters Junior High next fall. Sugar was still sick today seems to have tonsillitis and the poops. Agnes came in about seven o'clock tonight, she had been to Ellensburg with Chuck. No special news. Mom This is last day of May 1946. Joe came home late, and said Mr. Fox wants to buy 10 barrels. Dad said O.K. We got the barrels from Epperson's. Tonight we decided I wouldn't work out this summer but stay home and sew and can. Agnes gave me $4.00.

June 1, 1946 Saturday Hot

I arose at 5:30 got Jim off to work—then Joe, then Dad. Then fed the little kids—then Sissy & Agnes. Then done the washing and beds. Then Aggie and I went to Kent. There sure was crowds looking for meat and bread, but none could be found. Food is really scarce. Chuck and Aggie was chasing around looking for camera film, no 620, no luck. Chuck brought us all cokes at Guinsteads. I got 2 lbs hamburger 1lb link sausage at Pop Sebastian's Club Cold Storage. I bought 15 lbs spuds, 1lb shortening, 1lb substitute butter, 1lb cheese, 1 loaf bread at Safeway, 2 loafs bread at Stan's and Dee's. Agnes bought 1-loaf bread 1-pkg buns at Guinstead. Then Aggie and Chuck went to his sisters and I came home. My nephew Ed Brown gave me a ride up the hill. His wife Louise and two babies were with him. Tonight Bud Beall and Don were up. Don gave me $6.00. Jim gave me $5.00. Tonight Agnes went to a dance with Chuck. Jim to a show with George Rogers, Joe went to Sears Roebuck with Fritz. The rest are in bed. Dad is reading, I am ironing. Mom

June 2, 1946—Sunday—Threatening Rain

Well I arose late and worked all day but even so, everything went quite smoothly. Nothing unusual happened—no company. Joe went to Auburn with Gordon a neighbor boy. Jim went to Kent in the afternoon with George Rogers. Agnes never showed up all day. Pop and I went for a walk after dark. Then came home and had toasted cheese sandwiches and coffee so to bed. Joe took some pictures of the kids. Hope they are good. Mom

June 3, 1946 Monday Rainy and Sunny—Cool

Got up this morning up at 5:30 sent Jim to work by 6:30. Then watered garden sent Pop to work at 7:30. Then sent Joe to work at 8:30, then, fed the little kids. Made beds, washed clothes washed the dishes—swept floors—made a big pan Macaroni cheese. I had a small piece of lunchmeat left over from the lunches so I cut it in dices and put it in the macaroni and cheese. Sissy said it was delicious. I changed my clothes and hiked to Kent. I banked $11.25 for Jim. Then I met Pop at the other bank he gave me $20.00 for groceries. I bought Sissy some new shoes, a pair of brown oxfords size 3. I paid $2.50 for them. Then some bobby pins and socks, 35 cents. I had quite a time getting bread and meat, all the butcher shops were closed. All the stores out of bread. Finally, I walked home and cooked supper. All the kids except Joe are in bed, he is at a ball game. Agnes never came back. I am making Butchie a little white suit. Nothing unusual today. No news—no company. Mom

June 4, 1946 Tuesday

Jim woke up sleepy this morning but finally off to work at 6:30. Then Pop at 7:30, Joe at 8:30. I sent Sissy, Buzz and Sugar to Kent this morning to get bread and meat. No meat, so they bought fish. Agnes came at noon in a taxi, she ate lunch with us. She is keeping house for Chuck and his father. She left at 2:00 o'clock. Jim worked late tonight 12 ½ hrs today. I got a little sewing done today and ironing. Patsy, Yang and Gwenny played with Jimmy Houlns today. The other kids went to Swanson's. No mail today—no news, no nothing. Good Bye Mom

June 5, 1946 Wednesday

Today the two most outstanding things were. I received a letter from Peggy, she said at last they had a place of their own. A four room apartment and bath. The other, Mrs. McCullough came with the eggs and of course, we visited. The children started gathering cascara bark today, they are trying to raise a fund for carnival day. It was cold and windy today. I finished the little white suit I was making for Butchie. No other news. Joe was out late tonight. Mom

June 6, 1946 Thursday Cool

Sis, Buzz and Sugar-went down to Kent today and helped Mrs. McKinney, she gave them 60 cents. Agnes came up at noon by taxi. An old friend of Dads came up about 1:30 his name is Paul Radford. Agnes and I rode to Kent with him. I done some shopping, he brought me back up and I cooked supper. Now Dad and him are off drinking somewhere. All the kids are in bed but Joe he is out too. I am tired, I'm going to bed too. Good—Nite Mom P.S. A car just came, probably Pop and Paul. I will wait and see. Sounds like another car. I don't know what's cooking will write later. Well it was Pop and Paul and the other car was Bud and Don. Pop, Paul and Bud are pretty much drunk and how.

June 7-8-9 Fri Sat Sun

Well this is a fine howdy doo, have to combine three days in one. Can't remember much about Friday. Agnes came up and brought Butchie over for lunch, then she took him to Kent in the white suit I made him. Saturday I went shopping in Kent with $7.00 Jim Jr. gave me. Don bought a car today, a Ford V-8. $300.00 Pop lent him $250.00. Sunday morning Dons car wouldn't start, Dad, Jim and Dunc fooled around with it all day, finally Bud came up. Put a new gas pump in and some new spark plugs and now she goes. Pop and I went to a show tonight. We seen Clark Gable and Greer Garson in" Adventure". Sat afternoon a former schoolteacher of Sugars brought up four boxes of clothes. Saturday evening Mrs. McCullough brought over one box. I sure have sewing piled up, waiting for me now. A letter from Peggy Friday, I am putting it in the Diary as is. Rain—rain—rain to muchy rain now. Mom

June 10, 1946 Monday Hot

Today I washed clothes, scrubbed floors and went to town and done my weekly shopping. $20.00 worth. I received a chain letter am enclosing it. I answered it as requested and sent out five copies. Hope they all bite. Am enclosing letter and will wait results. Mom

June 11, 1946 Tuesday

Well this was quite an ordinary day. I washed, ironed and cooked. I cut out a dress for myself from two other dresses and the velvet trimmings are from another dress yet. Agnes came home this afternoon. No company today, and no mail. It was very warm today. Joe gave me $5.00 tonight. Mom

June 12, 1946

Agnes started to work at the hamburger express today. Mrs. Feroe came down to visit awhile this morning. Then Mrs. McCullough came with eggs this afternoon and we always visit. I made lemon pies today, yum-yum they were good. I also made ginger cookies. Don ate supper with Jimmie tonight, we had French fried potatoes—green beans—Spanish hamburger-onion—radishes—lettuce—pies. Tonight Joe is staying with Hessy. It is raining—lightning and thunder, a very wild night. Pops back license came today, also a picture of Peggy Ann, our little granddaughter in Cleveland Ohio. Well I stamped a lunch cloth to embroider for Peggy's birthday in Sept. I put Mexican Motif on it. Well, I'm going to sweep the floors sew a bit and go to bed. Goodnight Mom

June 13, 1946—Thursday

Today has been what I would call a rainstorm. Agnes and I went to Kent about 11 to get some meat but, couldn't find any. Finally, I bought a polish sausage. We ate beef stew at the

Bungalow Café, on Agnes. Finally, we came home. While we were away, Mrs. Rogers had been over to see why Agnes and Bud hadn't paid any money on Butch. For a wonder, Joe came home tonight he is getting to run around entirely too much. I've heard rumors that he is drinking. I am at my wits ends to know how to handle the situation. Agnes stayed out all night. Jimmy was out quite late. A Father's day card came for Pop from Peggy so I am putting it in the record too. Rain-Rain—Rain. Thunder—Lightening—Boom—Bang. Mom

June 14, 1946—Friday

Well today is past being a rainstorm, it's a down pour. A load of wood came today. One cord slab wood for $16.48. Mrs. McCullough came over in the afternoon with some Life magazines and a three pound jar of shortening. Something you can't buy in a store anywhere. We visited awhile then Donnie came and wanted me to go to Kent and sign for him to get a driver's license so I did. Jimmie is late getting home tonight. Joe is supposed to be going to a wedding shower on Joan tonight. I hope he is telling the truth, because I don't want him chasing around. Agnes is suppose to be working at the Hamburger Express. It has poured rain all day long and is still pouring. The kids are in an uproar. Tell you, it's awful when they can't get out to play. They tear the house to pieces also my nerves. No meat, no meat don't know what to cook, also no sugar and very little bread and nothing to put on what bread there is. No mail today. Mom

Have been doing lots of sewing. Made Agnes a blouse and Sissy some pajamas.

June 15, 1946

Today was cold, but the rain let up a little. I went to town and bought Father's Day gifts, a pair of pants a shirt to match and after shaving lotion. We all bought it together. I had a talk with Joe about staying out nights and drinking, but I don't think it done much good. He is living a fast life and one that will come to disaster. I shell have to take sharp measures with him I fear. Meat is still hard to get and bread has gone up. It is getting so hard to feed a family. Today I bought ¼ lb butter, the first I've had for about 8 weeks.

Mr. Russell and his wife—former neighbors came in last night. They had whiskey with them, they and Pop drank and talked until one thirty. I don't know why people drink, they look and act so silly. No Joe home tonight. That kid is getting me down. Mom

June 16, 1946 Sunday Father's Day

Agnes came in at 5 o'clock this morning, she had been drinking. Joe didn't come home at all, it now seven o'clock and there has been no word of Joe. I am really worried and I don't dare say much for getting Dad going on about it. The weather has been fairly nice today, no rain not too hot, just comfortable. Dad and the kids worked in the garden today, it sure looks fine. I have a terrific headache, a large ironing to do yet. So, all for today. Hoping Joe comes in soon. Mom

Joe came home about eight, he had been to Enumclaw, Buckley, Carbonado and Seattle. He gave Dad a box of cigars. Agnes got home 12 thirty, she bought Dad a card.

Monday June 17, 1946

I went to town today and done my shopping. Dad cut me down to $15.00 a week. Joe got a week's vacation with pay $24.00, he is going to Yakima. Donnie got his driver's license today. I am tired and unattached tonight, but I have a big ironing to do so I might as well hop to it. No meat in town today-no sugar—no butter, very little bread. Mom

Buzz and Sugar went to the ball game with Gary. Well this is still some more of June 17. It seems in place of going to Yakima, Joe picked up a kid named Quincy Drennan. They went to Auburn, rented a hotel room and went down to the ticket office and bought tickets to Ellensburg. Someone got the bright idea they were running away and notified Auburn Police. They went over to a restaurant to eat. The cops picked them up there and took them to the police station. They found $50.00 on Joe a $1.50 and Knife on Quincy. Well the Sheriff came and woke me up and asked me where Joe was suppose to be, and how much money was supposed to be on him. I told him, and they went back and called Mr. Murray and he said he gave Joe the money. Well finally, at one o'clock in the morning we went to Auburn and got the boys. In the mean time, Agnes came home from work and found all the lights on, us and the car gone. She got all in a dither and went back to Kent. She went to Harborview Hospital, Kent Police and Auburn Police and finally home at 5 in the morning. Boy, what a night and what a let—down for Joe. Mom

June 18, 1946 Tuesday Hot

The visiting nurse was here today in regards to Patsy. Agnes and I went to Kent this afternoon. I spent $3.00 on meat a beef heart, 2lbs liver and a 21/2 lb pot roast. I bought 5 lbs sugar, bread and bakery stuff. Agnes made me ride the taxi home. Joe isn't in tonight. I took $20.00 from him this morning. I put $5.00 in the bank for him. I'm sure worried whether they pick him up tonight, if they do its trouble for all of us and how. Agnes bought some cloth today too. The kids had a party in the woods today. They had cookies, Kool-Aid and watermelon. I should iron tonight but I am too sleepy. Mom

My last prayer is I hope Joe comes in. No Joe yet, Pop is getting hostile.

June 19, 1946 Wed

Well last night we went down to Kent and searched high and low for Joe, no can find, didn't sleep much. Anyway got up and worked, but didn't seem to accomplish much. Mrs. McCullough came with the eggs, they are up to 55 cents a dozen now. Mr. Fox came later in the day to tell me he would be up to get the barrels Friday. The milkman came today. Agnes bought two quarts of milk. Jimmie went to Lake Wilderness with the Roger boys tonight. Mom

June 20, 1946 Thursday

Arose early this morning and rode down with Daddy when he went to work. Sylvia and I went into Seattle to Harborview. We shopped all over town on Joe's money, bought Patsy and Yang some shoes. Several dresses, some flags for the 4th, some ribbon, some ric—rac a chemical garden. We came home on the three o'clock bus. We rode home with Dad when he came home from work. A card from Joe in the mail, he is in Ellensburg and O.K. will be home either tonight or in the morning. I might add I hope. Jimmie is out swimming again with the Rogers. I told him to bring me a bottle of pop, he said he would if he could find any. The kids won't go to bed tonight, they just want to hang around yap—yap—yap. Oh heck, I'm going to bed. Mom

Joe came home at midnight, he had been to Portland, Toppenish, Yakima and Ellensburg. He was tired and glad to get home. At two thirty, Chuck Groves came and knocked on the door, I went to the door and he was drinking. He had a quart of whiskey in one hand and a water glass in the other. He wanted to know where Aggie was, I told him in bed. He asked me what time she came home I said between 7 and 8. He finally went away.

June 21, 1946 Friday

Well it rained all day and I do mean rain. Kids ganged around the house all day. Agnes brought home some pink spun rayon,

I made her a blouse. The books I sent for came. Leave Her to Heaven and When The Sun Goes Down. That's all. Mom

Sat June 22, 1946

Well not to bad weather. Pop got up early. Jimmie worked with Mrs. Brown in the market at Seattle today. Pop is reading Leave Her to Heaven, Agnes went out with Judd Tallmadge. Joe went out with Gordon, Jimmie Jr. went to bed. Mom

June 23, 1946 Sunday

Today was neither hot or cold. Don came up at noon and so did Abbie Stark, he is in the Navy and only 15. This has been a very trying day. Everyone up late, that makes me a long time getting dishes and beds done. Went to Martins to get meat and there wasn't any. Bought $4.00 of other groceries. There was an earthquake at 9:15, quite a sever one. After dinner Mrs. Fox and her granddaughter came. Then it seemed liked I would never get my work finished, finally though I waded through it all and fed them supper. Then Pop and I started for the show, we met Aggie Brown, Jim's sister coming up Strawberry Lane. She told us Granddad Kessack was in a very serious condition, we took her home and visited about ½ hour then went on to the show. We seen, Scarlet Street. We finally came home at midnight, ate butter horns and drank coffee and to bed. Agnes came home after that. Mom

June 24, 1946 Monday

Rain—Rain. The boys could not work on the farm today, so they built a calf pen in the barn and put a lock on Jim's room. We went grocery shopping got $23.00 worth. Now Jim and Joe are remodeling their rooms. Agnes is working, Sissy and Buzz are off with Gary Cornell. The rest are playing wild furious games in the front room. Pop is in the bedroom reading. I am preparing to iron. I sent Grandma Kessack a card today. Poor soul, I feel sorry for, it must be hell to be old. Mom

June 25, 1946 Tuesday

Today was sort of a crazy day. I tried to hurry up things and get done, because I'll be gone tomorrow. As usual when you hurry, you accomplish just about nothing. Pop came home tired and cross. Jim and Dunc worked 11 hours today. Joe stayed all night with his cousin Bobby Brown. I did do a big ironing tonight. Took a hot shower and finally at eleven thirty went to bed. Mom

Wed—June 26, 1946

Well I got everything going early this morning. Took Gwenny and Patsy to Harborview Hospital in Seattle. We caught the 7:30 bus. Gwenny had two teeth pulled. We got back to Kent by one o'clock we ate lunch at Joe Blessings Café. Shopped around a bit. Hired the taxi and came home. Cooked supper, Spanish Hamburger—creamed cauliflower—tossed salad—boiled spuds, it was all good. Well I have more ironing to do tonight, I'm tired and I am canning a 3-quart jar of cauliflower then to bed. Mom

June 27, 1946 Thursday

Got up at 5 this morning and found Donnie in his car asleep in the yard. Guess him and Bud are not getting along so hot. Made lunches and breakfast for the boys and sent them all away to work, then I washed and worked around. This afternoon I made a white skirt for Aggie, it is trimmed in green and yellow rickrack. Tonight Donnie is staying with Jimmie, Joe is painting his room. Some of the neighbor's kids were over to play with our kids tonight. They sure had a good time. I am sleepy tonight, guess I will iron a bit and go to bed. Oh! Hum! Mom P. S. Jim gave me $6.00 for groceries.

June 28, 1946 Friday

Today was one of those days that make you wish you never heard of Washington. It poured rain and I do mean pour, all day long. I washed but couldn't hang the clothes out. The kids had to play in the house all day and believe me it was a mess and a racket. No, mail no nothing, a day so disagreeable I'd rather forget it. Mom

June 29, 1946 Saturday

Today was a mixture of rain and sunshine. I got the washing out, but not dry. The kids played out. I baked a pot of beans and everyone was in a little better spirits. Agnes is working tonight. Don-Jim and Joe went roller skating, the little kids are in bed reading comic books. Dad is reading When The Sun Goes Down. Two letters today, one from Olga saying Granddad is very ill. One from Peggy saying they are well and happy. I have ironing to do so—Tood-a-loo Mom

June 30, 1946 Sunday

The last day of June 1946. Agnes-Donnie-Jimmie Jr., Dad and I went to Carbonado in Donnie's car. Granddad Kessack is very ill. We spent the day with Jim's brother and his wife Olga. We sure had a good time. It was 10 o'clock when we got home. Sissy had the house cleaned up and the kids to bed. Joe spent the day at Lake Meridian with Fritz and Lillian. In the morning, Donnie laid down in his car and went to sleep with a burning cigarette in his hand. He set the car on fire. I really enjoyed myself today. Mom

July 1, 1946 Monday

Agnes and I walked to Kent. At noon, we had baked rib dinner at the 311. I bought $25.00 worth of groceries. The boys worked at Browns today. Pop at Epperson's—Joe at the store and tonight Aggie is working at the restaurant. Agnes bought me a new eggbeater and four yards of outing flannel today. It was nice weather today, not cold—no rain—not to hot, just right. Well I have a large ironing to do so to work I get. Mom

July 2, 1946-3 Wed-4 Thurs-5 Fri-6 Sat

Well, here we are four days behind. Time seems like there isn't enough time to go around anymore. Tues—I just worked and worked trying to get things shaped around for Wed. I took Patsy and Gwenny to Seattle. Pat to the clinic and Gwenny had the other two teeth pulled, then I rushed home, got supper cooked and ate. Pop said we were to go to Tacoma to see Granddad Kessack, in the St Joseph Hospital. So away, we went in Donnie's car. Thursday was the 4th. Dad and Red went with the boys fishing. Sis & Buzz went to Lake Tapps with George Rogers & Sleepy. Agnes laid in bed getting over a drunk the night before. I don't remember much about Fri. Agnes worked—Dad worked—Joe Worked—Jim & Dunc worked. Red came up in the evening and stayed all night. Sam Lee was up also. Mrs. Ashbaugh, brought one of Sugars teachers. Brought a crate of fresh raspberries so we all had berries and cream. Agnes came home sick. Saturday her and I went to Seattle. Sissy kept house again. I've got to quit chasing around and do more work at home. I canned 10 quarts of fruit and vegetable though. The weather is hot. Well I guess that leaves us caught up on things. So ironing—dishes and mopping to do yet tonight, and It's 10 o'clock. Mom

Sunday July 7, 1946

This was one of the easiest Sunday I've had for a long time. I slept until 9, then we had breakfast, and right away, I put dinner on. Everything was cleared away by 2 o'clock. The weather was warm so the kids played out. Supper was served all at one time and so to bed happy. Mom

Monday July 8, 1946

It rained and poured all day. Agnes called a taxi to go to work at 11 so I rode down with her to do my shopping. On my way home, I stopped in to see my friend Sophia Mc Kenny and found her sick in bed. Then on my way up the hill I stopped in to see Mrs. McCullough so home, a miserable day all day rain-rain. Mom

Tuesday July 9, 1946

The weather was clear and warm today. I washed and got some sewing done. I've been reading a book called When The Sun Goes Down. I never read such an out spoken book in my life. Agnes is working tonight. Donnie is out with his car and cousin Bobby Brown. Joe & Buzz and a friend of theirs is camping out in the orchard tonight. Red is expecting her calf any time now. So, so Mom

CHAPTER 4
MY DIARY VOLUME I

November 1964 to July 1965

November 15, 1964

Dear Diary, I am going to call this script my new adventure. I am a widow of three months—I have 12 living children as follows: Agnes Velasquez at Burien in Seattle. She is 39. This is her second marriage. Her husband is Don Velasquez he is 28 years old Spanish. Her divorced husband is Bud Beall he has the three younger children. Pat—Robin and Penny, they live in Kent. Two older children Butch is married to Judy, they have a little girl named Annette. They live in Skyway. Snooks is also married to Mike Fitch. They have a son named Rodney. Thus, you noticed I have two great grand children. Snooks and Mike are going to Colorado. Number-2. Child is Margaret Hudock, she is married to Andy Hudock. They have five children P.G. the oldest is married to Carl Zerker. They live in Virginia near Wash D.C. Tommy is in the Navy. The other three are at home. Charlie, April and Nancy. Number-3 child is Don Kessack he is married to Shirley, they have four children. Wendy, Butch—Linda and Scott. He works on a dairy farm in Renton. Number-4. Son James Jr. he is a Chief in the Navy, he is married to Beverly, they have three children. Jimmy the 3rd—Debbie and Gina. They live at Alameda California. Number-5. Son is Master

Sgt Wm Joe Kessack in the Air Force Germany not married. Number-6. Novella Bogue married to Marvin, seven children Vickie—Robert—Cindy—Patty Sue—Lorri—Twins Billy Joe—Candy Lynn. Live at Kent. [Known as Sissy] Number-7. George Kessack, married to Barbara have three children. Carolyn—Connie and Ronnie. He works on the State Highway lives in Renton-known as Buzz. Number-8. Alex Robert Kessack. Married to Judy, has one son named Bobby. Works on a dairy farm at Bothell. Known as Sugar. Number-9. Sylvia Hamilton, married to Harley, has four children named Bunny—PoPo—Duke and Holt. They live in White Center Seattle. We call her Patsy. Number-10. Geraldine known as Yang Yang. Divorced has three sons Stevie—and Jeff and the 1st unwanted. All have been adopted out. She lives alone at Kent. Number-11. Gwen Norris, married to Fred has four children. Kitten—Freddie—Kathy and the new daughter, I don't know her name yet. He is in the Navy, they live at the time in San Francisco. {New baby is Deborah Lisa}. Number-12. Kathy Geyman. Lives in Vancouver, has three sons Marvin—Ricky and Stevie James. We all call Marvin Boofy. Married to Marvin Geyman, who is presently in a prison camp at Washougal. She is called Dee-Dee. It is her I am going to live with. She is expecting a 4th child. I own a Chevy 57—that is. I still owe $486.00 on it. I am at the present time, at Sissy's house. I am in the process of selling my late husband property to Bogues. I have to have all papers signed etc. before I can leave. It is Sunday Sissy is bathing the twins. Vicki and Robert went to the Wigwam Store to spend their money. Vicki is going to a birthday party this afternoon. Marvin is out Elk hunting. It is a nice sunny day. Shirley Kessack was here for coffee before she went to church. I will write more tonight. At one o'clock Pat Beall came up with going away present for me and Dee Dee. He gave me a beautiful set of glass dishes. I don't know what

Dee Dee got. It was mighty sweet of him. Well Bob Brown was over for about an hour this afternoon. He was married to my late husband sister Agnes, she passed away about five years ago and is buried in the same cemetery Jim is. Hillcrest at Kent. Vicki went to a girlfriend's birthday party this afternoon and Sissy had to go get her. Then we had supper, mashed potatoes veal steak, hot dogs, pork & beans, green salad and milk. Shirley Fitch a friend and her two children Judy and Darrel were over this evening. It is freezing out. The kids are taking their baths and eating ice cream. Mrs. Geyman called tonight. That is Dee Dee's mother-in-law. She was going to come see Dee Dee but she has already moved to Vancouver. Well unless something else happens, this will be it for today. Novella Kessack

November 16, Mon 1964

Well today, I rolled up my little ball of yarn, so to speak. George signed the property papers. I took them to my lawyer, to send on to Gwen & Jim, then to Peggy and Joe. Then I went to Bowen Scarf and signed a new note on the car. Then to Seattle and got a death certificate and birth certificate on Dee Dee's three kids. Pat and I had steak dinners with Aggie at Rozies Café. Then I had the lights terminated. Then dash up to Sissy's. Shirley Kessack and her mother Thelma Smith, and Shirley & Elmer Fitch were there. We visited a while and then Yang Yang and I started for Vancouver. We got stopped at Castle Rock for having no tail light. Well I've finally made it. Now Yang is taking a hot bath. I sure like our new home. So to bed. Mom Kessack

November 17, 1964

Well diary my first day in my new home was very nice. We had cold cereal, hot rolls for breakfast. Dee Dee ironed this morning. I took an hour and half nap, for lunch we had meat loaf mashed potatoes, green salad, corn on the cob. In the afternoon we went to Washougal and Camas, we stopped at a second hand store. I bought a table and four chairs for $7.50, Dee Dee bought a bookcase for 75 cents. We then proceeded to a grocery store. I bought a small percolator and a cookie sheet. Dee Dee bought $23.00 worth groceries. We came home and warmed up what was left from lunch and also had ice cream. Now we all are having hot baths and pizza. It is a beautiful view from our front window. There is the highway, than a row of houses, then the Columbia River, and then the Portland airport, and we can see all the lights of Portland. I wrote letters & Postcards today. I asked Jim if I could borrow $20.00 until I get the property settlement. I sure hope he sends it. Well to bed. Later Alligator. Mom

Nov 18, Wed.

Well a fairly quiet day. Dee Dee washed, we ran out of heater oil. Ordered some, the oilman informed us with our heater we could burn diesel oil so they filled the barrel 45 gals was $7.65. Well now the darn kitchen stove won't burn, so Dee Dee is cooking supper on the electric frying pan and griddle. Marvin and Ricky got into a couple scraps with the neighbor kids, nothing serious. One neighbor down the walk is over efficient, her two small boys each have tricycles and a red wagon, which all must stay exactly put or else. I addressed Christmas cards this morning because I was really bored. I am going to have to find something to do. Dee Dee made hot cinnamon rolls this morning. I think we are having red snapper for super. I doubt if there will be any more news today, but if there is, I'll write about it in a postscript. No mail so goodbye. Mom

Saturday Nov 21, 1964

Well this has been one silly day. We decided we need some draino & a plunger for the toilet, gas for the car and some needed groceries. I had 3 paper dollars, we robbed Ricky's horsey bank and Boofy stood over us watching that we didn't touch his bull bank, which I know is pretty well loaded. We tried to find a shopping center and got lost, so went to Camas. The kids got some penny candy. We had sliced peaches & Tuna fish sandwiches for lunch. Waffles for breakfast. The mailman comes about 4 o'clock in the afternoon, I got a most interesting gab sheet from Sissy. A letter from Joe who has been very sick, also a nice letter from Bev & Jim they sent me a personal $20.00 check and said it was an early Xmas present. We went to Safeway Store in Vancouver and bought $8.00 of groceries including a 9 lb turkey for Thanksgiving. We came home and had a delicious supper. Breaded pork chops, mashed potatoes & a green salad. Dee Dee gave the boys a hot bath while I answered the letters. We will soon go to bed. Plan on going to see Marvin at the honors camp tomorrow. It looks like rain, kids played in the house today. Mom

Sunday Nov 22, 1964

Well this was one day and a half. Pouring rain. We went to Washougal Honor Camp to see Marvin, he seemed glad to see us but nervous as all get out. The kids were pretty good, but got kinda wound up so we left at 3. Got home about 4. Dee Dee fried chicken & corn and mashed potatoes. It was good but the kids were wound up and wouldn't eat. A special delivery letter didn't help any of us much. It was from Seattle welfare and it don't look good for either one of us. Hope we get our rent one way or another. We will go to Vancouver tomorrow and see what we can do. Boy, my fingers and legs and everything I got is crossed. Please lady luck be with us now. I have a headache. Go now. Mom

Nov 23, 1964

Boy this was a day. Better, not write about it. It poured rain all day, everybody was tense and got on each other's nerves. We discussed money problems. I wrote a letter to Huebanks to see if they would make me a $300.00 loan pending settlement of the property. I called Sissy long distance cost $1.90 and I am no wiser than I was. We don't know whether Dee Dee's welfare check will come here or not. If it don't we will be kicked out of here and that is for sure. Well to bed, rainy weather, broke and all. Sissy said Yang is running around with Bobby Evert's so there is no hope of sending the $50.00 she owes me on the car. Well Goodnight. Mom

Tuesday Nov 24, 1964

I'll start out no mail, no male, no nothing, oh, I'll take that back, rain-rain-rain. Well no relief in sight for rent. The oil barrel is less than half full, just enough milk for baby till morning. I have $2.00 in change, but Dee Dee said we would shake Boofy's bull bank tonight after he goes to sleep. If things get to bad, I'll sell the spare tire. We have all been in better spirits today. I read 5 little golden story books to the kids this morning. Took an hour nap this afternoon. The kids have been pretty good, they are playing trailer houses. Do—Do is asleep, it is 5 o'clock I suppose he will fuss tonight. We had fried potatoes wieners, macaroni and cheese, little green peas and peaches. At least we eat good. Mom

Wednesday Nov 25 1964

Well it's the day before Thanksgiving. We robbed the bull bank last night of about $7.00. We went to Camas today bought gas and oil with pennies. I baked bread rolls and pumpkin pies and made stuffing and stuffed the turkey. It has rained again all day. Guess we are getting use to it. Huebanks turned me down flat. Well I sure hope Dee Dee gets her welfare check so we can pay Dec. rent. I have a headache tonight and feel grouchy. No other mail. Anything happens tonight I'll sure let you know. Mom

Thursday Nov 26, 1964

Thanksgiving Day, quiet to the point of boredom. We had a nice full course Turkey dinner, lace tablecloth, candles and all. Dee Dee waited all day for Yang & Pat, but they didn't show up. It was very cold and rained, hailed and snowed all day. We watched Macy's big parade on television. We used the new dishes that Pat gave me. Stevie James is cranky tonight. Boofy & Ricky are happy, they helped Dee Dee burn rubbish outside. I have a twitchy eye and a headache tonight. Well if anything happens later, I'll sure let you know it is five o'clock. Mom

We played two games of scrabble, I won one and Dee Dee won the other.

Friday Nov 27, 1964

Stevie James cried all night, he was sick, cried most of the day. Had 103 fever. I went to the neighbors and borrowed soda. Her girlfriend and baby was there, we had coffee & gabbed. I came home, Dee Dee went to get a syringe so we could take down Stevie's fever. While she was gone, a woman came from the Vancouver welcoming committee and left some free coupons. This afternoon two punks came to the door looking for a girl that use to live here by the name of Shirley. Just after dark, I went looking for a milk box to leave a note for the milkman. The neighbors weren't home and there was ½ gal milk, so I took the milk and tore up the note. I felt a thousand eyes upon me, but done it anyway. Dee Dee got a nice letter and card from Geymans. I got a letter from Gwen. We had beef-aroni and toast for supper. It rained all day. The day of rent is drawing near and us with no money. Well who knows. I'll let you know. Mom

Saturday Nov 28, 1964

Well day of days. Stevie James was very, very sick this morning, so we all got in the car and headed for Vancouver. We found a doctor. He gave him a penicillin shot, he has a throat infection. We brought the kids home and fed them. Stevie slept most of the day. Dee Dee done the work and I sent her out with the $2.00 cash we had and the $1.00 free slip. I told her to sell the spare tire so we could get some gas, meat and stove oil. Nobody would buy it. We are almost out of oil. I tried to charge some and got nowhere fast. Well it looks like we will hit the dirt bottom before things get any better. I think I will call Buzz collect and get $8.00 and send me. There is still $10.00 in the bank acct. Stevie is lots better. We had creamed tuna fish, green peas and mashed potatoes for supper. I just made peanut butter fudge. Well anything happens more I'll write about it. Raining and no mail. Mom

Sunday Nov 29, 1964

Got up bright and early, had fried spam & eggs. Went looking for Clark County Hospital, we found it on T street. They gave little Stevie James a penicillin shot. We came home and Dee Dee went to see Marvin. Boofy & Ricky went to. Stevie and I stayed home. He was real good and is much better. They got home about four thirty, they had seen lots of snow and a deer. We had fish cakes, mashed potatoes and green beans. I mixed up cinnamon cookies but couldn't get the oven to work. We went to a nearby shopping center. I tried to call Buzz collect but no one was home. So called Sissy and told her to get a hold of him and have him send $8.00 airmail special delivery, so we can get stove oil and milk. I told her also to find out what's with my lawyer and the property deal. Sure hope Dee Dee gets her welfare check, it will help solve a few problems. Well Dee Dee is making popcorn think I will go to bed. Mom

Monday Nov 30, 1964

Another rainy one. We had $1.10 in pennies so went to the store and bought 1 can Simalac and 6 jars baby food. A man came around with free samples of Ajax washing soap. That was a good deal, we needed soap. Nobody home next door so we waited until dark and got that box too. Sure is something odd about next door. A woman with dyed red hair and two small children moved in and stayed two nights, took off in an old heap and never came back. She had Arkansas license. We had spaghetti for supper. We also got ½-gallon free milk from the Mayflower milkman, which came in a darn good time. I have been on the sick side today, poops, stomachache, headache. I took two aspirin and a rest, feel a little better. I received a letter from Joe offering his help, he has helped so much I absolutely won't ask for more. I'm on my own now, I've got to figure things out for myself. I expect my kids to help themselves and the least I can do is practice what I preach. Famous last words. I haven't the least idea when or how to begin. Thus another day. Mom

December 1, 1964

Well eight o'clock this morning special delivery letter from Barbara with the $10.00 in, boy what a relief the oil was on its last drop, we were out of baby food and milk. We hit for Camas and stretched that $10.00 bill, like it was made of rubber. The mail man didn't come until five o'clock tonight, but brought a nice newsy letter from Sissy so big in fact there was 8 cents postage due on it, and man the letter speaks for itself. Nice letter from Peggy too. Finally, Jim and Gwen have signed the papers and sent them on to Peggy who in turn will send them on to Joe. And speaking of Joe I finally decided to borrow $50.00 until the property settlement. I'm afraid things would be pretty bad around Xmas if I don't. Well I have letters to write. We had hamburger, mashed potatoes, green peas, black cherry jell-o. It's raining although the little boys played outside about an hour today while Dee Dee waxed floors. Our house is very comfortable. Mom

December 2, 1964 Wednesday

Well this was just a day, nothing lost, nothing gained. Rained all day. Dee Dee ironed, I did nothing just as blank as that. I wrote and mailed letters to Sissy & Peggy. We went up to the shopping center to buy four stamps. Boofy and Ricky each spent five pennies on penny candy. Kids have sure been good today. Well it's five o'clock if anything happens I'll let you know. We went over Dec. budget, it sure looks sick. Dee Dee got a letter from Marvin. I did make peanut butter fudge. We

117

had fried potatoes with wieners cut up in them and corn for supper. Mom

December 3, 1964 Thursday

Well today, the mailman was good to us. A card from Peggy, a letter from Judy, a very nice card from Joe with $20.00 in for Xmas. Well believe you me we hit for Camas. I filled the car with gas and got five gallons oil for the stove then $10.00 for groceries. $4.50 at the dime store. We had steak and salad for supper. Stevie James stood up alone today. I got some pillowcases to embroider for Joe when he gets married. We are making out Xmas cards to mail. Well things will be shaping up. Sure hope the welfare check comes tomorrow or Sat, otherwise the River of life rolls on. Mom

December 4, 1964 Friday

Well this was a day blessed by the Saints. The welfare check got here special delivery about 9. We went to a Vancouver Safeway and got $32.00 groceries, then over the tall bridge to Portland Oregon to a great big store just over the bridge. Spent $15.00 there, more or less on Christmas. Came home and had hamburgers, got our oil tank filled and paid our rent. The Landlady said her husband would bring us a Christmas tree and some holly. Later Dee Dee and the boys went to a shopping center and picked up a few items. We have had our supper—chili, garlic bread and peaches. Now Dee Dee is making an artificial fireplace for Xmas. So another page is written. No other mail, it is raining. Mailed a bunch of Xmas cards. Mom

December 5, 1964 Saturday

Dear Diary this has been a quiet day, more or less. We roasted a small turkey no particular reason, it just low priced and we needed meat. We mailed about 30 Christmas cards today. Got a letter from Gwen today. She wanted everybody's addresses. So I sat down and answered it. We went to the shopping center, bought a Xmas stocking for Stevie James and some scotch tape, also 3 small candy canes. I made chocolate fudge. The mysterious red head came back last night and moved out this morning in a blue car from Puyallup Wash. A black headed woman was driving. It's turning cold. The neighbor boys are putting lights on an outside Xmas tree. Well if anything else happens tonight, I'll let you know. Mom

December 6, 1964 Sunday

Well today, I baby sat Marvie and Stevie James. Dee Dee and Ricky went to see Marvin. It is very cold today. Our house is warm. I baked a white cake and made whipped cherry jello boiled spuds creamed leftover turkey and green beans. No company. A little neighbor boy named Mike played with Marvie a little while. So to bed. Mom

December 7, 1964 Monday

Well this was a pretty good day. I started to embroidery a pair of pillowcases. After lunch, we took the kids for a ride and bought them some ice cream and cupcakes. Dee Dee went to meet Marvin by the bridge tonight. She took him a bottle of wine. Well hope they don't get caught. I baby sat, the kids were good. We watched Little Beaver. Pouring down rain. Me & Dee Dee each got a Xmas card from Hamilton's, no other mail. Mom

December 8, 1964 Tuesday

Well we got up early and went to Vancouver to Clark County Welfare and requested that Dee Dee's welfare be transferred from King County to Clark County. It only took a few minutes. We went to Vancouver Goodwill and each bought a small article. We came home Dee Dee waxed floors and washed. We decorated the front window for Xmas. We had spaghetti and French bread, cherry jello for supper. We went for a ride after dark to look at the pretty Xmas lights people put up. I received a Christmas card from Stella Fox. Played scrabble so to bed. Mom

It's raining I have a headache.

December 9, 1964 Wednesday

Well today was a day, and I do mean a day. I got $50.00 money order and a letter. The letter speaks for its self. I was so mmmmad. I went to the shopping center and bought some groceries and a few Xmas gifts. Then I gave DD $15.00 and took $15.00 and came over to Seattle to wind up my little ball of yarn so to speak. I want also to find out who wrote to Joe. I called Shirley from the bus depot and she came and got me. So I am staying with them tonight. I called Buzz & Barbara also Aggie she is coming to get me tomorrow. I am visiting with Shirley and Judy. Mom

December 10, 1964 Thursday

I have had a very nice day. I ate breakfast with Don & Shirley, went out to visit Sugar & Judy. Aggie came and got me at 10. We went down to see Yang. She looks terrible. Aggie gave me a nice red and white overnight bag and took me out to roast beef dinner at Andes Café. Then up to Sissy's. I called my lawyer this morning and Hughbanks this afternoon. I guess the papers will be settled any day now. I will write a letter to Dee Dee and the boys now. Also to Kathy and Jerry Norns in Spain. Mom

December 11, 1964 Friday

A rather pleasant day. Sissy, the twins and I met Marvin by Harborview Hospital than went to Donahugh Loan Co to sign the papers, it will be about Tues before I get the check. We stopped at Benson Center on the way back. I mailed Dee Dee a letter, hope her and the kids are all right. Vicky went to her first dance tonight. The Jingle Bell Hop at Kent. She looked like a little doll. The other kids went to a puppet show, except Robbi went to Renton to guitar lessons. Sugar & Judy & Bobby Joe were up a few minutes. Mom

December 12, 1964 Saturday

I went shopping with Sissy this morning, she bought $60.00 of groceries. Spent the day until four o'clock at her house. Then Buzz came and got me. I am now at their house. We just had a very nice supper. It is bitter cold out. I called Mrs. Geyman, she is meeting me at Sissy's to give me gifts for Dee Dee kids. Mom

December 13, 1964 Sunday

When I woke up Barb, Buzz and their children were at church. I took my pills and waited for them. They came and we all had a breakfast visit. Barbra is making some very clever Christmas decorations. Like a gold wreath out of pinecones, a small Xmas tree for the table out of noodles, some angels, just real clever. We discussed my problems and they voiced their opinions and what I should do about them. In the afternoon, we drove out to Northgate to see Patsy & Harley on their Christmas tree lot. They are sure rolling in the dollars. They had us come back by White Center and pick up my Xmas gift at their house. We went back home, had hamburgers and canned peaches. Then I took a two-hour nap. I called Shirley to come and get me to stay overnight and see some movies they had taken. Don came after me and we ate fried chicken, baked potatoes, baked squash, salad, pumpkin pie with whipped cream. Then he took me to his place and we watched the movies. Pop was in one, it sure reminds me how alone I am. Well so, to bed, another day God has granted me to live. Mom

December 14, 1694 Monday

I ate breakfast with Thelma Smith, then had coffee with Judy. Then Thelma took me to Yang Yang's, then her and I went to Sissy's. Then we went to Renton and had our hair shampooed & set. Then we went and had coffee & hamburgers. Then we went to Woolworths and then Newberry's then back to Sissy's. Shirley Fitch was there and gave me a Xmas present and Snook's address. Now I am very sleepy and will soon go to bed. Oh yes, I heard from Dee Dee and the boys. She said they are O.K. Mom

December 15, 1964 Tuesday

This was a day for rattlesnakes. At 9 o'clock this morning, I called Hughbanks to see if there were any hopes of getting the check. WOW no. The wreck Sugar was in 5 or 6 years ago is against the place and that is just that. I was so darned upset, I walked to Kent and then to Yang Yang's. I found her so ill she couldn't stand up. I called Sissy, we got her to Dr. Phillips. He said it was ruptured Appendix. We took her to Auburn Hospital, she has been operated on. I called her landlady and told her. Bogue's brought her car up and drained it. I wrote Dee Dee a special delivery letter telling her, I talked to my lawyer he thinks he might be able to straighten things out. I have honestly given up. I hope I can pay the car off and settle my bills at least. I suppose if I have to, I can go to work and support myself. I have four pills left that I have to have daily. Maybe some sucker will let me charge some to keep going a while longer. Boy when your left alone you stand alone. God give me strength and show me the way. It's cold and snowing. We had Moose steak for supper.

December 16, Wednesday.

Well I talked to my lawyer twice today, he held out some hope. Bob Brown came over and visited today. Shirley Fitch took me to the hospital to see Yang Yang. She is very sick girl. I talked to Dr. Phillips on the phone. He didn't commit himself to much. She will be in the hospital several days he did say. It is very—very cold, down to zero. The water was frozen this morning. Bogue has been gone all day to a business meeting, will probably come home lit to the stars. Sissy baked cookies all day. We had roast moose tonight. I didn't feel too good today, to many mixed up emotions. I talked to Sugar on the phone, all I got was evasive answers. Mom

December 17, 1964 Thursday

Well Aggie came up this morning, I went with her to Penny's, she didn't find what she wanted there so we went to the Wigwam and bought a $8.00 radio for Penny. We had coffee and doughnuts at the A&H drug store. We came back to

Sissy's she gift wrapped the radio and left. I then went to Kent with Sissy. I left my medicine bottles at the Dr. Office and then Sissy gave me $20.00 for Xmas, we went to the Wigwam. I bought Yang a bathrobe and slippers, myself some sox's, a 5lb box of chocolates for Geymans from Dee Dee and the boys. We came home, I wrote a letter to Dee Dee and we went to see Yang Yang. She was cussing out the nurse and Doctor. She is a very sick girl. Well when we got back to Sissy's here was Dee Dee and the boys. Then this evening Shirley Fitch and Mrs. Geyman came, well it was a couple hectic hours then they left and Dee Dee & the boys went down to sleep at Dons house. It was 22 degrees and snowing. We had moose stew for supper, and a highball before we went to bed. Mom

P.S. Lawyer said to stand by, he has things rolling.

December 18, 1964 Friday

Well I spent the day at Sissy's. Dee Dee and the boys came up and we baby sat Bogue's kids while Sissy and Marvin went Xmas shopping. Then they watched Dee Dee's kids while we went to see Yang Yang. We found her very sick and very despondent. We came back and had fried chicken supper. Then Dee Dee and the boys went to Don's to stay. Sharon Gifford came up and baby sat Bogues kids, Marvin Sissy & I went to Kent. They bought Sugar and Judy a steam iron for Xmas. We went to the P&F Tavern, they had beer, I had loganberry wine. Then we went to the Pied Piper and had more of the same. Then went to the White Spot. Everywhere was very quiet and dead. We went to the Chinese Lantern and ate Chinese food and then home and to bed. It is still freezing and snowing. Mom

December 19, 1964 Saturday

Well miserable day, it snowed and snowed. Dee Dee drove up from Dunc's, she and Vicki baby-sat. I went with Sissy and Marvin to do their shopping. We couldn't go to the hospital, the roads were too bad. Butch and Judy came up and Dee Dee rode down to Dunc's with them. Now I don't know how she will get back up here. Sissy was baking cookies-cookies-cookies, so I went to bed. Mom

December 20, 1964 Sunday

Well if there is such a thing as a dead day, this was it. Snowed and blowed and nothing else happened. I read the Sunday paper an article on Xmas in Seattle 1909. Slept most of the day. Called Dee Dee she was at Donnie's house. We had elk burgers for supper, it was good. So that was it. Outside me phoning the highway patrol to find out road conditions to Vancouver. I was informed they had 9 inches of snow, which started to thaw and then froze and that traffic was impossible. Mom

December 21, 1964 Monday

Well I went with Bogue's three times today Christmas shopping. Dee Dee went home today, she called at four thirty and said she got home O.K. We had creamed tuna on toast and green beans and cottage cheese salad for supper. I laid down and went to sleep. Sissy and Marvin got real drunk on whiskey. At three in the morning, he took Billy Joe out of his crib and was going to take off with him. He also got Robert out of bed and dressed and was going to take him too. The argument went on until five in the morning, then Bogue conked out. No talk with my lawyer today. Dam I'm getting mad. Mom

December 22, 1964 Tuesday

Well this morning Sugar & Judy & Bobby came up. I just had coffee and my pills. They wanted me to go with them and so I did. We had breakfast at Meeker Café. I had 2 hotcakes, bacon, a fried egg and coffee. Then he took me to the lawyers. The lawyer said I was to sign a bunch of papers tomorrow. Like I don't have any adopted children, yes God with twelve of my own it sounds crazy. I have to sign that Dad don't owe no bills, and that the recent illness and funeral is paid. I won't get my check before Xmas, so I will go to Vancouver and come back again. Well then, we went to the Wigwam Center. Sugar gave Judy $28.00 to Xmas shop with. He bought her present in the drug store and had it wrapped. He also bought Bobby a red wagon. Then we came back to Bogues. Sugar left Bobby & Judy out to visit Lacey's. He and I took the presents to his house and then came back to Kent. We stopped at the Roadside Inn. He had a beer and I had a loganberry wine.

Then he gave me $10.00 on the upcoming bill. He then went to the liquor store and bought a bottle of Whiskey and a bottle of Vodka. We then went to Bogues and got Judy & Bobby and went to Auburn to see Yang Yang. He took Bobby with him and let Judy and I out at the Hospital. He said he would come and get us in thirty minutes. He came back in an hour and forty five minutes. He was mighty drunk. He took us to the Town & Country for dinner. He ordered the waitress around and yelled at Judy & Bobby. Well anyway, we ate, I had chicken fried steak. Then we went up to Bogues. I laid down for a rest and they left. Me and Sissy are going to town later this evening. Anything interesting happens I'll sure let you know. Mom

Sugar gave me $10.00.

December 23, 1964 Wednesday

Well this morning I went to the IGA Supermarket with Sugar and Bobby and done Judy's grocery shopping. She was home cleaning house. The groceries came to $63.00. Sugar said it was for two weeks. I came back to Bogues. Sissy was baking cookies. Vicki got a present through the mail from a boy named John. At one thirty, Sissy took me to my lawyers to sign more papers. "O" me it said we didn't have any adopted children, don't know why we would adopt any when we had twelve. Well Yang got out of the hospital today. She went to stay with Sugar and Judy. They will take good care of her. I'm going home tomorrow. Mom

Sissy gave me $15.00.

December 24, 1964

Well I got up at six thirty. I was informed, that Sugar is in Kent jail with $162.00 fine. I rode into Seattle in the little red truck. At nine I got the bus for Vancouver, man was it loaded. Stopped at Chehalis for coffee break. Between Kelso and Vancouver, a car had gone in the river and the highway patrol were trying to rescue bodies. I got into Vancouver at three o'clock, took the cab home. Cost me $1.60. I opened all the mail that had accumulated. Peggy sent me six one-dollar bills, which I put to one side to go back to Kent on after the New Year. Dee Dee and I took the kids to a shopping center and bought $15.00 of groceries. Filled the car with gas. We came home and had hamburgers and potato chips. The kids opened their presents and are very happy. Poor little devils, didn't get much but appreciated what they did get. Now I'm going to bed, Dee Dee's feet are terribly swollen. Mom

Xmas day 1964

We had a nice quiet day. Had scrambled eggs and toast for breakfast. Then I had a nice hot bubble bath. At fifteen to twelve, we went to Washougal Honor Camp to see Marvin. The roads between the fish hatchery and the camp were bad. We had a nice visit. Hot coffee, Ham sandwiches and potato chips. The cooks gave the boys each a sack of candy and nuts. There were three little deer's running around the grounds. Marvin made Dee Dee a jewelry box lined with red velvet and a nice planter with a plant in it, and play knives for the boys.

We got home about five. For supper we had fried ham, potato salad, fruit salad, hot pork& beans, pickles, olives, jello and Dixie cups. We had pop to drink. A very nice day. Mom

December 26, 1964 Saturday

Well this was a quiet no account day. I sewed on the pillowcases. Dee Dee cleaned house. We went to Camas this afternoon and got stove oil. We also went to our own shopping center. We got some minute steaks, soup, crackers and ice cream. We came home and had a nice supper. I took a nap. Then Dee Dee and I played scrabble, she beat. We are now watching television. I wrote a letter to Peggy. Mom

December 27, 1964 Sunday

Well it was a quiet day. Dee Dee went to see Marvin this afternoon. I watched the kids. I was happy to see her get out alone for a few hours. The kids were good, we read stories and played games. The boys went out and played Army games with the little neighbor boys for about thirty minutes. The Landlord came by and visited a few minutes. He has a davenport and chair he will sell us for $20.00. I told him I would get it when I came back from Kent. I had supper ready when Dee Dee got home. We had minute steak, green beans, spuds and left over macaroni. Dee Dee brought home one large Pepsi and cupcakes for a surprise. Rained most of the day, now it's turning cold so another day has past. Mom

December 28, 1964 Monday

This morning we hit for Vancouver Welfare. They told Dee Dee she could come to their office on the fourth and pick up her check. A lady will be out Wed and fill out her papers. It snowed like mad all morning. I bought a bus ticket to Seattle and gave Dee Dee what I had left. We went to Camas and bought five gallons stove oil. $1.00 in gas and 1-quart oil for the car. The rest went for Similac and baby food." Bong" we are broke. We had tuna fish and noodles, green peas and mashed potatoes for supper. We played scrabble and Dee Dee beat. The Landlord said he might bring the davenport and chair tonight. It quit snowing and has turned cold. No mail. Mom

December 29, 1964 Tuesday

Well I sewed on the pillowcases all morning. The rest of the day watched television. The landlord brought the davenport and chair, they aren't much but will serve their purpose very nicely. I can pay him later. It's turning cold. Hope our oil holds out. We had fried ham, mashed potatoes, creamed styled corn and jello for supper. No mail, no visitors, no nothing. So another day. The welfare women are due tomorrow. Mom

December 30, 1964 Wednesday

Well, quite a day. I had baked bread rolls and made Spanish rice. I went over to Jeans house and listened to the neighborhood gossip. It seems this Shirley lives with some guy and two Negro's, and they are all going to Kodiak Alaska. Well I called the oilman and he delivered a barrel of diesel and let us charge it. The welfare lady came out and made out Dee Dee's welfare papers. She said the check should be there by the 4th or it might be delayed. Now we are worried because Stevie is almost out of Similac and baby food, and every time we feed him from the table, he gets asthma. Dee Dee got a letter from Tommy and evidently, it was Sissy that wrote the wild letter to Joe. Well I don't know what she gained, but it might teach her not to gossip so much. It snowed all day and is quite cold. We played two games of scrabble. I sewed on the pillowcases. It is five o'clock. The kids have their pajama's on. Dee Dee is making popcorn. So another day. Mom

December 31, 1964

Well another day and another year. I baked some sick looking cupcakes, parker house rolls and a pot of beans. I finished the embroidery work on the pillowcases and started to crochet the edges. It has been rainy, cold and miserable all day. Dee Dee and the boys robbed the piggy banks and got two cans of Similac and one jar baby food for Stevie James, some penny candy and one pack cigarettes. Boy, big shopping day. It's really something to be left alone and especially with kids. Dee Dee got a letter from Marvin, there is two feet of snow where he is. I got a nice letter from Barbara. The gal across the way sent her boy over to see if I would baby sit eight kids tonight, I definitely said no. I stopped the milkman this morning and got two dozen eggs and one-gallon milk on credit. Well this is New Years Eve. We will probably just go to bed. And I don't think it's such a bad idea. I'm going to take a bubble bath. Big Deal. Mom

January 1, 1965

Well this was a slow day. I baked buns and made a big stew. We are down to fix what we can find. I had four potatoes one can sliced carrots, one can peas, one can welfare roast beef and a small can hot sauce. I simmered it all together, thickened the juice and it was good. We played two games of scrabble, Dee Dee beat. It rained all day. I don't know what we will eat tomorrow. Mom

P.S. A big blue station wagon turned over in the ditch by our house. The Vancouver Police and a tow wagon came and pulled them out. All this about nine o'clock.

January 2, 1965

Well another day of rain and boredom. I baked a clustered pie and made the kids cinnamon sticks. Dee Dee flagged down the milkman and got two quarts milk and one quart orange juice. Dee Dee scared up enough pennies to get a package of cigarettes, so we all rode up to the store. We got two letters, one from Peggy and one from Gwen. Peggy enclosed a letter she got from Joe about me and Dee Dee, that caused such an eruption. I should think with seven kids and a husband she would have enough to do minding her own business. I don't know why I feel sorry for Joe, Sissy or Dee Dee. I do know one thing I'm going to live my own life. I get along with Dee Dee and as long as I'm happy, what the heck? Mom

January 3, 1965 Sunday

Well we got up at eight thirty, had oatmeal for breakfast. I boiled a pot of Kidney beans with hot sauce. For supper we had instant mashed potatoes with creamed tuna fish some corn and beats and a can of sardines. Dee Dee washed today. The kids played in the house all day. We couldn't go see Marvin today because we are low on gas and are BROKE. I hope Dee Dee gets her welfare check tomorrow. I don't think she will, so we will have to sell something somewhere. Baby only has one can Similac left. I have to go back to Seattle tomorrow and I hate like H—to leave them broke. Mom

January 4, 1965 Monday

Well we left home at ten o'clock. We took the patio grill, the radio, a set of glasses and the sewing machine. We tried hocking them and got nowhere fast. We went to the welfare office and sat for 1 ½ hours to be told no check. We went to the second hand store and got $2.50 for the grill, radio, and glasses. I took the 50 cents and got out at the bus depot. Poor Dee Dee, I don't know how she is going to manage, but

I hope the good Lord takes a hand and does something. All the way to Seattle, we traveled through snow. At Chehalis, I bought two small doughnuts, cost me 21 cents. Got into Seattle fifteen to eight, the Kent bus left at nine thirty. I got into Kent and called Bogue. He came and got me and bought hamburgers and French fries. Boy, oh boy it tasted good. So to bed. Mom

January 5, 1965 Tuesday

Well I called my lawyer this morning, he informed me I have to sign a note for the other lawyer and that it will take five to ten days to get my money. I sure didn't figure on it taking that long. I talked on the phone to Barbara and Patsy and Aggie. Aggie and Don were in a bad wreck in a snow blizzard down by Eureka Calf. It took them forty-eight hours to get back home. It should have only been about sixteen. I had a quiet rest today. I made two hot mats. I'm sure worried about Dee Dee, and the boys with no money or food. Aggie came up tonight and gave me a check for five dollars. I'll cash it tomorrow and send her $3.00, it ain't much but better than nothing. I had a nice supper but kept wondering if the little boys had any. Sure, hope she gets help soon. Mom

January 6, 1965 Wednesday

Well Yang showed up at nine thirty. We went to Kent. I cashed the five-dollar check at Safeway, I went to the post office and mailed $3.00 to Dee Dee special delivery and gave Yang $1.00

for gas. We went to White Center and had lunch with Patsy. She had fish cakes, corn, hash browns and macaroni salad. And piece cake. We then came back to Kent. We went to the Chinese lantern and had coffee. Left Dee Dee's Social Security number and address so George could send her income tax thing. Came back up to Sissy's. Oh yes I stopped at Penney's in Kent and talked them into letting me have $15.00 credit. The man say's well what is it you need? I said well a change of underwear and a birthday gift for Patti Sue. He actually blushed. I got a pink and white check housedress, a slip, panties, anklets and six yards of flannel, an umbrella for Patti Sue. I talked to Barbara on the phone and Buzz called me later. We had fried chicken for supper. I would sure sleep better if I knew Dee Dee and the boys are O.K. Mom

January 7, 1965 Thursday

A good day all around. I hemmed five diapers for Dee Dee's expected baby. Yang came up, we went to my lawyers at eleven thirty. The office girl said come back at noon, so we went to Andies Café, had hot soup and milk went back to my lawyers he said come back at four thirty. Man I love this crazy run around. We went down to Judy's and Sugar's. They got the $5.00 from Dee Dee so I know now she got her check. What a relief on my mind. I just mentally relaxed. Came back up to Sissy's and watched the Secret Storm on T.V. Looks like Amy might hang on to Kip or else he is a good liar—like most men are. We had coffee then back to my lawyer. I signed the last of the papers. I should get my check next week. O.K. blessed thought. Then back to Sissy's we had pot roast with vegetables. I really enjoyed my supper. I talked to Jim long distance and I enjoyed that too. He invited me down and I accepted. As soon as my business is settled. Well I watched Peyton Place at nine thirty so to bed. Mom

January 8, 1965 Friday

Well I received the enclosed letter from Dee Dee. She sent back the $3.00 that I sent her. I went shopping with Sissy and the twins. Sissy bought groceries and birthday presents for Patti Sue. Yany Yang, Judy and Bobby were up a little while. We had hamburgers for supper, fruit salad, pork & beans. I laid down to rest after supper. Ed Brown called that Bob had died and his funeral will be Monday. Well another of us is sure to go before long. Things always goes by three's. Mom

January 9, 1965 Saturday

Well everything at Sissy's was in an uproar today, getting ready for Patti Sues birthday party. Vicki and Carol Lacy decorated then took off for the show. I gave Vicki 50 cents, I told her not to tell. All the kids came and so did Shirley and Elmer Fitch. Elmer and Bogue are drinking whiskey. Buzz came and got me. I had a nice afternoon nap and then supper. Meat loaf, baked potatoes, coleslaw and peas. Then we played pick—up sticks and believe it or not, I won. A very pleasant day. Mom

January 10, 1965

Buzz, Barb & children went to church. I read the Sunday paper and laid down and rested. When they came home, we went up to Alex & Olga's dairy farm. We had coffee and fruitcake and a nice visit. Then we drove back to Buzzy's. We had roast pork, mashed potatoes, salad and green beans, chocolate cake pudding with whipped cream. We played Pic-up Stixs and I won. I'm going to try this game on Dee Dee, she always beats me at scrabble. Mom

January 11, 1965 Monday

Well Buzz and I went to Bob Browns funeral today. It seemed a very cold funeral to me as if it was just a matter of getting it over. After that, I came up to Sissy's. Aggie was here for a few minutes. She said Pat was on his way to Vancouver to see Dee Dee. Sissy was cleaning house after a wild weekend, which I am glad I missed. We had chili, French fries, parsnips and cottage cheese salad for supper. Shirley Fitch was here to visit a short time, also Virginia Lacey. Well if nothing of interest happens tonight, I will have to say ado to this day. See you later Alligator. Mom

P.S. Yang came up after work and visited and paid me $5.00 on the car, she just might get that car paid for yet. Just $45.00 balance now.

January 12, 1965 Tuesday

Well this morning was slow going, nothing to do. Aggie called and talked awhile. Dee Dee called from Vancouver and said Pat wanted her to drive him back over here but I don't know when I will get my check to go back over there. She said that she had seen Marvin Sunday, but they had not got along at all but she didn't say why. Yang came up at noon we ate lunch at Tonkins Cafeteria in Renton, then we went to Bennett's Beauty School and had shampoos and hair set. They put a true steel rinse in mine. Then we had coffee. I had pie, Yang had a hamburger. Then we went to Newberry's. Yang bought a new coat. Then we went to Sugars and Judy's and had supper. Hamburger, fried spuds, beans, lettuce and sliced tomatoes. Then back up to Sissy's and here, I am. Mom

January 13, 1965 Wednesday

A slow drag of a day. My lawyer called and said I should get my check Friday, to check with Hughbanks. I called them and they said yes, call Friday morning. That did make me feel a lot better. I talked to Barbara on the phone. Candy the little twin pulled the fish bowl over and squashed one little fish to death. Sissy had to change everything she had on and Candy thought it was funny. It rained all day. I watched T.V. and napped. Mom

January 14, 1965 Thursday

Well Patti Sue forgot her lunch this morning, so I took it to the school, then I walked to the A&H Drug Store. I got Sissy two scrapbooks. She wanted four but there was only two left. I bought two magazines to read, so I read and slept most of the day. Sissy seems all on edge today, maybe she is tired of me hanging around. Well I'll soon be gone and it will probably be a long time before I come back and will probably be never. Yang came up about four, she was on her way to work. She had ripped the Chinese sheath she wears at work. Sissy mended it. Yang said the Don at Richfield Station had been giving her a bad time over some money she owes him. I had her take me down and I told him I would pay him, and I didn't want no more trouble. He looked a bit nonplus but it makes me mad. I also went to Bowen Scarf to see what my bill is and to reassure them I'd be in. Then I made an appointment with Yang to take me around Mon. & Tues. to settle my affairs. I'm supposed to get paid tomorrow. I wonder what will happen this time. I wonder how Dee Dee and the boys are. Mom

January 16, 1965 Friday

Well after five months of waiting and hoping, the property check came through. I went to settle and picked it up. I put $500.00 in Federal Saving and Loan Bank. That pays 4 ½ interest. I gave my address in care of Buzz at Renton. I bought the twins some outfits. I bought Boofy& Ricky some jeans and shirts and a storybook. I packed all my bills but the lawyer and Totem Pole. I'll send them checks from Vancouver. Dee Dee called from Patsy's, she is going to pick me up at two tomorrow and we are going home to Vancouver. Sissy and Marvin and I went to the Mandarin last night and had mixed drinks. Then to the Pied Piper and had beer and wine. I called up Dunc and Yang and they joined us. Then we all went to the lantern and ate. Mom

January 17, 1965 Saturday

Well this morning Bogue's and I went to a lawyer in Renton. He sign a note quoting that he owes me $1600.00 to be made in two payments of $800.00 each. Then I went to Kent and got 60 days' supply of medicine. Then back to Sissy's and had ham and eggs. Then I waited until two and Dee Dee came and got me and now we came back to Vancouver. A letter from Marvin saying the parole board would not parole him to Vancouver. We will go to Washougal and talk about it tomorrow. Mom

January 18, 1965 Sunday

We went to see Marvin at Washougal Honor Camp. The boys wore their new clothes and were very well behaved, even though they were sick with head colds. He was glad to see us, anyway he seemed so. We discussed his parole and such as. We came home a four o'clock and had supper and went to bed early. Mom

January 18, 1965 Monday

Dee Dee and the kids all woke up with chest colds and fevers. We went to the welfare clinic, they sent her to a special children's Dr. He prescribed medicine for them. I bought my car license and banked $600.00 in a bank in Vancouver. I got money and paid all the bills except the lawyer and the davenport. I went to a shopping center and piled up on groceries. I got Marvin & Ricky a couple toys and a coat for Stevie James and diapers and shirts for the new baby. I am babysitting while Dee Dee meets Marvin at the bridge. Kids have had their medicine and seem to feel a little better. If anything else happens tonight, I'll write about it. Been a nice sun shiny day. Mom

January 19, 1965 Tuesday

A quiet day. Dee Dee washed and cleaned house. I hung the clothes big deal. At supper, we had pork chops, mashed potatoes, applesauce, salad and hot rolls. Well any way we took the kids for a ride to Vancouver. We stopped at a Safeway and got a case of hot sauce and potato chips. Home to bed early like. We got our barrel full of stove oil. We have a new neighbor two houses down. They are Mexicans. The big kid looks like one of the Beatles. Dee Dee made an appointment by phone to get her hair done tomorrow. The weather was nice. Mom

January 20, 1965 Wednesday

Well just a day. Dee Dee went to Vancouver and got her hair done. It sure looks a lot better. I baby-sat the little boys. Boofy put on cowboy shows for us and we all just had a ball. Dee Dee made spaghetti. We played two games pickup sticks, she won them both. No, mail No visitors, Blah. Mom

January 21, 1965 Thursday

Well I went to Vancouver today and got my haircut, tinted silver mist and set. I ate downtown and lingered around awhile. Came home and ate supper, steak and then we went up to Richfield Station and bargained to have the car serviced tomorrow. I got my lawyer bill today. $150.00. We went to Washougal and sent money order to pay it. We got a high chair for Stevie James, it cost $11.65, came home. Also a letter from Peggy, which speaks for its self. Rainy. Mom

P.S. Judy and Leona came over last night, we drank coffee and watched Peyton Place on T. V. and listen to their gossip. Judy is 21, divorced, has four children and is living with someone else's husband. Leona is older divorced, has one boy six named Mike. She was living with a man in the neighborhood but he kicked her out without her clothes and such as. She moved in with Judy. Big Deal.

January 22, 1965 Friday

Well the man from the Richfield Station from the shopping center came and got my car today, and completely serviced it. I went over to Jeans this morning. Judy and Leona were there. I drank coffee and listen to them. Discussion on men and kids. They brought the car back at one, cost me $12.50. We went to Vancouver and made a Dr. appointment for Dee Dee on Monday. Then we went to Portland. I bought gifts for Jim, Bev and the kids and some for Fred, Gwen and kids. We came home and had barbecued chicken, corn on the cob and fried potatoes. I rested awhile, now we will play pick—up sticks and scrabble. I got a birthday card from my sister Helen. Mom

January 23, 1965 Saturday

Well it sure rained today. Dee Dee washed and washed. I mailed Scott and Nancy late birthday cards with dollar bills. We didn't get any mail. Marvin sure is giving Dee Dee the cold shoulder treatment. We went to Camas this afternoon. I got a new slip and new panties. Dee Dee got a new bra and a smock that was on sale for $1.00. We then went to Washougal. We stopped at a bakery got raisin pie. I dozen rolls and one dozen potato rolls. Then we went to Washougal shopping center, got a beef roast and 1lb wieners and some vegetables. There was a guy taking kids pictures. Stevie was asleep but Boofy and Ricky got theirs taken. So home. Had supper and played scrabble and pick—up sticks. Mom

January 24, 1965 Sunday

Had a real nice day. We went to Washougal laundry mat and dried our clothes. Then we went to the Honors Camp and visited Marvin for two hours. It was nice and sun shiny when we left. Then we went through rain, it was snowing at the camp. Marvin was quite agreeable. I asked him if I could take Boofy to California with me, he didn't know what to say but finally he said OK. We bought hamburgers and fries on the way home. Tomorrow I will baby sit while Dee Dee goes to the Dr. and then at six thirty Boofy and I will take the Greyhound bus from Vancouver to Oakland, so I won't write tomorrow but next day at Jim's. Mom

January 25, 26, 1965 Mon & Tues

Little Marvin and I had a nice trip down. We drank some 7 Up in a little hamburger joint. I also bought a cheese sandwich and potato chips to take on the bus. We ate the potato chips in the Portland bus depot, after I called Jim. We ate the cheese sandwiches on the bus. There was a small baby on the bus that cried quite a bit. Marvie slept pretty good. We had cake two o'clock in the morning. We came through a snowstorm. We had breakfast at Redding six o'clock in the morning. Marvie ate two fried eggs and we took a maple bar on the bus he ate it about eight. We got into Oakland at twelve, Jim and Bev were there to meet us. They took us to Gwens at Hunter's Point in San Francisco. We are having a nice visit. She is moving to San Diego Thursday then Marvin and I will go to Jim's. We had Spaghetti and rolls for supper. Marvie liked that. Mom—I wrote Dee Dee

January 27, 1965 Wednesday

Gwen and I had a very nice day together. At one we took the kids to Wilma's house, she baby-sat. She owed Gwen some babysitting. We went to the laundry mat and Navy exchange. We got givin a green bedspread and a pink blanket and a white bathroom set. I got some pretty postcards and wrote on them to this one and that. We brought the kids home and fed them hamburgers, french fries and pork and beans. We tried putting them to bed, Freddy and Boofy won't go to sleep. Gwen is trying to pack so she can move to San Diego tomorrow. When Fred gets off at eight or nine we are suppose to get a baby sitter and go to Jim's, it is his birthday. I hope Boofy goes to sleep so he won't know I am gone. We got a letter from Dee Dee today. There will probably be a postscript to this. Mom

January 28, 1965 Thursday

Well Gwen packed and fussed all day. The place has to be spotless and pass inspection. People were in and out all day. Her place did not pass inspection. Kitten and Freddie had the poops all day. Fred was in and out with orders all day. About six we started for Jim's. The car is haywire, generator troubles, keeps cutting out. I don't know how it will ever make San Diego. Well any way Boofy and I are at Jim's. Bev had potato salad and hot dogs, sure tasted good. We had a nice rest. Mom

January 29, 1965 Friday

Sure spent a lazy day doing nothing. Boofy had a wonderful day playing with Jim's kids. Jim babysat tonight and Bev and I went to the show. We seen I'd Rather Be Rich. I think I laid around too much, the longer I slept the worst I felt. Mom

January 30, 1965 Saturday

Well Jim wanted Bev and I to go with him and Jeff to Reno today, but Bev wouldn't go. So we decided to go to the San Francisco zoo. Well Debbie developed a fever so Bev said no. So Jim and Jimmy Jr. and Boofy and I went and another sailor wanted his wife to go because she loves animals, so away we went. We stopped along the way and seen the ocean. We had a good time. Boofy got a letter from his momma today. I gave Bev $20.00 today and told her to buy the kids something they needed. Gina was sick yesterday, today Debby is. Boofy played with Jimmy Jr. and the neighbor boys this morning. He seems to be quite happy. Mom

Today was my birthday I am 57. Bev and Jim gave me a red overnight bag.

January 31, 1965 Sunday

Bev, Jim and the kids all went to Church, except Debbie, she is sick. In the afternoon, we went to what they call a penny fair. It's a drive inn theater. People bring whatever they have for sale and set it out on card tables and you pay twenty-five cents a person to get in and walk around and bargain for what you want. Believe me they have everything from soup to nuts. Bev bought a pair of skates, I bought a target game and toy gun. The rest of the day, we laid around and either watched television or slept. Got a special delivery letter from Gwen. They got to San Diego OK, and want me and Boofy to come down, and I think we will. I wrote to Dee Dee and Marvin if they don't phone and say no we will go by train Wednesday morning. Mom

February 1, 1965 Monday

Jim took off on a flight today. Jimmie Jr. and Gina went to school. Bev took Debbie to the Dr. and got home at twelve fifteen. She has tonsillitis and got some medicine to take. Bev, Boof and I went to downtown Alameda to shop. Bev bought the kids some things with the $20.00 I gave her. Boof bought some valentines and a tooth brush, and some Gleam. Bev and I had pie and coffee, Boof had ice cream and grape juice. Bev bought some knitting needles and is at the neighbors learning to knit. It is five o'clock and I am hungry. Mom No mail Boofy is talking about Stevie James and Ricky today so I guess he is home sick.

February 2, 1965 Tuesday

A very dead day. We went to the Mitchell's for coffee in the morning. Jim came home for lunch, we had chili. Boofy wouldn't eat. After lunch, we went to the Oakland Goodwill. Boofy bought two little cars. Bev bought some dolls and hand craved chessmen. I took Boofy across the street and bought him a tuna fish sandwich. Jim talked me out of going to San Diego, so I think about Saturday we will go home. Boofy got a letter from his momma, she said she has a surprise for him when he gets home. I can't imagine what it is. Jim went to school tonight. Bev is learning to knit. Mom

February 3, 1965 Wednesday

Jim flew to Albuquerque Mexico today. The kids all went to school and Bev spent the morning at the neighbors and now she is at a meeting. Boofy is playing around. I'm so damn lonesome I don't know what to do. Well Bev came home and we went to the Goodwill this afternoon, otherwise nothing. No mail. Mom

February 4, 5, 1965 Thurs, Fri

Well not much doing really. Bev is getting ready to serve at a Bishops dinner. We visited a woman in Alameda, she had a little boy five that Boofy played with. Fred called and wanted Jim to come to Frisco Friday evening and pick him up. We did and then he couldn't get off the boat. Boy was he mad. Boofy sure got excited over that big boat. Friday afternoon Bev took us to Oakland, I bought some frying chickens so we had fried chicken. Dee Dee called long distance last night and I sure was glad. Her X-rays turned out OK. I guess Stevie James is sick. I also have been advised that big Marvin is concerned about Boofy being gone so long. Well at least I'm glad he is concerned. It rained Thurs and Fri. Bev went to the show while we were gone. Mom

Feb 6, 1965 Saturday

Jim was home today and we had a nice visit. I also decided to go home tonight. There is a bus leaving at ten-ten. Jim is going to be gone flying all day Sunday and Bev will be at the church all day. So bye—bye Grandma bye-bye.

Sunday—Boofy and I traveled all night on the bus, got into Vancouver at eleven thirty. Took the cab home. Dee Dee is gone, guess to see Marvin. I have some birthday cards and a scarf from Buzz and Barb. Cards from Bobby Joe Sugar & Judy—Peggy. Dee Dee rearranged the bedroom, and has new blue curtains and bedspread. It sure looks nice. She will be surprised when she gets home, because she don't expect us until Tues. Mom

February 8, 1965 Monday

Well Dee Dee worked around the house until eleven or so. We loaded the kids in the car and headed for Vancouver. Bought a whole lot of valentines. Well then, we went to the Lotus Café and had dinner. Kids had hamburgers and fries, Dee Dee had fish and fries, I had roast pork. Then we went grocery shopping. When we got home I had a letter from Gwen. She wants to borrow a $100.00. I guess I better lend it to her. We played scrabble and pick-up-sticks and Dee Dee won them both. I sent valentines to all my kids and grandchildren, also my sister. I sent a real nice one to Joe, even if he is mad. The bible says if somebody slaps your face, to turn the other cheek and let them slap that too. So I'm sticking my neck out there. It is real cold here but clear. Mom

P.S. I told Gwen by long distance I would send the money. Also went to Washougal and bought a car jack for $6.50.

February 9, 1965 Tuesday

Didn't do much today. We went to Vancouver this morning and sent Gwen $100.00. I also drew $100.00 for personal use so I don't have to go to the bank again for two months. {Famous last words} It was a beautiful day, we stopped at the Goodwill and got two cheap tricycles. The kids had a ball outside with them. All the little neighbor kids have them. Dee Dee went to the Dr. today. We went to the shopping center and got angel food cake and marshmellows and had hot cocoa before we went to bed. No mail. Mom

February 10, 1965 Wednesday

Well didn't do much today, mended a pair of Boofy's pajamas, got the clothes out of the cleaners. Bought a Teflon frying pan and a nylon turn over. Dee Dee made spaghetti, hot biscuits and a cherry pie. We played scrabble and pick-up-sticks.

Went to bed early. Kids played outside about two hours. No mail. Mom

February 11, 1965 Thursday

Well not much of a day. Dee Dee washed and cleaned all morning. I fixed a roast beef with mashed potatoes. We had an early dinner and went to Camas. Bought some clothes pins, liquid solder and a pair of pliers, $8.00 of groceries. No mail. We played scrabble and watched Peyton Place. It appears our neighbor Judy is quite suddenly moving, we haven't found out why yet. No mail-rain-period. Mom

February 12, 1965 Friday

It rained all day, very gloomy. Shirley came and borrowed Dee Dee's iron and ironing board, she was helping Jean iron. They didn't bring it back. Judy came and asked Dee Dee to drive her to Vancouver, so she did. We went to the corner shopping center, baby food was on sale eight cents a jar, we bought eighty jars. We both got valentines from Bogue kids. I got a bill from a card company, no other mail-nothing but rain. The neighbor boys had a wild drinking party with girls tonight. Well, so another day. Mom

February 13, 1965 Saturday

Well Dee Dee and I both got up with itchy palms. We scratched them on the table leg and laughed, because where in the world would we get money. They continued to itch and we also continued to laugh. Dee Dee changed all the sheets and washed them. We played a game of scrabble, she only beat by two points. Well then, the mailman came and what do you think happen? I got a valentine from Peggy with five one-dollar bills in it for my birthday—Dee Dee got a letter from Snooks with two one-dollar bills in that, she had owed for five months on a lamp. Well so much for itchy palms. We went to Camas, I bought a pair of dress shoes, and a angel food cake with coconut frosting. We had a nice ride and a good time. It rained all day. Mom

February 14, 1965 Sunday

Valentine day and a nice one. We got up late, had hot rolls and scrambled eggs. Packed sandwiches and cookies and oranges and went to Washougal Honor Camp to visit Marvin. There was about three inches of slushy snow and real cold, but we had a real nice visit. So then we went home and ate, and me and the kids got in our P.J.'s and Dee Dee went back to meet Marvin by a side road. He gave her a real nice zenith radio. So to bed. Mom

February 15, 1965 Monday

A not so bad day. Dee Dee washed and I hung it out doors. We watched the Secret Storm on T.V. Went to the store I bought some birthday cards and a few groceries. We came home, had some ground round and fruit salad. It was a nice afternoon. Kids played out all the time. Boofy was terribly temperamental this morning. But Dee Dee stuck to her guns and won the battle. We played scrabble. The kids got valentines from Geymans. No mail for me. Ha—Ha. Mom

February 16, 1965 Tuesday

A dull good for nothing day. Rained, everybody out of sorts. No, mail-no company-nothing, just blank. Mom

February 17, 1965 Wednesday

Well it was a real nice day. The sun shone all day. The kids sure enjoyed it. We even put Stevie James out in the high chair. Done a big washing and hung it outside. We went to Hazel Dell to get our surplus foods, stopped in Vancouver and got some outing flannel at thirty-three cents a yard, going to make some nighties for the new baby. Played scrabble, I beat by fifteen points. A valentine letter from Gwen. Goodnight. Mom The neighbor man brought home a motorcycle and all the kids got turns riding around the block. Marvin and Ricky sure enjoyed that.

February 18, 1965 Thursday

Another nice day. Dee Dee took the boys to get dental appointments. She came home and we got the washing on the line. She fried chicken and we packed a picnic and went to Camas City Park and ate it. Then we stopped at Safeway and bought a case of Similac for Stevie James and some bananas, hamburger and hot dogs. Came home, the kids played out on tricycles with the neighbor kids. Stevie took a long nap. Me and Dee Dee played scrabble—I won once anyway. She got a letter from her ever-loving husband. I as usual got no mail. I'll be darned like a sock if I'm going to write any more letters. Mom

February 19, 1965 Friday

Just a nice, sunny pleasant day. We didn't go anywhere, but the weather was sunny. The kids played all day with the landlady's kids. Dee Dee and I both got letters from Patsy, which we both were glad to get. A fuller brush salesman came yesterday evening, I thought he would never quit giving us things. He gave the boys each a comb and shoehorn. He gave us a vegetable brush, pastry brush, soap stops, combs, bottle stoppers, a spoon caddy and crème sachet samples. I ordered hand lotion—fancy soap—and hair crème for the boys. Dee Dee baked cherry supreme cup cakes. Well another day is on its way. Mom

February 20, 1965 Saturday

A real nice day. We got our work done in the morning. A beautiful sunshiny day, we went to Portland and shopped and then to Washougal and then home. We had pork chop dinner, played scrabble. No mail, just a sticky med bill, Dee Dee owed McMillan St in Kent. I mailed letters to Hamilton's and the Earl case family in Renton. I write enough, just don't get answers, guess I'm writing to the wrong people. Oh well time will tell. Mom

February 21, 1965 Sunday

Well it rained all day. Dee Dee went to see Marvin, I didn't go this time. I baby sat so she could go alone. He wanted her to meet him at night too, and she did and got caught. We don't know whether they caught him or not, only time will tell. The kids were good. No other news. Mom

February 22, 1965 Monday

Well this was a state holiday, on account it was George Washington's birthday. We didn't do anything of any mention. It would rain and then the sun would shine. The kids were in and out. We discussed what would happen to Marvin and would they do anything to Dee Dee over them getting caught outside the prison camp. She wrote him a letter to see if he will get it or will it come back. We went to the store about seven and got some cough syrup, Dixie cups and candy. I finished a little nightie for the new baby and started a little blanket. No mail delivery today. We played scrabble. Mom

February 23, 1965 Tuesday

Well it was a really nice day, weather wise. The landlady gave me the names of two heart doctors in Vancouver, in a clinic. One of them just lives across the highway and down a block. It was really sweet of her, but she is an unusually swell person. We went to Vancouver this afternoon and I went to the bank and got $75.00, then we went to the clinic and made an appointment for tomorrow afternoon at three. We stopped at a Safeway and shopped. The mailman was here when we got home, but he didn't bring us any mail. I told him he was fired, he thought that was funny. I don't, but there is only one conclusion we are writing to the wrong people or we would get answers. We speculated more on what is going to happen over the meeting at the camp. We played scrabble and Dee Dee made hamburger for supper and Fritos, we ate off the coffee table in the front room. Oh yes when we backed out to go to town, we ran over the neighbor's cat and killed it. Mom

February 24, 1965 Wednesday

Well, what a nice sunny day. I went to Jean's this morning and called Dee Dee's Dr. and made an appointment for her Friday morning. Jean was giving a friend of hers a permanent.

Kids played out all morning. I kept my medical appointment with the heart doctor, named Dr. Price he knows Dr. Hogan in Kent. He looked me over and listened to my heartbeat, prescribed some medicine that cost $14.00. We came back home and the only mail we got was a wedding invitation to my brothers boy in Michigan, well big deal. Dee Dee was very disappointed over not hearing from Marvin, but they probably won't let him write. I hope and pray she won't get in trouble over it. Jean came over and asked we could take her to school at seven, we told her yes. On the way she told us, Shirley is pregnant, she also said she hoped the baby is white. I guess babies these days are like everything else, the come in colors. We bought ice cream on the way home. Dee Dee don't feel well she is bleeding at the bowels. She is also worried about Marvin. Well it really hurts, the kids don't write. They sure can when they want something. HA Mom

February 25, 1965 Thursday

Well, a nice sunny day. Kids played and had a good time. About one o'clock we drove to Washougal second hand store to see if they had a playpen, they don't, so we drove to Vancouver Goodwill. They had two but wanted $8.00 each so we didn't buy one. When we got home, there was a letter to Dee Dee from her ever-lovin husband. He is in Clark County jail. She will go see him tomorrow. We went for a ride after supper to see where the jail was at. It is on the top floor of the Courthouse. We stopped at a bakery and got some brownies, doughnuts and cinnamon rolls. I sure hope and pray they are not going to arrest or involve Dee Dee in this deal. She will find out what they said to Marvin when she sees him. I got a note from Gwen, she has the flu. Mom

February 26, 1965 Friday

Well we got an early start today. Dee Dee went to Vancouver to see Marvin and they wouldn't allow her any communication at all, no messages or nothing. So she came home and we all went with her to see her doctor. Me and the kids waited in the car. After she came out, we decided to go to Seattle and see Patsy. We packed some of the surplus dishes, the books, some bedding and things to store in Patsy basement until we find a place to move to in April. We went to the big Goodwill looking for a playpen. They didn't have any but we bought a car bed for eighty-five cents and a stroller for ninety-five cents and a cowboy town for Boofy for fifty-nine cents. We got to Patsy about five, had steak. We ate on our way through at Toledo, we had to go four miles out of our way to eat but we sure had a good meal. We played Parcheesi till eleven. The baby cried off and on all night. I called Sissy on the phone. Mom

February 27, 1965 Saturday

Well a rainy day. Harley was trying to sleep and the kids kept waking him up. I called Aggie and had a long talk with her. She is painting her kitchen lavender with white cupboards and pink curtains, and had her cat operated on and she don't know where Pat is. I called up Yang Yang, she came up to Patsy's. She had bought a Chevy for $75.00 and is selling the ford to

Sugar. She had a new blue coat with black fur collar, has been working long hours and has a new boyfriend. She went to work at noon and said she was going to drive to our place in Vancouver tomorrow. We had bologna sandwiches and potato chips for lunch and started out for home. We ate sandwiches and pop at Castle Rock, and bought groceries at Safeway in Vancouver. Bought Salisbury steak TV dinners for super, everybody was tired. We went to bed at eight. Mom

A letter from Barbara

February 28, 1965 Sunday

Not much of a day, sunshine then rain. We waited all day for Yang Yang and she didn't show up. We baked potatoes and boiled corn on the cob, made macaroni and cheese and Dee Dee baked a cherry pie, which was delicious. We discussed this and that, mostly moving and what is going to happen to Marvin. Today is Aggies's birthday, she is forty, it is also Vicki Lee Bogues she is thirteen. We watched Lassie and the Martian on T.V. and went to bed. Our neighbor boy Mike got fresh with another little neighbor girl. Mom

March 1, 1965 Monday

Well old March came in roaring like a lion. We done housework and packed all surplus things we could and stored them in the bathroom ready for moving. I called Clark County jail to see if Marvin was still there and he is. Leona came over yelling because we told Jean about Mike getting fresh with Mary's little girl. She was quite hostile at everybody but Mike. I guess mothers don't like to face the truth. Dee Dee got a letter from Snooks. I wrote Barbara a nice long letter. Mom

March 2, 1965 Tuesday

A typical March day, the wind really blew. Dee Dee washed and waxed floors. I baked bread buns period, I haven't been so lazy in a long time. No company, no nothing. I received the enclosed letter from Dora my sister in-law in Michigan. At least I'm welcome there. I haven't heard from my sister, I hope she isn't sick. No word from Marvin. No letters from all these kids of mine. Well if I'm not important to them tra-la-la. Mom.

March 3, 1965 Wednesday

Well good old March and its wind. I went over and had coffee with Jean and we gossiped mostly about Leona. Had sandwiches for lunch. Dee Dee's welfare check came. We went to a big Safeway and bout $50.00 groceries and went to Portland. Yang called long distance, she will be here tomorrow. Mom

March 4, 1965 Thursday

Well Yang Yang arrived about one o'clock, we had fried chicken dinner ready. We ate and she wanted me and her to go get our hair shampooed and set, so I called the beauty parlor and got a two o'clock appointment. After we got our hair fixed we drove around Vancouver and then over the bridge to Portland. I had a Banana Split, she had a coke high. We shopped, she bought steak for supper. We came home. She took a nap and we ate and she wanted me to go to Vancouver Cocktail Lounge with her. I had already bought pink champagne and we had drank half of it. Well I got dressed and we went. We went to the Red Lotus, she had three coke highs and I had one vodka Collins then we went to the Clipper Room. I had another vodka Collins, she had three coke highs. Then we went to the Frontier where they had a live band and dancing. I had a crab louie, she had a burger basket and another coke high, she danced. We stayed there until midnight and we drove to Camas and Washougal then went home and went to sleep. Mom

March 5, 1965 Friday

Well Yang started off for home about ten o'clock, she had to be to work by three o'clock in Auburn. We just didn't do much today. It was one of those days that the kids run in and out and got into fights with the neighbor all day. We went to Portland in the afternoon and got some birthday presents for the boys. I had coffee at Jeans today, she sure has her hands full with all these kids. We had TV dinners for supper. Roast turkey, the kids wouldn't eat the turkey. Dee Dee got three bills in the mail. I as usual got nothing. Believe you me when we move

I'm going to get out and make some new friends. And that is that. I'm not ready to be a forgotten nobody at fifty-seven. We shall see. Mom

March 6, 1965 Saturday

Well not much doing today. Nice weather, usual washing. We went to Washougal and ordered the boys birthday cake. Then went to Vancouver and priced trailers. They sound reasonable if Kathy can handle one. Stevie has a bad cold or stomachache or something. I received a letter from Aggie and a very nice Easter card from Joe. Maybe he isn't as mad at his mother as he thinks he is. Well I bought some magazines to read and a pair of pillowcases to embroidery. I sent Lorri Bogue and PoPo Hamilton each a birthday card with $1.00 in. I also mailed a wedding card with $5.00 in it to David Midkiff. Mom

March 7, 1965 Sunday

It was a sunny day with nothing to do. We took one short trip to the shopping center. Dee Dee bought some bread and liquid aspirin and Pertussin for Stevie James. He has an awful bad congestion. The neighbors next door planted flowers and Ricky and Marvin were under their feet all day. They didn't seem to mind. I had coffee at Jeans this morning, and old boy friend of hers was there. This was the joke they told; A sister was walking in the park and a man grabbed her—dragged her in the bushes and undressed her and raped her. When she was, getting dressed the man said—oh sister I'm sorry, what are you going to tell the Father at confession? She replied—I'll say I was walking in the park a man grabbed me, pulled me in the bushes, undressed me and raped me twice if you got the time. Well I sewed on a pair of pillowcases and read a story. Dee Dee was spotting blood tonight and I was worried in case she would land in the hospital. Mom

March 8, 1965 Monday

Well I had coffee with Jean, she is taking birth control pills. It was a sunny day. The kids played out, but they were in and out. Kids fighting, a dog bite, just something all day long. We went to Woolworths and Dee Dee bought a yellow blouse to wear home from the hospital. We called Patsy and asked if we could bring up another load of stuff and store it in her basement, she said yes. So we loaded the car. A letter from Patsy to both of us. No other mail. Went to bed early. Mom

March 9, 1965 Tuesday

We got up early and went to Seattle at Patsy's and left a load of stuff in her basement. She had clipped some for rents out of the paper. We looked at a three-bedroom house on 21st S.W., but the bedrooms were up a steep stairs and we wouldn't want that with the kids. I called Sissy while there and told her Joe had sent me a nice card. She said Vicki had—had her birthday party and had got seven pairs of nylons and ten records. Patsy wanted us to stay overnight but we came home, the kids sleep better. Two bills in the mail for Dee Dee. Mom

March 10, 1965 Wednesday

It was a nice sunny day. We took the boys to the shopping center and got their haircut. We then went to Camas and got the boys new tennis shoes and prizes for the party. We came home and the kids went out to play. From then on, it was hectic. A kid named Butch beat Ricky up. We brought him in and got him settled. Then him and Carol Lyn the little neighbor girl got on the road behinds Jeans, and Jean paddled him and brought him home. We put on his pajamas and listen to him fuss till bedtime. No mail again, well I love you too. I'm going to find me some pen pals to heck with the dirty dozen and boy do I mean it. Mom

March 11, 1965 Thursday

We had trouble letting the kids play today. Finally, we went to Vancouver to Buster Brown shoe store and bought Stevie James some shoes. Then we went for a long ride. I don't know what supports Vancouver but they sure have the mansions to live in. Dee Dee was a nervous wreck by evening, almost hysterical. She tries so hard and the kids won't mind. It sure worries and upsets me. No end, finally everything calmed down and we went to sleep. NO MAIL. Mom

March 12, 1965 Friday

Well things went pretty nice today. Everybody's kids got along, the weather was good. We went to my bank and got some money and then to Portland. We came home, I went over to Jeans and called Clark County Jail. They took Marvin to Monroe on Wednesday. Dee Dee decorated the house with crepe paper and balloons. At four o'clock, she went to Washougal and got the cake. It sure is pretty, it has three cowboys riding horses in a fenced corral, it has all their names on. Gave the boys a hot bath and went to bed early. No mail again today. That just does it, I'm changing my ways. I'm writing to three lonely-hearts clubs and I'll fine me somebody to write too. One in Chicago, one in Texas and one in Seattle. We Will See. Mom

March 13, 1965 Saturday

Well little Marvin was five today. We had the boys combined birthday party at one o'clock. Nine little neighbors' kids came and brought presents. Two mothers were here. We had the cake with cowboys and horses on—and Jean sent over a revolving stand to put it on that played Happy Birthday. The pinned the tail on a donkey and all got prizes. Had ice cream and fruit punch. Everything went nicely. We cleaned up the house afterwards and had fried potatoes pork and beans and little sausages for supper, and went to bed early. A letter from Barbara believe it or not. Dee Dee got a food card. No word from Marvin. I mailed letters to three lonely-hearts clubs today. Mom

March 14, 1965 Sunday

A beautiful morning, sun shiny birds singing, food in the cupboards, no sweat either which way. A lazy day, kids played outdoors all day, and we done absolutely nothing, just laid around. Most of the neighbors went somewhere. The kids dug a hole by the back door looking for the Devil. Well that's it. Mom

March 15, 1965 Monday

Nothing much today, the weather was good. Dee Dee took Marvin and Ricky to the dentist. They pulled a tooth for Marvin. Ricky came home and said his teeth were going to be full of silver. Received the Renton paper from Buzz and Barbara, it looks hopeful, we might find a house around auburn. Marvin, Ricky and Stevie James each got a birthday card and a $1.00 bill from Grandma and Grandpa Geyman. They put their dollar in their banks. No word from Marvin. Dee Dee decided to write a letter and send it to Monroe and see what happens. This is Stevie's birthday, he is one. Mom

March 16-17-18-1965 Tues. Wed, Thurs

Well we decided to go to Kent and find a place to live. We also decided to go at night because the kids sleep and it's easier to drive. We packed a lunch and started out. We got about three miles this side of Castle Rock and something went wrong with the car. We pulled over and tried flagging down cars to send for help. Five different cars stopped and said they would but they didn't. Finally a tow truck came. We got into Castle Rock, they said they would put in a head oil seal the next morning. So they took us to the Walsh Motel and we stayed there until noon the next day. They brought the car back and I paid the bill. Then we got along fine to Tacoma and something went wrong with the brakes, we stopped three places and they couldn't help us. We struggled to Kent and left the car there to get the brakes fixed. We took a cab up to Sissy's and they brought the car up when it was finished. We went to Algona and looked at a house, it looked too big to heat, it had a deep ditch near it so we looked at one in Auburn. It was near the street. We stayed at a motel in Kent, and next morning we started out and went to a place in Des Moines, didn't like it. We went to Renton looked at duplexes and a big house, almost took one duplex then changed our minds. We almost gave up then decided to go to Tukwila. Every time we would slow down and turn it sounded like the whole steering system was coming apart. Groan and screeched. Well we went up to Foster and found a perfect set up. We liked the house, completely furnished, fenced yard and all. We talked them into signing the rent receipt from April 5, to May 5. We went back up to Sissy's and rested awhile and drove back to the brake place and told them. They found a bolt loose that was making the trouble. So we started home, got as far as Federal Way and the generator light turn on. We went to a gas station, he said that we would make it. We got five miles this side of Challis and poof everything died. Well we went back to flagging down cars. Finally, one stopped, he was going to Portland and offered to take us home. In the mean time, the Highway Patrol came along. He said he would have the car towed in. I could phone the next day to find out where it is, so home. Mom No word from Marvin.

March 19, 1965 Friday

Well I called the State Patrol at Challis and they told me my car was at a Shell Station on the freeway exit. I called them and told them to fix the generator and call when it was ready. So they did. I gave Jean the money and her and Eddie went and got it for me. Dee Dee got a letter from Marvin, he is in Walla Walla State Pen. She is pretty upset, but that is the way it is. Nothing else of importance. Mom

March 20, 1965 Saturday

Nothing much today. Nice weather, we went to a shopping center. Dee Dee bought dye to put her hair back dark, it is pretty dark such a change from blonde. I bought a new purse, mine busted out on the side, a few groceries and came home. I didn't feel good today so I mostly rested. Mom

March 21, 1965 Sunday

Well spring is sprung, so the calendar says. Well the sun was shining. We were all invited to Jeans, to Shirley's little girl's birthday party. Her name is Dee Dee and she was one year old. We gave her a pink dress with panties to match, and a little stuffed clown. Then we came home and played scrabble and wrote letters. Dee Dee wrote to Marvin and Patsy. I wrote to Snooks and the Parole Board. I asked Snooks if she knew anyone that could move us. We asked the Parole Board for mercy. Well it looks like rain. I suppose spring showers are in order. Mom

Dee Dee beat at scrabble the brat.

March 22, 1965 Monday

Showers most of the day. I honestly didn't do anything. Dee Dee worked all day. Kids had to play inside all day. I did work on the pillowcases a little bit, and wrote a letter to Federal Savings for $700.00 check. No baby yet, and no mail. Mom

March 23 1965 Tuesday

Well it was a nice sunny day. Marvin and Ricky played out all day. The neighbor kids are out on Spring vacation. Dee Dee got her hair cut and went to the Dr., he gave her a card to get into the hospital with. He said it wouldn't be long now. I wrote a letter to Buzz. I asked if he was interested in a moving job. I'll find somebody. No mail as usual. I love the way my children write. Mom

March 24, 1965 Wednesday

This morning was real cold. Kids didn't get out to play until almost noon, then it was fairly nice. Dee Dee jumped around doing crazy exercises trying to start her pains, she hurt everywhere but where it counts. We didn't do much this morning. Around noon, we were playing scrabble. Jean came over a few minutes. The welfare lady dropped in. I heard from Bowen Scarff they are a bunch of squirrels. The insurance co sent papers to be filed. Federal Savings sent the check for $100.00, so we went to Vancouver Safeway and bought $18.00 of groceries. We forgot to get Aprils birthday card and Gwen's anniversary card. We'll get that tomorrow. No mail from my ever—lovin dozen. Well so what? Mom

March 25, 1965 Thursday

Well not much doing, it was snowing when we got up and was mixed snow and rain all day. Kids played inside all day. We played two games, I won both games. We went to the shopping center and got a birthday card for April Hudock and anniversary card for Gwen and Fred. Dee Dee made Spaghetti, I finished the pillow cases, and had coffee with Jean. She told me about her capers with Jim the landlord. My sons and daughters really made life worthwhile with all the nice letters they did not send. Guess I'm being punished for something I done wrong. No visitors, no mail. Mom

March 26, 1965 Friday

Well the weather was better today. The kids played out in the afternoon. Dee Dee was awful, out of sorts today. I crocheted hot mats to take up my loose ends. Sent Dee Dee and the kids to the store in the evening to get tea, bread and cookies. We got a nice letter and Easter card from Patsy. Nobody has answered to say if they would move us. Heck for that matter, nobody else wrote period. Mom

March 27, 1965 Saturday

Dee Dee felt real good today. We done our daily jobs, played scrabble. We went to big shopping center, got some frozen food and minute steaks, even bought a basket of fresh strawberries, 29 cents a basket. Dee Dee got a letter from the parole board, a real nice one. She also got a letter from her ever—lovin Marvin. I had coffee at Jeans, while there Jim the landlord came. I suggested he let Jean use his pick-up to move us. He didn't say anything one way or the other. Jim and she would talk to Eddie about a truck. Mom

March 28, 1965 Sunday

A not much doing day. Mostly played scrabble all day. It was pro and con, she would win and then I would win. Kids played out. The weather would rain then sunshine. We went to the store and got some sugar sliced ham and candy Easter eggs. I baked parker house rolls. Late afternoon I had coffee with

Jean. Tony followed me home. He played with Boofy in the bedroom. Marvin threw the darnest fit you ever saw. He got a spankin for his trouble. It didn't seem to help much. This Tony is a stinker. Mom

March 29 & 30th 1965 Mon & Tue

We decided to go to our new house with a car load of stuff. Get the gas and lights on and clean some. We had a nice trip up, and the kids just love the house. We went to White Center and ate supper in a restaurant then went to Patsy's and got a load of our stuff. Duke had the measles. We stayed overnight in our new house, it was so quiet and nice. We went shopping in the morning, then about eleven we left. We stopped at Dunc's but he wasn't home. We went to Sissy's and she wasn't home. We then went to Judy's, there was everybody. Aggie, Sis, Snooks, Shirley Fitch, Virginia Lacey all having an Avon party. We stayed a bit then went to Kent laundry matt and done our washing. Then went to Auburn to the Mandarin where Yang works. We had dinner then went back to Judy's to get $25.00 she owed me. We met Buzz in front of the laundry, he said he would be down Sunday to move us. When we got home, there was mail from Peggy and Gwen. Mom

March 31, 1965 Wednesday

Well a nice day, kids played all day. Billy came in and had coffee and stayed about one and a half hours. We went to Vancouver at three. Dee Dee went to her Dr. the baby is real low but just won't come. We went to Penney's, they were suppose to have bedspreads 2 for $5.00 only had one left, and it was yellow. Came home and had TV dinners. I got a coat in the mail from Peggy, and a cute letter from April. Went to bed early. Jean came over at ten to say Yang had called and wouldn't be down this week. She hinted that I babysit while she took Eddie home. But I didn't bite, I went back to bed. Mom

April 1, 1965 Thursday

Well April fool's day was quite a day. Marvin, Ricky and I walked to the shopping center and got SOS pads and Spic & Span. Got the boys balloons and popcorn. Came back and Dee Dee started house cleaning. We took the washed clothes to the dryer and went to Ft Vancouver High School to a rummage sale. Dee Dee slipped on a cement down grade and fell with Stevie James on top of her. We decided to get for home. She was having pains. But up till seven nothing happen. She got upset and I called the Dr., he said bring her to the hospital so he could see her. Jean took her and brought her home. Mom

April 2, 1965 Friday

Well nothing unusual about today. Showers in the morning and sunshine in the afternoon. Marvin Jr. got a hold of some matches and lit a field of grass on fire and got scared and ran. Dee Dee caught up with him and paddled his behind, and he threw a toy through the window and broke it. When he cooled off, he was a pretty good boy. We went to a drive-in for supper. Dee Dee sure don't feel good. She got a package of clothes from Peggy. Mom

April 3, 1965 Saturday

Dee Dee got up bleeding this morning. I sent her to the doctor's he said her pains should start, they didn't. Well one minute she consents to stay here and have the baby the next minute she is going to Seattle with us. Well she is a very despondent mood. I can't reach her, guess she is scared, well so am I. Her check came. We went to Portland. We came back, bleeding started again. I called Dunc & Shirley to come and get me and the kids tomorrow when Buzz moves us. One minute Dee Dee is going then she starts bleeding again and says will stay here. I sure don't know what to do. Mom

April 4, 1965 Sunday

Well, what a day. We got up Dee Dee was bleeding again. I sent her to the hospital. They kept her awhile and released her, but it was too late to call Shirley. Buzz and his brother in-law Don showed up and moved our stuff, we waited one hour for Shirley and decided to start out. We watched for her, we passed five miles so off to Chehalis. Tried to stop her but couldn't. Well is she mad or isn't she. I haven't seen her but I left $15.00 for her trouble and my sincere apology, but it will take awhile. We paid Buzz $30.00. Well Yang showed up and took me to a store and bought hot food. Mom

April 5 1965 Monday

Well got up and had breakfast. I finally got Dee Dee off to King County Hospital to make arrangements, they wanted to keep her, she wouldn't stay. The boys were good until they seen her coming, then they really let loose. Sissy, Vicki the twins Judy and Bobby came for coffee in the afternoon. The kids were good, seemed like Bobbie was wound up. Dee Dee got home about five, we had supper. Buzz and Barb came in the evening. Marvin acted like an idiot, Dee Dee had to take him in the bathroom and paddle him. She was so embarrassed. Makes me think of a few times her and Gwennie embarrassed me, and they were much older. It rained some today but seems to be clearing up. Mom

April 6, 1965 Tuesday

Well Dee Dee got up at six and got off to the clinic by seven. She got home by eleven. We had lunch, I had made a big pan of beef-aroni. We decided to go get some groceries and go to the big Goodwill and look for a playpen so Stevie could get outdoors on nice days. We got half way in there and she started pains. She insisted on finishing our job. We didn't get a playpen but we bought Ricky a little red wheelbarrow, we got our groceries and came home. We had supper and Yang Yang came by, this time the pains were for real, so Yang took her to the hospital about seven thirty. Yang came back by at ten and said she was in the delivery room. She also told me how mad Shirley is. Well I'm always in trouble with the relatives.

Strangers are more understanding. I refuse to let it get me down. Dee Dee got a letter from Marvin. Mom

April 7, 1965 Wednesday

Well I got up this morning and fed the kids. I went to the landlords and called the hospital and Dee Dee had another boy. The kids played outside all day. Ricky washed my car with muddy water, boy. Marvin peed on Ricky. Otherwise, the day went pretty good. Sissy and the kids came up about six. While they were here, Yang and Judy came. They had been to see Dee Dee and then Patsy's. Dee Dee is disappointed over having another boy. Well that's the breaks. Weather, pretty good. Food card, a bill and a letter from city light for Geyman. Naturally, none of my darlings could write. Sissy is having a lunch and baby shower for Dee Dee next Thursday. Mom

April 8, 1965 Thursday

Dee Dee brought me home today. I was glad to see my little apt. I may have to babysit tonight if they call her to work. I called Sissy, she said she might come down. I hope she does. Agnes came and had lunch with me. We had turkey noodle soup and sweet rolls from the bakery. We had a nice visit and she gave me a nice blanket for Mother's Day. Sissy and the kids and Judy and Bobby came down around five. They brought Yang's clothes down. I will have to try and find a way up there next week. Sissy invited me up for supper, so I went, we had fish & chips and salad. Buzz called while I was there, he stopped by and got my key and came down and painted my front room. Shirley called Judy and they got in a fight over two calves. Then I came home. Buzz was still painting. Dunc and Wendy came with a nice plant for Mother's Day. Wendy had bought a dress for Shirley's birthday. I sent the nice pillowslips I had made. No mail. Mom

May 7, 1965 Friday

Got up at eight, the sun is shining. Who knows what this day will bring. Well later on, I will let you know. Well Dee Dee came at eleven thirty, she was headed for the welfare office in Seattle. She left Stevie James and little Donnie with me and took Marvin and Ricky. The babies were good. She got her check and food voucher too. She went shopping and took Judy and Bobby with her. She got some plants and took up to Grandma German. They took movies of the boys and gave them a puppy. Dee Dee got back about four thirty, she gave me $7.00 and a lavender rug for Mother's Day. During the afternoon Sissy came down with my curtains. Boy with this nice paint job and curtains it really looks nice. Well after everybody left I went to the new Shop Rite got my orchid and signed up for the door prize. Got some groceries and brought them home. Then went to Meeker's Café and ate a hot beef sandwich. I sewed on my quilt until eight thirty and went to bed. Mom

May 8, 1965 Saturday

Got up at nine and ate breakfast, 2 boiled eggs, 2 pieces toast and two cups coffee. Done the dishes, shampooed my hair and set it. Cleaned house and here I am. I'm scared to look in the mailbox because I hate to see it empty all the time, so I guess I'll take my garbage sack down stairs and then come back and sew. Well its one thirty, I finished the quilt top. I fixed a can of chicken gumbo soup for lunch. Just finished the dishes and Sugar dropped in for all of five minutes. At three o'clock, I went to the Goodwill store and got a ten-cent piece of material for quilt blocks. When I got back, Dee Dee and the boys were here. We went to Sugars, he wasn't home but Judy and Bobby were. Tom and Sherry were there but they left. We had coffee and the boys got there dog. Came back home. Dee Dee gave me some baby nighties for the gal down the hall, I took them to her and had coffee. I came back and fixed fried potatoes and pork & beans for my supper. It's six o'clock. Auntie and Uncle came between 7 and 8 o'clock, was sure glad to see them. NO MAIL. BLAH Mom

May 9, 1965 Sunday

Mother's Day. Shirley and the kids came about nine with a card and box of chocolates. They invited me for dinner and spend the day I accepted. We went to their place, her and the kid's cleaned house and fixed things for dinner. Took the kids to the show at one thirty and Shirley and I went to visit Hamilton's. Before we left Dunc's, Buzz and Barbara and the kids stopped in and gave me pictures of the kids and a stainless steel canister set. At five, we came back and Shirley fixed dinner then went to get the kids. Don came home we had dinner. Baked ham—potato salad—green salad—hot rolls, cottage cheese—buttered asparagus—cheese—pickles—green onions—jello with fruit salad. Then they brought me home and gave me a television. Mom

May 10, 1965 Monday

Well at nine, Judy came and got me and we took Yang's things and went to see her. She was in a screaming rage when we got. They gave her a shot and she calmed right down. She sure looks wild. We ate a hamburger on the way home. Finally, I got a letter in my mailbox. A nice card from Hudock's with $2.00 in it. A telegram on my door from Gwen and Fred. Not a word from Jim and Bev. I wonder what I done wrong down there. I am resting and watching T.V. I am taking the 4:40 bus to Dee Dee's. I am supposed to babysit tomorrow. Shirley and Judy Fitch, Snooks and Rodney and Dee Dee and her 4 came. We visited a while and Shirley& Snooks left. I went home with Dee Dee and had supper. Judy and Bobby came and they took me home. I went to phone Sissy but she isn't home so guess I'll just rest and go to bed. No word from Joe or Jim. Mom

May 11, 1965 Tuesday

Well I got up and had breakfast. Cleaned the apt up and waited for Dee Dee to show with the kids. She hadn't shown by noon so I had tea—brown bread with raspberry jam and cheese for lunch. She came about one and she left to job hunt. She was gone two hours, the kids were good. She starts at the Mandarin at eleven tomorrow. I will take the 8:40 bus to her place and babysit. After she left I called Sissy. She is going to come and get me and I will have supper up there. I walked over to Spouse Ritz dime store and bought a piece of flannel, a storybook and some cards. I came home and wrote letters. Now I am waiting for Sis to show. Received a letter from Yang. No mail from Jim or Joe-Rah Rah. Well Sissy came and we had fried ham-fruit salad—green beans—new potatoes and gravy. Then we went to Shirley Fitch's and had coffee. Judy and Bobby were there. Elmer was in a grumpy mood. Then home and to bed. As I said, tomorrow I babysit. Mom

May 12, 1965 Wednesday

Got up at seven had breakfast, sat down to write and broke my glasses, it's the frame. Will be leaving in a few minutes to take the bus to Tukwila. It looks like rain, just my luck when I babysit. Write later alligator. Well it's seven thirty and I am home again, I finally heard from Jim and Bev a very nice letter and $5.00 for Mother's Day. Dee Dee worked six hours and paid me $3.00. Judy came out there, so she drove me home. Mom

P.S. I answered the letter.

May 13, 1965 Thursday

Got up had coffee and pills, ate a cookie and banana and rode the 7:15 bus to Tukwila, but Dee Dee didn't work today. So I watched the two babies while she took Marvin Jr. to the school and register him for kindergarten. Ricky went with them. Then we went to Auburn and she got her surplus food and went to a Trade well and done her shopping. She let me out at my apartment and she went home. I started out for Benjamin Franklin's dime store to get some glasses so I can read and sew. I seen Sissy's car at the doctor's office so I went in. It seems Candy runs a high fever all the time and the Dr. don't know why. Well I stayed with her until she went up the hill, then I went to the store. I ciped the glasses{ I think this means she stole them} and bought Rodney a birthday present. Then I bought a turkey sandwich and came home and ate it with hot tea and ½ cantaloupes. I finish the baby quilt and took it down the hall to Elaine. I visited and had coffee with her. Then I went to the meat market and bought two wieners and one pork chop it cost me twenty-five cents. I boiled two white potatoes and one sweet potato and boiled two weenies with a small can of sauerkraut and ate the whole works. Sissy said she might be down. Well who knows, I'll tell you later. It is six o'clock now. NO MAIL If anything else happens today I will add a postscript, otherwise I'll take a sponge bath in lilac soap and call it a day. Mom P. S. Buzz and Barbara and the kids came after while, they gave me an iron and a little suit for little Donnie. Buzz painted the second coat on my front room and it sure looks nice. We had coffee and doughnuts and a nice visit. After they left, I took a hot bath with lilac soap. A sponge bath in my big old dishpan. It serves its purpose, I am clean. Mom

May 14, 1965 Friday

I got up at eight, had two doughnuts-a banana—my pills and two cups of coffee. I'm going to the store pretty soon and get a ball and some colors so older children will have something to do when they visit me. It is on the cool side this morning. Dee Dee is suppose to come and get me at three o'clock to babysit while she works. More, after-while. Saturday—Well she came and got me, she went to work at six and worked until four in the morning. The kids slept pretty good, after I got them to sleep. But boy they all got up early and wouldn't let her sleep and it poured rain all day. My head sure was aching. They told her to come back at midnight, but her knows that either one could take it. She called her boss lady and she said to come in six o'clock Sunday morning, so we all went to bed and had a good sleep. She got a letter from Marvin. Mom

May 16, 1965 Sunday

Dee Dee left for work before me and the kids woke up. I fed them breakfast, bathed Donnie and done the washing. I cooked up a pot of beans and wienies and a pot of new spuds and made some stuffed eggs. The kids were good and ate good. Dee Dee got home before three and took me home. She works four hours tomorrow so the kids will stay here at the apt. I went to the eighty-eight cent store and got a beach ball and some cards for the toy box. I called Sissy she said Yang was home for the week and so I told her to have them stop in when she goes back. I called Aggie and told her I couldn't go

Wednesday on acct—of babysitting. She said she would stop by tomorrow. Sissy says Candy has the bad measles. If there is more news, I will let you know. Mom

May 17, 1965 Monday

Well I got up, ate my breakfast, watched out my window for Shop Rite to open, went over when it did and got coffee, bread, eggs and doughnuts. Came home cleaned the apt up. Dee Dee got here early with the kids. I told her how Yang was tearing her down in front of Judy. Dee Dee said this family will never be satisfied until they get me and Marvin divorced. Well anyway, I watched the kids while Dee Dee worked. When she came, I watched the two babies while she took Marvin and Ricky to the store. Then when they all left, I walked to the Arctic Circle and got a taco and French fries. On the way over, I called Sissy, it sounded like a mad house. When I got home, I found a note, Aggie had been here and a package from Peggy it was a two-piece dress. I took off again and bought two storybooks, a magazine, some hamburger and buns. I came home and flopped. A letter from Gwen. No money. Mom

May 18, 1965 Tuesday

Well now, this was a day. I was waiting for Dee Dee to bring the kids for me to babysit while she worked. She came but complained of this lump in her right breast, she decided to go to the clinic. We went and picked up Judy and Bobby. I watched Marvin, Ricky and Stevie James. They took little

Donnie and Bobby. It was a nice day and the kids played outside. They got back at five thirty and Dee Dee either has cancer or a tumor, anyway it has to be removed. She goes to surgery next Tuesday. It was then decided that she go get her pay and tomorrow at midnight, she go round trip by bus to see Marvin.

May 19,1965 Wednesday

I'm going to a big fashion show and lunch that Aggies's club is putting on today. Then Judy will pick me up at ten tonight and take me to Dee Dee's and take Dee Dee to the bus in Seattle. I will babysit until she gets back. I'm wearing my green dress today. It is raining. No mail. Mom P.S. I went and enjoyed it. I called Gwen had a nice talk.

May 20, 1965 Thursday

Well Dee Dee took Ricky with her so I babysat the other three. Stevie has a black eye. Donnie sleeps better since he gets cereal. Shirley Fitch came and got us at noon and we went too little Rodney's birthday party. The kids were good and it was fun. Sissy brought us home at two. Sissy is yowling because Yang wants home for the weekend and Judy won't go and get her. Personally, I don't blame Judy. Yang uses terrible language, is obnoxious etc. If Sissy is so warned, let her keep her a weekend. Dee Dee got back at eleven thirty, she looked so tired. Judy and I went to Riva's and had french fries and deluxe hamburgers. Bobby sure was wide-awake. Mom NO MAIL

May 21, 1965 Friday

Well I got up at nine, I sure did sleep. Had coffee and pills, went over to Kent bakery got some bread and rolls, went to Kent meat market got six slices of bacon and four slices of bologna. Came home now I am just sitting here. I can't decide whether to get on a bus and go help Dee Dee or just sew. I see the mailman went by and there is no mail in my box. Well about four o'clock Dee Dee came. We went to the Arctic and got some fries and hamburgers and came up to the apartment and ate them. The kids wanted to go to Sissy's so we did, but they were not home. We decided to go to Patsy's, going through Kent we saw Yang Yang. She wanted a ride up to Sugars so we took her. We visited a few minutes then went up to Geymans, Dee Dee told her about things but she never said anything about the kids or anything. I stayed overnight with Dee Dee. Mom

May 22, 1965 Saturday

We woke up late. Dee Dee is very disturbed about what to do with the kids. I suggested Lily Hamilton. I called her on the phone, she said she would take them. Monday afternoon, for one month and Dee Dee is to pay her $100.00 from her welfare check. Well we went up to Sissy's for a while. Billy Joe has the measles. Then we went over to Sugar's and stayed a long time, even for supper. Tom and Sherry was there and Sugar came in with four drunk milker's. We left shortly after that. Mrs. Thatcher from down the hall came and visited a while. Then Lily Hamilton came and asked a few questions about the boys so she could take better care of them. Then to bed. I received a letter from Joe. Mom

May 23, 1965 Sunday

It was a lonely quiet day. I walked a lot and bought a Sunday paper and sewed and slept. No company. Mom

May 24, 1965 Monday

Lily came at twelve thirty, we went to Dee Dee's and Lily and Becky took the little boys. I knew Dee Dee would panic so I told her to load up Susie and we would go to Sugars and Judy's. We did, Yang was there she has to go to court Tuesday night. We visited a while and went to Sissy's to see the new colt. We went to my apartment and got the wreath I bought to put on Papa's grave. We went to Auburn to return the money belt Dee Dee had used at the restaurant. Then we went to Meeker Café and had dinner. Then went to Sugar's and got Yang Yang and went to the El Rancho drive in. We seen a racial picture, To Kill A Mocking Bird. And Twice Around. We got home at two thirty in the morning. I stayed with Dee Dee. Mom

May 25, 1965 Tuesday

Got up at nine, nothing in the house to eat but we did have coffee. I brought the clothes in off the line, and picked the toys up out of the yard. Then we waited for Holdar and Louise to come and they did we all had coffee and then went to the hospital. Dee Dee was sent to surgery clinic. We waited quite a while. They sent her to O. B. clinic to get some pills. They sent us to get the pills and then to admitting office to get admittance papers for Sunday, then to X-ray. At about four-thirty, we were done there. We then went to Kresses downtown and ate. We then got on a Auburn bus to Tukwila but they wouldn't let us off until we go to Kent. Dee Dee wouldn't stay with me. I don't know why. She started hitch hiking to Sugar's. Judy picked her up on the road they were taking Yang to court in Auburn. They left her off and came back to my apartment and had coffee. They left to find Sugar. Then Yang came and had a sandwich and coffee. She left and was headed for a tavern to see if she could catch a ride home. NO MAIL Mom

May 26, 1965 Wednesday

I got up at twenty minutes to ten, and had my breakfast. I am supposed to go with Judy and Dee Dee to Western State Hospital to take Yang back today. It will probably be around noon. I have a pot of split pea soup on cooking. The girls are always hungry. I'll write more later-alligator. Well about one o'clock the three girls showed up, but Yang wasn't headed for Western State. Judy was taking Dee Dee and Yang out to Dee Dee's to get the car and Dee Dee was suppose to buy gas with her last dollar to take Yang to Puyallup to work. I was to go with Judy to show her where the Orthopedic Hospital was so she could bring Sugar home from work. So away we all went. Then we all landed at Sugar's for ham dinner. O. K. but Yang didn't work. One of Sugar's calves were gone so he sent Judy up to call the Sheriff. He said he knew Dunc took it and was going to jail for it. I had Dee Dee bring me home. I put $1.00 of gas in the car and listened to a triad from Yang on my neglect as a mother. NO MAIL Mom

May 27, 1965 Thursday

Well I got up about nine and ate split pea soup for breakfast. I went for a long walk from one end of town to the other. I talked to Sissy on the phone. Her and Shirley Fitch came down about one and had coffee and split pea soup. Just as they were leaving, Dee Dee came. She is in one hell of a mood. We went to Lela Gifford's a few minutes then we went to Snooks then I came home and she went back to Sugar's. I went to the Arctic Circle and got a taco and a order of fries. I came home and ate that and took a nap. Then Dee Dee and Yang came and Yang and I really got into it. They wanted me to go to Judy's so I did. Eight o'clock and Sugar wasn't home for supper yet. Finally, at eight thirty they ate without him. Dee Dee wanted me to go stay overnight at her house so I did. We seen Sugar's car at the Colonial Tavern. We got to her place, she had a letter from Marvin, little Donnie's birth certificate and a bill. We had a good sleep. NO MAIL Mom

May 28,1965 Friday

Well got up at twenty after ten, At Dee Dee's. I put the coffee on to perk and hung up the clothes she had run through last night. I boiled the eggs and toasted the bread I brought with me. She wrote to Marvin and mailed some cards to the little boys. Then she brought me home and went to Judy's. I haven't seen her since. I went the bank and got $4.50. I went to Safeway and bought $2.50 in groceries. I bought a soup bone and vegetables and made a roaster full of vegetable soup, been eating every since. I talked to Sissy on the phone, she said she would see me later. Well it's seven thirty now and no C Sissy. I sewed on the silk quilt and took a nap. Two punks went up to Slax's apt 2. And he went and bought two and one half cases beer and was about to put them in one punks car when who should see him but a Kent cop. He talked to the punks then went up to Slax's apt. The punks left. NO MAIL Mom

May 29, 1965 Saturday

Got up at nine o'clock ate breakfast and cleaned up the apt. So far, nothing has happen but as I used to tell the girls, you never know what's just around the corner. After while crocodile. Well at ten o'clock Dee Dee and Yang came by. I'm sure I don't know which one was the goofiest. They were headed for Dee Dee's to leave the Chevy, while she is in the hospital. When they left, I went and called Lilly to see how the boy's were. She said they were fine except Stevie is running a tempture but not bad. I said hello to Ricky and Marvin. I went to the bakery and bought some rolls and came back. Now I am going to sew on quilts. My mailbox is empty and the mailman has gone. THAT IS IT I will write NO MORE LETTERS. More later alligator. It is almost eight o'clock no one else has been here. I can see the hill from my window that Papa's grave is on. No one has been to say they took flowers up. Tomorrow is Memorial Day. Guess they all got short memories. They sure forget I'm around and I'm still alive. Well if anything happens tonight, I will let you know. Mom

May 30, 1965 Sunday Memorial Day

Well as I have said before Diary old pal, you never know just what is around the corner. Well it started out pretty drab and dreary today. I sewed and dawdled around. Then I took ten pennies out of the cookie jar and got a dime at the drug store and phoned Sissy. See if I could come up, she said yes if I could stand it. So I guess Bogue, Elmer and Sugar were all there drunk. So I said never mind I'll go for a walk, so I did. Buzz and Barbara were buzzing around through town and picked me up. I had them take me up to Sissy's. Well WOW they were plastered. Shorty was there too. We all got in a big fat argument over Philip Alf. Shorty went home. Then yang came over and she got drunk and called Don Heinz and asked him to take her out. Her and Sugar got in a fight about it and went home. Shirley came and took Elmer home. Bogue got Robert in the car and took off. Dee Dee called and wanted someone to come and get her at the hospital, because they aren't going to operate until Tuesday. I told her to call Geymans. I asked Shorty to bring me home, he did. That is one guy I would like to nab. We are all supposed to go to Sugar's tomorrow. Mom

P.S. Dee Dee hitched hiked to Judy's. Her, Judy and Yang were all down about ten o'clock at night. Mom

May 31, 1965 Monday

Well I got up and put a roaster of baked beans on, we are all suppose to go to Sugar's today for dinner. It looks nice and sunny out. I burned two fingers on my left hand this morning. Judy is suppose to come and get me at eleven thirty today. Well Sugar and Dee Dee came and got me and I spent a nice quiet day with lots of food. Then Judy, Yang and Bobby and I all took Dee Dee to the hospital. When I got home, I found a note that Patsy had been here. I called Aggie, she is coming for me tomorrow at eight thirty to take me to Seattle. I feel awful uneasy and disturbed tonight about everything. I don't know why I just do. Mom

June 1, 1965 Tuesday

Well got up at eight, Aggie came at eight thirty. We went to her place and had coffee and rolls. Went to her bank in Burien, then she let me out at King County Hospital at ten o'clock. I went through the screening Doctor, he said I needed medical and surgery. He wrote me out a prescription and then I was sent over to Social Service. They told me I would have to sell my property note at a loss and take care of my own medical until it was gone. I went up to see Dee Dee, she had already been through surgery. She hadn't eaten. They tried to get her up but she was faint. She gets out tomorrow afternoon. I called

Patsy, she said to come out and have supper and they would get me home and I did. We had steak, mashed potatoes, green beans and shred pineapple, sure tasted good. Harley brought me home. I got a letter from Peggy. Mom

June 2, 1965 Wednesday

Well it's nine thirty. I have had my breakfast and made my bed etc. I am waiting for the bank to open. I want to ask them about my selling this $1600.00 note I have. I am also going to look around car wise. If I can get Dee Dee a car that runs and clear $100.00 on mine, I am going to do it. I wonder what Yang and Judy are up too, if either one of them thinks' they are going to get money out of me they are nuts. I'll give Judy $1.00 to go get Dee Dee outside of that, Poo. Well it's a nice sunny day. I love my little apt. This morning my plants are looking up, I have roses and sunshine in both rooms. I kind of feel peaceful like. I am also mailing a letter of inquiry to Social Sec to see if I can get a disabled benefit before the age of 62. Well Judy and Bobby came and I gave her $1.00 for gas to go get Dee Dee, she gave me a note from Yang Yang wanting $6.50. I wrote back and said NO. We went to Dee Dee's and her and I came to Kent. Ran into a wild Yang. Well bogue it seems is going to pay me $500.00 in 30 days so that takes care of me. I stayed all night at Dee Dee's. Mom

June 3, 1965 Thursday

Dee Dee got her check from welfare. We went shopping to Renton and she got $40.00 of groceries. Then we went to Enumclaw and got her kids, she gave Lilly $35.00 but she wants $50.00. Well Dee Dee said I'll have to give you the rest next month. We got to Auburn and had a picnic in the park. Then I came home and Dee Dee took her kids and went home. The kids all looked good except Stevie James, he has lost weight and didn't look happy. I got my first gas bill it was $1.35, sure is cheap for one month's cooking. I seen Sissy and Yang at Harold's Drive-In. Yang got a dollar off me, also Gwen's phone number. Well I had cold sliced turkey and a salad tonight. The turkey comes in little jars. My salad consisted of lettuce-onion-tomato-kidney beans and Roquefort dressing. I had bacon crackers with it and crème soda pop. Mom

Yang wanted Gwen's phone number, I gave it to her.

June 4, 1965 Friday

I got up fifteen to nine, had my coffee and pills and done my house work. I went to the rummage sale and bought three pictures, one a snow scene on a farm, one a cool lake in summer and a little baby sleeping in a high chair. I then went to the dentist and got Dee Dee and the boys appointments. Then I walked around town and came home, and waited for Dee Dee to come and take me to my shower at Judy's. She was late and then we had to go to White Center and get Patsy. Then they had to stop at a Wigwam store. We were two hours late to the party. Well we had a good time anyway. I got two lamps—two sets of bowls—two sets of glasses, lots of terry cloth dish towels a cute little note thing for my door, a set of salt and pepper shakers. We had a nice lunch. I also got a whistling teakettle. I stayed at Judy's and watched Dee Dee's kids while she took Patsy home. Dee Dee had car trouble on the way back. Oh yes I got a covered butter dish too. NO MAIL. Today I am kinda tired. I ate a cold turkey sandwich for supper. Mom

June 5, 1965 Saturday

I woke up at ten this morning and made a big bowl of hot mush and ate. I cleaned up my apartment and walked all over town. I went to the Goodwill and bought two cereal bowls and four spoons. I came home and had a letter from my brother Frank and sister-in law Dora. I took off again and ran into Snooks and little Rodney. We came up to the apartment and had lunch and then went to the rummage sale-Goodwill-and a dime store. She bought me a dustpan, we had fun together. She is in case you have forgot, my granddaughter. Now I have had a rest. While I was gone, Judy and Yang were here and left me gifts from Lois Lawrence and Sherry Hill, Fred Norse sister and Mother. It was a set of tablemats and a set of measuring spoons. It is quite warm today, but my apartment is cool. I am suppose to call Patsy at seven to see if they are going rock hunting tomorrow, if they are I get to go. Will write more later alligator. I called Patsy twice and a baby sitter answered. So I guess I won't be going there. I am lonesome tonight. Actually, wish I had a boy friend. Guess that's all, it's nine o'clock. Mom

I miss Dee Dee and the kids, but I know they have to live their own life's.

June 6, 1965 Sunday

Well I got up at ten this morning and I really should have gone to church, but I kept thinking some of the kids might show up and I should know better by now. I called Patsy but no one was home. I also called Sissy, but no one was home. I called Aggie, she was cleaning up after company. So I came home and went to the launder matt by Safeway and done my washing. I came home and ironed. I baked some potatoes and heated some carrots and beans, then I slept a couple of hours. I just had some coffee and bread and jelly. And, I Am LONESOME, don't do you no good to raise twelve kids for company. I wonder if Dee Dee went to Geymans today. I wonder if Yang went to work. Well next Sunday I will get up and go to church. I don't know which one yet. Maybe I will make some friends. No use going on this way, might as well join Pop at the cemetery. Well maybe somebody will drop by this evening but I doubt it. Sure let you know if they do. Mom

Well nobody came, I went for a long walk about twenty blocks. I ate a banana split at Meeker, cost me.65 cents. Some smart character yelled at me from a car.

June 7, 1965 Monday

Well last night I visited with my neighbor lady in Apt 3. Her name is Amelia Thatcher, she is a practical Nurse and earns her own living. She goes to the Seventh Day Adventist Church.

They have their Sunday on Saturday, she invited me to go with her and I probably will. Don woke me up at nine this morning and we had coffee. They are leaving for California next Saturday morning. I walked around town this morning and came home and sewed. I think I will take the four-fifty five bus to see Dee Dee if she don't show up before then. Maybe I should call her landlady, I am thinking that over, she is probably waiting for them to deliver her freezer. I wonder if she will get it. She sure was in a sour mood last time I seen her. It is hot today. The morning mailman did not bring me any mail. I am getting low on money and food. I will have to eat what I got for a while. I boiled a potato and some green beans at two o'clock. It is about three thirty. More news later alligator. Well at four fifteen I went to the bus depot and had lemon pie and coffee and went on the bus to Dee Dee's, I stayed overnight. Mom Joe was supposed to get married today. Mom

June 8, 1965 Tuesday

Well I played around with Dee Dee's kids and she took Ricky to the hospital with her. She got back about three thirty. She hasn't heard from Marvin since his mother wrote him, she don't know why. She got home and we went by Sugar's. Yang was doing the work Judy was out job hunting. I came home. Sissy had been here so I called her. I bought French bread—bologna—cheese and lettuce and had soup and sandwiches for supper. Bogue and Sissy came down and gave me a check for $500.00 on the property note. Boy what a relief. Yang came while they were here, had coffee and bummed them for 50 cents. Now I'm here alone. I got a letter from Gwen. Mom

I visited with Amelia Thatcher my neighbor in Apt 3. I was asking her if any used clothing was available at the church that would fit the two little Lyons girls. She said she would find out and let me know.

June 9, 1965 Wednesday

Well got up at nine fifteen, took my glasses to Greer the Opt. He said frames would cost me $17.00. I left them to get fixed. I called the phone company to see about getting a phone. It's ten to install and a $35.00 deposit which I would get back in nine months. It's $5.00 a month. I think I will wait until I hear from Social Security. I went to the bank and deposited $450.00. I went shopping for badly needed groceries. I came back, and Dee Dee came and we went to the Mc Ness party. I bought shampoo—spice and vanilla and said I would have a party July 13. Got home about three thirty and decided to start painting my kitchen. Done 1 ½ walls. Amelia stopped by and said I could go with her and pick out clothes for the little Lyons girls. I think I will get some for Bobby Joe too. Yang and I went to Meeker Café and had something to eat, and went to 88 cents store and got some things I needed. I called Aggie, she is real sick with bleeding ulcers. Came home and here I am. Mom NO MAIL

June 10, 1965 Thursday

Well I woke up to a nice sunny day in a nice sunny feeling. I finished painting my kitchen went out banging around town and bought a few things. Elaine came down the hall and had coffee with me. Dee Dee and the boys came about four and wanted me to come stay overnight but I had promised Amelia to go help them tonight at the church and pick out some clothes for the little Lyon's girls. I called Sissy and invited her and Shirley down for lunch tomorrow. She said they would come. So I got salad material and red salmon and apple pie. I went with Amelia and met some nice ladies and help sort clothes for a rummage sale, and got some clothes for the girls. I also got four pair of pants for Bobby Joe. When we came home, it was raining. Mom

NO MAIL P.S. Elaine gave me a rocking chair but out of one of the other apartments.

June 11, 1965 Friday

Well diary I got up a sane and sensible person, now it's three o'clock in the afternoon and I doubt whether I got a good sense or not. I got an invitation in the mail from the girl Joe is going to marry. In Colorado Springs on June 15th. Well I had Sissy and Shirley Fitch down for lunch and they talked me into thinking I should go. I actually went to the bank, and got $100.00 and called the Greyhound bus depot in Seattle. I would have to leave Seattle one thirty Sunday. Well darn me anyway. I guess I might go. I am supposed to go stay overnight at Dee Dee's and the boys tonight. An old fool like me ought to have sense enough to stay home. I'll write more tomorrow, when I get back from Dee Dee's place. Well dear diary old pal, I didn't get back until June 19. Judy brought me down, I changed my dress grabbed my suit case, went to Seattle Trail ways bus, climbed on and went to Colorado. I sure did surprise Joe. He had a nice wedding in the Air Force Chapel and then a big reception in N.C.O. Club. Food—dancing—drinking, they left to California on their honeymoon. I started home Wednesday afternoon. My bus got stalled in a tornado, we waited two hours for it to stop and then the floods came. Bridges washed out in front of us and in back of us. We waited by a raging river that had everything floating in it,—houses-furniture—cars—trucks—animals and people. We were there eight hours without food or water, not knowing what was going to happen to us. There was three buses—four trucks and about fifty cars, about three hundred people. Finally the Army helicopters came. Four of them and took us to safety, eight at a time, where the Highway Patrol cars took us to Fort Carson until the next day then they sent us on our way, a different route. We had to leave all our luggage but I guess we are lucky to be alive. What a shaking experience. I am glad to be home. Dee Dee and the boys were here for supper. She is so unhappy. The baby's toes are grown together and Marvin has not written to her. She is getting along financially, but is very unhappy. I don't really know what to do for her. Well I am tired and glad to be home. There is a letter from Peggy. Mom

June 20, 1965

Well I got up and had breakfast and cleaned up the apartment and went to the launder mat by Safeway and done my washing. Came home and ironed. Went to the drug store to see if I could get my medicine bottles filled. I got one but have to wait till Monday for the rest. Came home and shampooed my hair and set it. Hamilton's came at noon to visit and the Buzz and Barbara came. I left with them on a picnic at Crystal Mountain. When leaving, here comes Dee Dee with her little kids. Stevie James had fell and cut his tongue open. I wanted to go and help her. But she said no, she would get Yang. I feel so badly about Dee Dee and her little ones but seems like there isn't any end to it. We had a nice time and stopped at Alex and Olga's dairy farm on the way back. They had just got back from Lake Tapps. I caught a cold and don't feel so hot. Mom

June 21, 1965 Monday

Aggie was suppose to come to lunch at one o'clock, so I fixed mashed potatoes—creamed chicken and buttered asparagus and got apple turnovers from the bakery, but Aggie didn't come. Shirley Fitch did, so she ate with me. Then Yang and Dee Dee and the kids came. I cleaned the place up and went home with Dee Dee. I have a rotten headache. Mom

June 22, 1965 Tuesday

Stayed with Dee Dee all day. Her welfare worker came out. It has been eleven days since she heard from Marvin. Kids and I took long walks. Stevie is off the bottle. He sleeps better but don't eat much. Mom

June 23, 1965 Wednesday

Went to Shirley Fitches to a Fashion Frocks Show. Had a good time. Ordered a garter belt—slip—and three pair of nylons. Came home took a nap. I am going to wait until five thirty to see if Fitch shows up to go out and eat. She didn't come so I ate out alone. Mom

June 24, 1965 Thursday

Today started out kinda dull and draggy. I done my work, sat around and sewed quilt blocks. Around noon, Shirley Fitch and Snooks dropped in for coffee. Snooks drank tea and I told her fortune. Shirley came and got me at three thirty and I had supper at her house, and I really did enjoy it. We had pork steak—fried potatoes—Brussels sprouts—cottage cheese and a Swedish pudding. After supper, Elmer and her and I went to Renton to get a muffler for the car. Then Shirley and I went to Snooks Mc Ness party, she invited twenty people and six showed up. Anyway, it was fun. Elmer put the muffler on the car. So home at nine thirty. NO Mail Mom

June 25, 1965 Friday

At eight thirty, Shirley Fitch and Snooks and Rodney came and got me. We were headed for the Airport with some luggage for Leonard Fitch in Alaska. Shirley says don't eat breakfast, we will eat out and then go visit Aggie. Well half way out of Kent the new muffler fell off. We had to stop and get that fixed.

Then we go to Des Moines and the distributor cap went poof. Well that took a bit of fixing. So we walked six blocks to a restaurant and ate breakfast. Then by that time, Shirley had spent all the shipping money and there wasn't any use of going to the Airport so we went to Aggies. She had a HANGOVER, she had burned her hair the night before with a permanent. Snooks told her she looked like hell. We had coffee and left. Our muffler came loose on the way to Kent. Well I came home and took a nap. Its three o'clock if anything else happens I'll say so. Dee Dee came and got me to stay overnight. Mom

June 26, 1965 Saturday

Got up and took the kids for a walk. They chased a black chicken all over the school ground, came home and had breakfast, took another little walk. Dee Dee is in the blackest most unhappy mood I ever saw in my life. She is scared of him coming home, I think. I just can't figure things out, but she is certainly in an unhappy panic over something, and all she talks about is him. Poor kids don't understand. Well anyway then we took a big long walk and Stevie James went to sleep, and slept for three or four hours. Then we went to Sugar's, things were odd there, like a black cloud before a storm. I finally came home. Yang Yang went to spend the weekend with Dee Dee. I gave them $2.00, it was all I had. I am supposed to go to Dee Dee Monday night so she can take Donnie to the clinic Tuesday morning. I suppose today I won't forget. I got a letter from Social Security informing me no money. Well OBOY guess I'll either have to find a job or a husband. Either one don't sound good. Mom

June 27, 1965 Sunday

Well the sun is shining this morning. I put a pot of split pea soup on. I wonder if I'll have company today. It is nine o'clock, I will let you know later. Well at eleven o'clock Shirley Kessack and the four kids came. I went home with them and had lunch. I done a little bit of ironing for her. Then we went to a Box Social with Wendy, it was held outdoors. We ate and the kids went on a scavenger hunt. The women went in the house and had coffee while they were gone. Oh what a beautiful home. I sure do feel like I missed a lot in life. Oh well too late now. At least I have my own apartment. We then went to Rachel's house. She is a friend of Shirley's and real active in the church. She has been married twice and has three or four children, but she seems to be very capable woman and keeps a nice home on welfare. We then stopped at Sissy's a few minutes. Then home. Quite a full day. Mom

June 28, 1965 Monday

I got up and cleaned house today. Barbara Kessack and her mother and children were here. I was real glad to see them. We went downstairs and looked at the apartment, what a dump. I was real happy to get back upstairs. They left and I took a rest and Dee Dee and Yang came and the kids. We went to Auburn. Dee Dee went in and got Yang's money and also four shifts a week for herself. It's all weekend, Friday night all night, Saturday night till two in the morning, Sunday and Monday five hours day shifts. It's a man killer but what can I do? She needs the money and I do too. Well we will see. She is still fighting with Marvin, so I guess he won't be coming home after all. I went home with Dee Dee and stayed all night. NO MAIL. Mom

June 29, 1965 Tuesday

Dee Dee got up and took little Donnie and Ricky to the clinic. Marvin and Stevie and I went on two or three walks. She got home at noon. We fixed the kids up and went to Auburn Park and had hamburgers and fries. The kids went in the pool and seemed to enjoy it. I had left the gas on, and was it ever hot. I opened all the windows and cooled things down. Amelia stopped in and we had a nice visit. I sure enjoy her, we can discuss life and problems and people so easily. NO MAIL. Mom

June 30, 1965 Wednesday

Well I got up at nine well rested. My knees are giving me a rough time. I went to the laundry mat and done my washing and phoned Sissy. I came home and went to the Goodwill and bakery. At the Goodwill, I bought a pillow-a picture—a cake plate—an ashtray—and some hankies. At the bakery, I bought $1.00 mixed cookies. I came home and made orange cool aid, I hope I have company. I met Slax on the street and asked him if I could use the chest of drawers that is downstairs, he said yes. He would bring it up. Good deal. Its twelve thirty, I will write more later. Well it is now ten to seven, nobody came. I seen Dee Dee and the boys drive by. I flagged her down and asked her up but she wouldn't come up. She was very-very bitter, she had got a letter from Marvin but was very unhappy with it. I think her bitterness is going to ruin her life and her little sons. Well I don't know what to do. NO MAIL. Mom

July 1, 1965 Thursday

Well it's eight o'clock, the sun is shining, it's a new day and a new month. I hope both turn out well. I couldn't get to sleep last night thinking of Dee Dee and her troubles, and there just isn't anything I can do to help. I hate to see her eat her heart out in bitterness, it's bad for her and bad for the kids. I prayed to God to take a hand last night. I feel so useless. Well I wonder what will happen today. I haven't much to do but sew. Will write more later. Well it's close to five o'clock, Sissy came down with the twins-Cindy-Patti-and Lorri. We had Kool aid and cookies. I went and got Elaine's little baby and showed them. After they left, I called Barbara and her and Buzz are coming to visit this evening. I done a little shopping today. I got teaspoons and remnants at the Goodwill. A yard of print and some eyelet at Penney's. I made a round pillow for my bed. I called Wendy and told her I couldn't go to church Sunday because I would be working. I mailed Cindy—Jimmie Jr.—and Butch Kessack birthday cards today with quarters glued to them. Well guess this is all unless something unexpected turns up. Mom P.S. Dee Dee and the boys came, Shirley Fitch came, Buzz and Barb and kids came. I got a letter from Seattle Bus Depot, my suitcase is there. I will get it tomorrow.

July 2, 1965 Friday

Well I got on the eight o'clock bus and went to Seattle and picked up my long lost suitcase at Trail Ways bus depot. Then I went to Dee Dee's and babysat. She worked all night, got home seven in the morning. Mom

July 3, 1965 Saturday

Well Dee Dee slept until eleven. The kids were pretty good. The welfare check came. She went house hunting, found one in Kent. A duplex at $70.00 a month, no furniture, just stove and refrigerator. She took it. I watched Stevie and Donnie in my apartment while she shopped and paid bills. Well she paid me $20.00, part babysitting and part some she had borrowed. She went to work until two in the morning. She brought Yang home with her. Her landlord found out she is moving and came over and raised the devil. Mom

July 4, 1965 Sunday

We all got up and had breakfast. Yang and I took Boofy—Ricky and Stevie, and went hunting for a store that was open. We found one. Yang bought $6.00 worth of groceries—chicken—potato chips—watermelon—candy etc. We went home, Dee Dee left to work at one. Yang slept until four. The kids were good, it was hot. Dee Dee got home at nine and brought me home. I slept like a log. Mom

July 5, 1965 Monday

Well I had a good rest and feel much better. I took a hot lilac sponge bath and put on clean clothes. I am going out to see if I can find an open store. Dee Dee is going to move today and I will have the kids. So more later alligator. Well I had to shop at Meeker Cafe, nothing else was open. I had the kids from ten till six, they were real good but I was sure tired when they left. Amelia visited with me a few minutes. Dee Dee got Yang and Pat to help her and rented a U Haul Truck and got moved. Old Smoltz is sure mad at her. Well I wonder if she will be satisfied here. I hope she at least stays until he gets home. I phoned Aggie last night, she was drunk. Mom

July 6, 1965 Tuesday

Well I woke up at six, ate two boiled eggs, coffee and my pills and went to the laundry mat and done my washing. I phoned Barbara and gabbed. My place needs cleaning up, but the kids will be here all afternoon while Dee Dee goes to King County Hospital and gets the birth control deal. So more after while crocodile. Well Dee Dee didn't go. She came over with Marvin—Ricky and Suzie the dog about two o'clock. We went grocery shopping for her. The new landlady said the dog had to go. Ricky was screaming about it. I told her get some gold fish for them. So she did. We took Suzie up on the hill and turned her loose. Well Ricky was so upset I said let me take him home overnight, so I did. He was just fine until bedtime, then he wanted home. There was a big three car crash under my window about five o'clock. Well more tomorrow. Mom

July 7, 1965 Wednesday

Got up at ten. Ricky and I had breakfast. Donnie came and had coffee with us. I walked Ricky home at noon. Dee Dee had just got up. Boy was that place a mess. Man. She wanted some pink plastic to put new seats on her chairs so I told her I would go get it and come back in an hour. I went and got it and was going to stop by my apartment, and here was Sissy and the kids. Well we were having coffee, and here comes Shirley Fitch. We all had coffee and I paid Shirley $8.00 for the bed. Then we all went to Dee Dee's, she still wasn't dressed and the place was still a mess. We stayed a few minutes and left. I went to the bank and got $25.00. I ate a roast beef dinner and had my haircut. I came home and painted my cupboards and two chairs. Scrubbed floors and waxed them. I went to the laundry mat with my rugs. Dee Dee came, we drove to Tukwila to see if she had any mail, just a bill. We came to Kent and had root beer and French fries. So to bed. NO MAIL. Mom

July 8, 1965 Thursday

Got up at ten, had boiled eggs and fresh raspberries. It is cool today. My apt sure looks sharp and clean. Well I wonder what will happen today. I go babysit at nine tonight until two—tomorrow. Well now it is six o'clock, I have been here and there all day. No mail as usual. I called Gwen long distance, she sounded hilarious. She said why don't I write. I told her when I get a letter to answer I would. It is cooling off, it looks like rain. Naturally. If I go babysit a weekend, it will rain. I don't like this weekend bologna. I would like to go to church on Sunday and visit the other kids that work all week. But darn it anyway, I do need the money so what am I going to do? I wish Dee Dee had a husband that would support her and keep her busy and happy so I wouldn't get so involved. I would like a life of my own. Mom

July 9, 1965 Friday

Well me and the kids got up at ten thirty. Dee Dee got home fifteen after eleven. Tired and crossed. She got to bed about twelve and slept till three with a couple interruptions. She got up cranky as a skunk. I came home. I have to have a few hours to myself to stand it. Stevie James was asleep when I left. The other three were awake and just as cranky as her. I wonder what it takes to teach her she can't raise four kids and work twelve-hour shifts. I went to Meeker Café and had liver and onions, came home. NO MAIL I laid down and slept 1 ½ hours. I made $4.00, but I am beat. Well I go back at nine tonight and try again. Darn kids stay up until midnight. Mom P.S. I signed the car over to Dee Dee today. Probably never get anything for it, but the insurance is up and I don't want the responsibility.

July 10, 1965 Saturday

Well a very dull day, I slept most of the time. I walked home from Dee Dee's at nine o'clock, she didn't work last night. So I spent the night with no pay. She went to Renton to see Yang and ran into Ronnie a friend of hers. They were out a while. He wants to buy my car for $150.00 cash. I'm going to sell it if he does. I mended and washed sox's today, six pair of them and sewed one quilt block. Dee Dee came over about three and I went with her grocery shopping. Her and the kids came up to the apartment a few minutes. She is an OLD GROUCH, the kids were wound up. She wants me to babysit tonight. She says she is going to work, I don't know. If I do, I expect pay tonight. I would rather stay home and go to church in the morning. Snooks came with my floor wax from the Mc Ness party. It's raining, its six thirty. NO MAIL. Mom

July 11, 1965 Sunday

Well not much stirring today. I got home from babysitting at one o'clock with $4.00 pay this time. I slept a while, walked the floor a while. I ate a can of chilled apricots and the rest of the split pea soup. About five o'clock I started out for a walk and ran into Sissy. She took me up the hill. They are painting Vicki and Cindy's room, lavender and coral rose. I visited a while and came back home. It seems Sugar has another car, a Buick, he got from old man Fowler. That makes six and none of them run. Well no other news I guess. Tomorrow I babysit the kids at my house for ten hours with pay. I wonder how me, the kids and the apartment will live through that? Mom

July 12, 1965 Monday

Well up and bright and early. I am waiting for the stores to open so I can go to the bakery and order cupcakes for my party tomorrow, and get some stuff for lunch today. As I will have four little boys for ten hours. I am also expecting Aggie and Shirley Fitch and maybe Sis for a few minutes and maybe Yang part of the time. Man it sounds wild. More later alligator. Well the boys did not come so I guess Dee Dee didn't wake up. Snooks—Robin—Penny—Rodney and the two little boys she babysits came down and had lunch with me. Shirley Fitch and Judy came down and we went over to Dee Dee's. Now I am back home. Shirley and Elmer might trade cars with her and $90.00 to boot. It would be a good deal and I hope it goes through. Twenty minutes to three, more later. Well Buzz came at five and took me home to dinner and I sure enjoyed that. I sold my car to Shirley Fitch for $100.00 cash, and a 52 Chevy for Dee Dee to drive. Now I am free and clear of that headache. NO MAIL. Mom

July 13, 1965 Tuesday

Got up and got things lined up for my Mc Ness party tonight. I babysat Angel from eleven to four thirty. I took her over to play with the boys a while. Then Aggie came and brought us home, and had lunch with us. She gave me a $5.00 order and booked a party. It is six thirty, one hour and my guest will begin to come. I hope it is a success. I have cupcakes—jello with fruit—cookies—punch and coffee. Also dishes of candy.

NO MAIL, well more later diary. Well my party was a huge success, I get a nice rug for my trouble. Thelma Smith was here and said she had been to see Marty, and he had remarked that they better get Geyman out soon, or some of them lifer's were going to kill him. I remarked, maybe they would be doing Dee Dee a big favor. None of the Geyman's showed up. Mom

July 14, 1965 Wednesday

Got up about eight. Cleaned up the apartment and sewed on quilt blocks. Snooks and Dee Dee came about one. They left me and little Donnie off at Shirley Fitches for Darrell's birthday party. They took the other kids and Judy, and Bobby to the better clinic on highway 99. They were gone all afternoon but I had a nice time. Sissy and her seven were there, May Lyons and her seven were there. Sissy has a badly swollen jaw from a bad tooth. When the girls came back, they had cake and ice cream and then took Dee Dee and her kid's home. She got a letter from Marvin. Then Snooks—Penny—Robin and I got hamburgers and came up to the apartment and ate them with cupcakes and jello and kool aid. After they left I put on my Moo Moo and just rested. NO MAIL. Mom

July 15, 1965 Thursday

Got up at seven thirty, Sissy was here at eight thirty and her jaw sure was a mess. Dr. Rigg, dentist across the street, opened at nine. She went over and had it pulled. Dunc was here at noon and had coffee. They are foreclosing on his house and he is glad of that. He wants to dump it. but the renter in it—signed a year's lease. So I don't know legally where that leaves Dunc. It is two fifteen, Aggie was supposed to come today but as Snooks says, don't depend on it. Wonder what Dee Dee is doing? I have been sewing quilt blocks and sleeping. I had ground round—boiled spud—and wax beans for dinner. More later. Well Dee Dee came over at four, left Stevie James and Donnie, took Marvin and Ricky to Auburn to shop and get her pay for Jeanie. She came back at six thirty and had Yang. She said she was going to work. Well it made me raving mad, with her on welfare they could throw us both in and I told her so. Well it ended up her not going. Mom

July 16, 1965 Friday

Sis was down at eight thirty this morning. She looks a lot better. I am not feeling good today. I think it was a reaction from fighting with Dee Dee last night. Darn that girl, will she ever settle down? She knows damn well if she gets caught, working on welfare what the results would be. They would have me for aiding and abetting. I tell her go out and kick up your heels once a week, they can't throw you in jail for that. Well I got a headache and upset stomach. I can't take this old jazz any more. Its eleven thirty. Well at three thirty Dee Dee brought the kids over, the two babies had the poops, so she asked me to take the two boys to the dentist, so I did. They had appointments O.K. but the nurse informed me the slips were no good, they should have been used in May. It just didn't hit me right and I told her so. I told her the whole set up was squirrely. I brought the bys home. They played for two hours with Angel. Elaine came down for coffee. Ricky fell down the back steps and skinned his face and side. I took them home at seven o'clock. Dee Dee was watching for Ronnie and he didn't come. Boy was she mad. She had a nice letter from Marvin but was not interested. She went over to Esters a while. I stayed overnight. Mom

July 17, 1965 Saturday

I walk home from Dee Dee's at eight o'clock. I had coffee—a butter horn—and a piece of cantaloupe and my pills. Laid down and slept, now it is ten minutes to ten. I think I will go get something to sew. I will let you know later. Well its fifteen to eleven. I just took a walk over to Benjamin Franklins to get a pair of pillowcases to work on. When a parade of old fashion cars drove up and stopped, about 75 of them dating back to 1915 or more. The people in them were dressed according to the date of their car. What a sight. I wished little Boofy could have seen them. They never get up in time to see anything. Well it's cold today. I am going to sew on the pillowcases, more later. Dee Dee came over and wanted me to ride to Sugars and pick up Yang. Then it seems Ricky wanted to stay overnight with me, so I said O.K. Well we went to Dee Dee's until time for Yang to go to work. I watched the kids while she took her to Renton. She brought home a watermelon and then brought me and Ricky home. Judy invited us up for dinner today, we said O.K. now Dee Dee won't go because Sugar is mad, because I sold the Chevy to Fitches. Well I was the one that sold the car and I'll damn soon tell him so. He has seven heaps in the yard now. Don't make no difference what I do somebody is mad. So Whoopie, to heck with em, they are all spoiled brats. NO MAIL. Mom

July 18, 1965 Sunday

Well Ricky and I got up and ate a light breakfast at eight, and at nine walked over and got Dee Dee up. We ate pancakes and got ready and went to Sugar and Judy's by eleven thirty. Judy and Dee Dee took Marvin—Ricky and Bobby to Safeway so Judy could shop. I watched Stevie and Donnie. Sugar and Yang were asleep. Well they got back about two and fixed dinner and we all ate. Then we left Dannie D with Yang and the rest of us went to Buzzy's. Hamilton's were there, we all visited and Buzz cut Sugars hair. Then Sugar—Judy—Bobby—Dee Dee, the boys and I all went to Geymans and visited about two hours. Then back to Sugars. They brought me home and here I am. Tired but I had a nice day. Sugar paid me $5.00 on the note, that makes $15.00 he has paid and boy it's O.K. Well to bed I think, I am tired. More tomorrow. Mom P.S. Bogue's bought a station wagon and went to Yakima today.

July 19, 1965 Monday

Well got up at eight, ate a peach—cup of coffee and my pills. Went to the laundry mat and done my washing. Went to the eighty-eight cent store and bought five coffee cups, all pink and a wedding anniversary card for Dee Dee. Went over and watched her kids while she went to the dentist. When she got back Judy and Bobby came and Snooks—Rodney—Penny and Robin. I rode home with Judy. I got a letter from Peggy. I talked to Sissy and Aggie on the phone. I ate cottage cheese and sliced tomato for lunch. I slept from one to three. Dee Dee and Marvin Jr. came and we went to Auburn and back. She went home and I went to Meeker Café and had a hot beef sandwich and dinner salad. It is now six o'clock, guess I will answer Peggy's letter. Any more news I'll let you know. Amelia was in and visited a couple of hours tonight. Mom

July 20, 1965 Tuesday Last page Volume 1.

Well its nine o'clock in the morning and its pouring rain. Just my luck to babysit today. Dee Dee goes to Seattle to get that birth control deal in her. At least there won't be anymore. At ten, I am going to the bank and get some money. I am going to buy a three-quart soup kettle with a lid so I can make big pots of soup. I am going to get some stuff for old fashion vegetable beef soup. More later you old horn toad alligator. Well it is fifteen to twelve, I got the money. I bought a five quart soup kettle at the Goodwill, went to Safeway and bought vegetables and meat to fill it up. I'll be eating soup for the rest of the week, but it's good. At twelve I am to go to Dee Dee's, it's raining more or less. I didn't get any mail, big deal. More later. Well I got to Dee Dee's, kids and her were still in nightgowns and Yang in bed fighting like mad. Poor Boofy, got paddled three times before she left. They just went out the door and here comes the welfare worker. Well they came back in and got that settled, then left. I got the kids dressed and cooled down and cleaned up the house. Boofy got hurt in the afternoon. After she got home, that pig Ester came. Mom NO MAIL.

CHAPTER 5
MOM KESSACKS DIARY 1965

Volume 2, 7-21-1965 to 8-11-1965

July 21, 1965 Wednesday

Well I woke up at eight, had to wait thirty minutes to use the bathroom. Now I am having my pills and coffee. I am supposed to walk over and watch the kids while Dee Dee gets her driver's license renewed. Then watch the babies tonight, while she goes to Geyman's to Agnes's birthday party. Hope she is up and dressed and in a better mood. It's cool and looks like rain. Well Shirley Fitch and Judy came down, we had soup and doughnuts. They left and Sissy and the kids came down. The twins are a year old today. They are having a party Saturday. Well we had soup and doughnuts and went over to Dee Dee's. Shirley and Judy were there and so was Snooks—Penny and Robin. Well we all left there. I came home. Got a letter from Gwen finally. I went back to Dee Dee's at about four thirty and babysat while she shopped and ate supper. Then she took Marvin and Ricky and went to Geyman's. I watched Stevie and Donnie. She got home at eleven thirty, with chow mien from Long acres Café where Yang is working. I stayed all night. Mom

219

July 22, 1965 Thursday

They are having sidewalk sales in Kent today, Friday and Saturday. So I will be going up town. Well I didn't see any bargains so I came home and sewed on the pillowcases and took a long nap. I got the things I ordered from Fashion Frocks through the mail today. Sure is a pretty slip. Eileen and her baby came down and visited this afternoon. She has a swollen jaw from a bad tooth. Snooks—Dee Dee and kids came and got me at five o'clock. We bought Barbecued chicken dinners and ate on Dee Dee's lawn. Snooks went home at six thirty. I stayed until nine and Dee Dee brought me home. She seems to be in a lot better spirits. Well not to bad a day. Mom

July 23, 1965 Friday

Got up at eight. Crocheted a while, finished the pillowcases. Then walked over to Dee Dee's and watched Marvin—Stevie and Donnie while she went to Auburn. Shirley Fitch came while I was there. I rode home with her. I got a letter from Peggy. I watched Elaine's baby while she went to the dentist. Dee Dee came by, said she was headed for the post office because she wasn't getting her mail. I know how she feels. I had the same trouble until I raised the devil. It is real hot today. Dee Dee said come on over, she made spaghetti, but my apartment is so cool and her house so hot and there is six blocks between us. I want to watch the street dance at nine. Maybe around six I will walk over there. It is five now. Well I walked over and Yang was there. Dee Dee was in one of her nasty moods and Boofy was just as bad. Ricky had, got black top all over him and was a mess. The house was hot. Sure wished I had stayed home. Yang brought me home at eight. I walked around town, at nine came home and went to bed. Mom

July 24, 1965 Saturday

Got up at eight, it's going to be one of those hot days. Went up town and bought a spool of thread, been sewing on a quilt. Elaine came down and borrowed some soap. Dull day, no mail. Suppose to go to the Twins birthday party at two, if Dee Dee comes and takes me. Well she came at eleven and we went to her place. A neighbor girl came over for coffee. Then Dee Dee—Marvin and Ricky went to get birthday presents for the twins and Penny. Then we went to Sissy's to the party and stayed until five. It was real hot today. We came down to my apartment and ate split pea soup. Buzz stopped by and gave me $5.00. They had been to Point Defiance. After Dee Dee left, I went to Shop Rite and got some food for $3.90, came home and Amelia visited for ½ hour. I sewed on the silk quilt, in fact, I finished it. I took a sponge bath. It is eight o'clock. I'm tired. NO MAIL Mom

July 25, 1965 Sunday

This is Sunday, I didn't' wake up until ten o'clock. I had my breakfast, swept the apartment and hall and made my bed. I took the clothes across the street to the laundry mat. It is real hot today. I wonder if I will have any company. If I don't, I will sew on some baby quilts. I will have to iron my clothes when they are done. Amelia was in last night. We both know so many people from years back that we find lots to talk about. Well it is eleven o'clock, will write more later.

Well Dee Dee came and said, let's go get Yang and go to Auburn Park, I said O.K. and went. We took Judy and Bobby too. We had root beer—hamburgers and French fries and everyone enjoyed it. We took Judy and Bobby home and Yang bought a watermelon. I stayed until seven and Yang brought me home. Dee Dee is in one of her terrible moods again, and her and Boofy go round and round. It's terrible, he was going to run away this morning. I wonder how this is all going to end. I think CALAMITY is the word. Mom

July 26, 1965 Monday

Well it hasn't been much of a day. Ester woke me up at seven thirty, wanting me to babysit Shelly. I didn't want to and didn't. I went to Dee Dee's at one so she could go get the car in her name. Aggie came on over. I made two beds and hung up the clothes while she was gone. Yang was there sleeping, she got up and brought me home. I stopped at Elaine's apartment, because she wants me to babysit DaWanda, while her and Slacks takes Angel to the circus. She had noodles and beef so I ate there. I finished sewing the baby quilts today. I gave one to Elaine. The other two I think I will keep around to use on my legs and visiting children. No mail, oh boy some people. Mom

July 27, 1965 Tuesday

Well what a goofy day. I got up at nine, ate a banana and doughnut for breakfast. Started out to Safeway to buy some groceries, stopped at the phone booth and called Sissy and along came Shirley Fitch and her kids and Snooks and Rodney. Well we all went to the rummage sale. I bought cushions—a sweater and a bedspread. Then we went to the Goodwill. I bought three forks—three knives—a pillow—a piece of cloth. We came to my place, I fixed beef and gravy—mashed spuds and green beans. Then we went up the hill. Snooks took all the kids swimming, we went to Sissy's and then to Dee Dee's. Then I came home and washed the dishes and mended sox's. Laid down to rest and Yang came and said Dee Dee wanted me to babysit. Well I did, then we took the kids to Auburn Park and then had fish and chips at the A&W. Now I am home and Elaine and Slax want me down for steak supper. Well I'm going. I went to Elaine's and Slacks had fixed a nice steak dinner. I enjoyed it and had a nice visit. They are all good friends. NO MAIL. Mom

July 28, 1965 Wednesday

Well I'm up at eight twenty, the sun is shining looks like it's going to be hot today. Am supposed to go to a Tupperware party at Snooks today. If, someone comes and gets me. Well Dee Dee came and got me, her landlady and neighbor was with her. We had a good time, I ordered a bread container. Went to Dee Dee's afterwards and listened to her landlady yack yack till my head hurt. Snooks came by so I rode home. It's hot today. Am home, I think I will take a nap. Its ten minutes after four. More later you nasty gator. Well I slept till five fifteen, got up and went to the butcher shop, bought six eggs ½ lb ground round, came home and boiled a spud and cooked half the meat and sliced a tomato. Yang dropped in with a raspberry pie and some ice cream. She ironed her apron and took off for work, she sure looked cute. Well cleaned up my apartment, put on my muu muu and went to sleep. NO MAIL. Mom

July 29, 1965 Thursday

Shirley Fitch—Snooks and Rodney woke me up at nine. We had coffee and pie. It is going to be hot today. We got in a hot discussion on how stinky the Alf's are. Well they are gone now, Wonder what else will happen today. It's ten o'clock. Well its four o'clock and it has been quite a day. At eleven o'clock Sissy and her seven—Snooks and Rodney—Shirley Fitch and Betty Blaylock and Heather came, we all had pastries from the bakery—coffee and lemonade until one thirty, then everybody left but Sissy. We went to Steel Lake for about an hour. So now, we are all planning a picnic there tomorrow. I seen Yang at the Post Office when we drove through Kent. I yelled at her to come up but so far she hasn't. I think I will fix beans and weenies for tomorrow. More later alligator. Well I walked over to Dee Dee's and they were all content. She was making kitchen curtains. I visited and played with the kids and ate supper and then they brought me home. It is now twenty five after eight. I will call it a day. NO MAIL Mom

July 30, 1965 Friday

Well it is nine twenty and it is shaping up for a hot day. I ate two doughnuts had coffee for my breakfast. I mopped my apartment and hallway. If things go as planned Bogues—Fitches—Geymans and I are all going to Steel Lake at noon. I am going to buy a dollar box of goodies at the bakery to take. Well I'll write more later. Well it is ten twenty five. I have been all over town this morning. Just got home in time to see Patsy. They have been salmon fishing. They left me some salmon and Patsy said she might come out on the bus to Dee Dee's birthday party next Wednesday. Well more after while you lousy crocodile. Well we all went to Steel Lake and had a ball. The twins played in the dirt and got dirty. Stevie James didn't feel good. We all ate and ate. Came home, went over to Dee Dee's with the salmon steaks, stayed until after eight, had Yang bring me home. Sure was hot. Now here this for a bit of news, No mail. HA. Mom

July 31, 1965 Saturday

Well it is ten after eight and hotter than blazes already. I have had my breakfast. I wonder what will happen today. It's like looking at the cover of a book and wondering what the story is like inside. Well after while crocodile. Well its eight o'clock and been a busy day. Elaine came and Shirley Fitch—Snooks came and Thelma Smith and her Aunt came and it's just been a ball. Dee Dee came at four to get me to babysit Stevie and Donnie while her and Marvin and Ricky and Ester and Shelly went swimming at Steel Lake. I did and Yang came to Dee Dee's while they were gone. Dee Dee and Ester are going out tonight. I guess I'll babysit. Well someday alligator old pal this old gal is going to find somebody and go out too, and I'll tell you something else, it ain't going to be long now. I'm getting to old to waste any more time, ole pal o mine, so as the song says, there's going to be some changes made around here. No mail as usual Mom

August 1, 1965 Sunday

It is eleven o'clock I just woke up. I walked home from Dee Dee's at seven this morning, took my pills and ate a cup of soup and went to sleep. It is hot again today. Ricky cried in his sleep all night. I think he has leg cramps. I wonder what will happen today. Well I'll tell you it was hot. All I done was lay around. I did go to the laundry mat. There has been a man in a white shirt running around town looking for a room to rent. I first ran into him at three and it is eight o'clock and he is still looking. If Slax and Elaine were home, he could probably get the front room. He is from Las Vegas and is going to work at Heath. I talked to Sissy on the phone. I wonder how Dee Dee and the kids are. I wish this heat would break, it's so hard on little ones. Well no company today. I should have gone and helped Dee Dee. I was just too damn tired to move. I walked around town with this man a while, he bought me a pop. Seemed funny even talking to a man. I don't even know his name. Guess I'll go talk to Amelia. Moms

August 2, 1965 Monday

The Lord helps them what help themselves. Now read this before you answer me. Well this has been one day and a half. Sissy came at nine, we had coffee and a nice visit. It seemed cool so I walked over to Dee Dee's to see if she wanted to pick beans. She wasn't up, so I came back home. I had coffee with Elaine and Slax, it seems the man I was running around town with slept in the front room last night. Then this morning he moved to an apartment. He told Elaine he had to have a place where he could entertain women. Elaine said he gave her $10.00. She gets to keep $8.00. He told me he was from Las Vegas and he told her he was from Chicago. He had three suitcases and a wallet full of money. Well at eleven Snooks and Shirley came. We went to Renton. Shirley said tomorrow we would go to Seattle. So I went to the bank at ten to three and drew $25.00. The banker left a $50.00 bill laying there and I snitched it. The bank will have a hard time figuring the fifty-dollar deficit. Sis didn't think much of it, but Sis isn't in the world alone trying to exist. What better place to get it from than a bank. They got lots of money. I've got my apartment ready for Peg and Andy, guess they are in Calif. Somewhere. I called Bev she said they aint there yet. Called Gwen she wasn't home NO MAIL. Mom

August 3, 1965 Tuesday

Shirley and Snooks were here at eight thirty this morning, and I was ready to go. We went to Seattle Goodwill. I bought a nice wool skirt for $1.00 and a sleeper for Donnie D for .39 cents and a pair of shoes for .39 cents. We stopped at a Wigwam store. I bought a few things there. Then we went to Andies Café and had dinner. Shirley had roast turkey, Snooks and I had roast beef. Came home and guess what, there was a letter in my box, the gas bill. BIG DEAL. I went to Dee Dee and watched Donnie D while her and the boys went shopping. Pat came home with her so I walked home. Laid down and took a nap. No other News I guess that is nothing personal. It is seven thirty now. Don't suppose anything else will happen today. Mom

August 4, 1965 Wednesday

Well this is Dee Dee's birthday she is 22. We are having potluck lunch and birthday party for her. It is cool today which is good. Will write more later you scaly old gator. Well its twenty minutes to nine, it has been quite a day. I went to Dee Dee's at ten, she went and got her driver's license renewed. Then everybody came for her party. Vicki and Robin got in a fight. Old Smotzes, Dee Dee's old landlord from Tukwila came and threaten her. After everybody left, we took a ride to Auburn. Kinda looked along the way for bean picking, but didn't find any. I got out at my apartment. I visited Elaine and went up town. I ate turkey at the Moonlight Inn. I bought some pink material, I'm going to make pink pillowcases with lavender pansies on it. I asked Amelia if her friend Juanita Epperson would hire Dee Dee to pick cucumbers, so she called her up and she said yes. So I went over to tell her, Marvin and Ricky were up the road two blocks away. Zelma was at Dee Dee's, yack—yack—yacking. Geymans came with cake and ice cream, Dee Dee just sat there like a dummy. I had to come home and babysit for Elaine. Don't know what happened. NO MAIL. Mom

August 5, 1965 Thursday

The alarm rang at five, I shut it off and fell back asleep until ten to six. I jumped up and headed for Dee Dee's. I had my coffee and pills over there. Her and the landlady went cucumber picking. They picked from seven to twelve. They get 1 cent a pound, didn't make much. To boot the landlady lost $20.00 out of her bra. Spent a quiet afternoon. Maybelle Evans is picking Elaine and I up to go to Buzzy's and Barbs to a toy party. If anything else happens, I will let you know. I got a card from Patsy. I have to get up in the morning and go babysit. Dee Dee is going to try beans tomorrow. Mom P.S. Went to the party. Barbara had to be taken to the hospital in an ambulance, she was having a miscarriage. Bonnie her sister fainted and Maybelle went to pieces. Otherwise, toys were sold etc.

August 6, 1965 Friday

Got up at six thirty, walked to Dee Dee's her and Pat and the little neighbor boy started out bean picking but didn't get to pick. So Dee Dee brought me home. I washed at the laundry mat and done my ironing, then went to Safeway. Came home and put some butterbeans on to cook. I laid down and feel asleep and burned them. It is now fifteen to twelve, guess I'll sew on my pink pillowcases a while. Well its eight o'clock. I went to the Goodwill, bought a blanket—a meat platter—a iron. Then went to the second had store. Bought a toaster for .50 cents. Haven't done much today laid around mostly. I am defrosting the refrigerator. Went to the store with Elaine. She said she might be down after awhile. Slax is going to watch a game on T.V. It was 84 today. Well I suppose Hudocks will arrive this weekend. Hope Barbara is O.K. Mom

August 7, 1965 Saturday

Well it has been quite warm today. I stayed at home until noon. Cleaned up my apartment then walked over to Dee Dee's. Yang was there, then Amelia came and then Sugar. I hung up the washing, then Sugar and I went to Arctic Circle and bought hamburgers and milkshakes. Then we went back to Dee Dee's. Sugar was drinking beer. We went to Auburn and got Dee Dee's pictures out. Stopped at the Silver Slipper. Sugar had a schooner I had 7-Up. Sugar bought half a case of beer for a bean picker. We came back to Dee Dee's and Carol and Mrs. Smith were there. We visited a while. Sugar invited us all up for dinner tomorrow and took Ricky home with him. It is two weeks and a day since Dee Dee has heard from Marvin, she's quite upset. I came home and Elaine was down. Then Amelia Thatcher came. There is going to be a baby shower at the church for a woman with seven kids, so we got busy and finished up a baby quilt for her. It has been hot today. NO MAIL. Mom

August 8, 1965 Sunday

It's Sunday morning, ten after nine, and hot already. I crocheted on the one pink pillowcase. I wonder where Andy and Peggy are at. Am suppose to go to Sugars for dinner today with Dee Dee and the kids, and to a baby shower at the Adventist church with Amelia to night at seven. Well we will see about all these things later in the day. Well I walked over to Dee Dee's and helped her get ready, her yacking landlady was there. We finally got going. Judy fixed fried chicken—macaroni salad and corn on the cob. I came home at four because I had called Jimmies and Bev said Hudocks would be here by six. Well they came at five thirty and we had a supper and went up to Sissy's. Mom

August 9, 1965 Monday

Well the day started out with Aggie coming and cooking up a get together for Sunday at her place. Then Peggy and I went to Shop Rite and got some groceries. Peggy made cabbage rolls. Sissy and her kids came down and Dee Dee and her kids came over. Also, her ex-landlord came barging in raising hell. Well otherwise, it's been an ordinary day I guess. Its seven o'clock and I'm here alone, I don't know where anybody is. A young couple named Barbara and Mike are moving in downstairs. They are friends of Elaine's and Slax. Well I don't know what's cooking tonight but will let you know. Well Bogue and Sissy, Andy and Peggy, Tommy and I went to the Colonial Tavern and then Duncs. Sugar and Butch had been down earlier and were {something} to the girls. We came home about eleven thirty and Peggy don't know it, but Tommy sneaked out to Dee Dee's. Mom

August 10, 1965 Tuesday

Bogue came after Tommy at seven, suppose to be working. Went to laundry mat and then Dee Dee's, she was in one of her black moods. Then we went up to Sissy's. Well we are back home. Peggy is making chili. More later. Dunc and Shirley were here today. They all went to Bogues. I watched little Donnie Dee while Dee Dee took Charlie and the boys to the drive in. She had their hair cut today, even little Stevie James curls. NO MAIL. Mom

August 11, 1965 Wednesday

Well Aggie came before I was up. I got up and her and I took off to Auburn to get a can of Van Camps Pork & Beans for the dinner Sun. Then we went to Sugars to see Judy. Then to Shirley Fitches and Snooks and they were not home. Then we went to Renton to the Beacon and had a steak dinner and vodka Collins. Then home. I took a nap and then went with Hudocks, house hunting. Then at six went to Dunc and Shirley's for steak dinner. Buzz and Barb came down while we were there. Tommy took pictures with a Polaroid camera. Had a good time. I called Gwens and Georgia answered. Gwen is sitting out three days, car fines. Well Bev called Sissy's and said Jim would fly up Friday. A letter from Dottie. Mom

Chapter 6

Volume 2
Aug to Oct 1965

August 12-13 1965 Thurs & Fri

Don't remember too much about Thursday, we had corn on the cob—fresh tomatoes and pork chops for supper. But man Friday the 13th I got up at six and walked to Dee Dee's and babysat while she and Charlie went bean picking. Charlie earned $3.00 she earned $7.00. When I got home what a shock, a letter from a collection agency trying to sue me for Dee Dee's rent in Tukwila. Boy, I went down to Chief Lee and told him my troubles, he said to call him if any of them bother me again. We went up to Sissy's and here is her and the kids on the road crying because he is taking off with Billy, well we took off with her and the kids. OH I HATE MEN THE DRUNKER SODDEN BEAST PERIOD. Mom

August 14, 1965 Saturday

Well I didn't get up until ten. Dunc came Andy left with him and Sugar came and went with them. It's eight o'clock at night and hadn't seen them since. Buzz, Barb and Diane came. Shirley Fitch and Snooks came. She brought my Tupperware.

Barb brought the toys I bought. After everybody left Peggy and I went to Renton Beauty Parlor and got our hair shampooed and set. Then we went to Dee Dee's. Something was wrong with her car. We took Tommy to get the parts so he could fix it and get Dee Dee's groceries. I paid Nov & Dec rent today and stocked up on canned food. I will be O.K. until Jan 1. Then I don't really know what is going to happen to me financially, but I'm not going to worry yet. I got a letter from Gina today. I also mailed her a birthday card and a pair of pretty pants. Am writing a card to Gwen. Well Tommy seems to be staying with Dee Dee, hope no stinking trouble comes from that. Mom Well Sugar came in drunk at ten and fell across my bed. Andy came in drunk at eleven, we put him on the floor. UG—do they stink.

August 15, 1965 Sunday

Well we all got up and went to Aggie's. Bogues—George Kessack —Don Kessack—Sugar—Butch & Judy—Hamilton's—Mike & Snooks—Penny & Robin—Dee Dee and the boys and her neighbors Arleen & Marvin. We had barbecued chicken— weenies—beans—salads—scalloped spuds—sandwiches— birthday cake for Dunc and watermelon. Pictures were taken, food was eaten, beer was drank and it is now eight o'clock and there is still a poker game going on. I am tired so Snooks brought me home. I am going to lay down and I hope I sleep a little bit at least. Mom

August 16, 1965 Monday

Well it is one-year today that my husband died. I thought about it all day. This morning we took the clothes to the laundry mat and went over to Dee Dee's. Stevie James had just spilled a jug of syrup. Tommy was sitting there already. What a situation. Little Donnie is his child, and Dee Dee's Nephew. Wonder how Tommy and her must feel, wonder how it will all end. I know her conscience is driving her crazy. He looks pretty nonchalant about the whole thing. We went up to Sissy's, little Billy Joe has pneumonia went to Patsy's for supper at seven. We ate outside and had salmon steaks etc. It was fun No Mail. Mom

August 17, 1965 Tuesday

Well Tommy woke us up at six o'clock. He put on his white navy uniform and left, supposedly to Seattle. To see about a hop to California and he says his shoulder hurts. Well who knows. More later you snoopy gator. I went to Kuvara, a lawyer and he is writing old Roy Schmultz that I am in no way responsibly for Kathy's rent or damages. Boy someday I will learn to keep my nose out of my kids business. It seems a shame I can't help her without getting in legal messes. But I guess you get bruised if you get in the wrong box of apples. Dee Dee came and got me at twelve to babysit while she went to Harborview to get her coil to prevent pregnancy, well At least I am glad about that. Her house looked like a cyclone. I got it and the kids in order, it took a bit of doing. Peggy & Andy came over and had coffee and doughnuts. At four we, all went to Sissy's for a cook out. Auntie and Uncle were there—Fitches—Shortie and his mother—oh that charming Frenchman, he is the most. Grandma seemed to enjoy everything. Lots of pictures were taken. Poor Sissy, Billy Joe is so sick and upset. Well its sure hard raising so many little ones, no one knows better than I. But once they grow up you forget all the frustration. Then its big problems you can't handle. No mail. Mom

August 18, 1965 Wednesday

Well Peggy-Andy and the kids left for Ohio today about eleven o'clock. Dunc stopped by and said good-bye. They gave me $50.00 cash for which I was very grateful. I applied for a babysitting job starting Sept 1st. Sixty dollars a month, five days a week from 7 to 4:15. Two kid's one girl 10 in school all day and 1 boy 5 in school ½ day. I hope I can do it. I went to Dee Dee's, Tommy is there. BIG HEADACHE. Yang came with a tape recorder. We took Marvin and Ricky and went to Patsy's. I brought them and Stevie James some sox's and tennis shoes. When I got back, I bought her $8.00 of groceries and ate supper there. Then baby-sat while her and Tommy went to Sugars. They really disabled Sugar's car and he is unhappy. Well I did come home and get a good night's sleep. I am glad to be alone again. I enjoy my little pad. My cupboards is full of groceries, my rent is paid to Dec 27, and I have $40.00 cash. I have to say I am thankful. No mail but you can't have everything. Mom

August 19, 1965 Thursday

I slept until nine, got up and went to the store. Had breakfast and washed out a few things. Called Sissy—Barbara and Aggie. Am going to iron and later go to Dee Dee's. I sure don't like her relationship with Tommy. He is supposed to leave tomorrow and I hope he does. More later ole alligator. Well I had some fun with Elaine, we unlocked and snooped in the closets that are up and down the hall. Found an old padlocked trunk in one, according to the dates it had been there for twenty years or more. We pried it open and had ourselves a ball. We found all kinds of things. After that, I went over to Dee Dee's and brought Marvin and Ricky home with me to stay overnight. We went to the dime store in the rain and spent $1.20 on toys then to Meeker Café and had hamburgers and fries. Then home. Amelia was in and visited a while. Me and the kids slept on the davenport. No mail. Mom

August 20, 1965 Friday

Well the boys woke up. I fixed them French toast and eggs. They wanted to go home so I took them. Tommy was still there. Judy and Bobby were there, everything was a mess and uproar, so I came home. Tommy and Ricky came, I fixed Tommy some breakfast. Elaine came down with banana bread. I done my washing, then Tommy took Ricky home and came back. We went to the Moonlight Inn, coffee shop and had lunch. Then we went to Dee Dee's. She had the house cleaned up, I hung up the clothes for her and took Stevie James for a ride in the stroller. When I came back, Tommy had hickies on his neck. Oh boy, does it get me down. I came home. You can see what mail I got. I hope it is the end of that little item. I'm getting tired of being sued for other people's bills. Well I came home and slept for thirty minutes. My iron don't work so I'm going out and buy a cheap one. Mom

P.S. Tommy is supposed to go to Whidbey Island tonight and fly to Jim's tomorrow. I went and bought an iron.

August 21, 1965 Saturday

Well last night I went with Bogues and took Tommy to the Whidbey Island Ferry at Mukilteo Bay near Everett, he got there just as the ferry was loading. He's probably at Jim's now. Yang came at four o'clock in the morning with chicken and shrimp chow mien, we ate it with hot coffee and went to bed. I got up at ten this morning and went to the store and got milk and bread. It is five after eleven, a hot day weather wise. Yang is asleep, I guess I will snoop around town a little bit. Well diary is this the outer limits, Dee Dee wants to dump Marvin. Sell out take the kids and go to California. Man this is way out. I don't blame her in a way, life with Geyman is hell. However, I am afraid she is depending on Tommy, which is no damn good. She cannot get welfare in California nor credit. Here at least she has both. I am supposed to help her down there and then come back and send her October check. Well here, we go again. Wonder what kind of mess I'll get into this time No mail. Mom

August 22, 1965 Sunday

Got up at ten and fooled around. I got Dee Dee's furniture for sale signs in the laundry mats. Went to the railway station and it was closed. Went over to Dee Dee's and no sooner sat down than Buzz and Barb came and wanted me to go with them, home to roast beef dinner and then to Patsy's. I did and it was fun. Lilly was at Patsy's. Everybody agrees that Dee Dee should leave Geyman, BUT stay here and face the facts. I kinda agree she is going to lose an awful lot going and probably the kids down there. BOY I pray the good Lord in his heaven to put an obstacle in her path to stop her, because I sure can't. Well we will see. Mom

August 23, 1965 Monday

Well I sewed a bit, it is raining. Dee Dee came over and I went with her, Yang and Stevie James were sleeping all day. Yang don't look good, she looks awful white. Dee Dee went to Rottles and got $50.00 worth of clothes for the boys and charged them to Marvin. Sugar and some punk were at Dee Dee's when we got back, drunk as hell. I got them out of there by saying I had to go. They gave me a wild ride home and headed for Auburn. Yang said she wanted to look at the apt in the building, I told her O.K. and am waiting for her now. I fixed potatoes and eggs for supper. I still wish Dee Dee wouldn't go. Dear Lord up in heaven, I pray you take a hand and change her mind. Well Yang came but don't like either apartment. NO MAIL. Mom P.S. I called Jim and told him to find out how long it would be before she could get on welfare down there.

August 24, 1965 Tuesday

Well I got up and called welfare here and they said she had to have one year residence to get welfare in California and all they would do is send her back here, minus her luggage and then she would have a ninety day wait here before she could get help. Plus she can't get nothing for her furniture. Well Aggie came and we both talked to her, she said she wouldn't go, so I came home relieved. NO MAIL. Mom

August 25, 1965 Wednesday

Took the kids to the dentist but it is wrong day. I got on the bus and went to White Center to spend overnight with Patsy. Looked in Seattle for a Patti Duke shop for Vicki but can't find any. Had salmon—salad—and fried spuds. Bought three pair stamped pillowcases. Mom

August 26, 1965 Thursday

Got up at nine and realized I didn't have my pills. Aggie came and got me at ten and took me out to dinner in Burien. I had fish & chips. I came home and got some groceries. Then walked to Dee Dee's and went with her to O'Brien school to register Boofy. Now that crazy girl wants to leave him with me for three weeks and her and the three little ones go by bus to San Diego. I swear the girl is crazy. I pray to you again dear

God make it impossible for her to go-please be with me now and do something. I have faith in you dear Lord for the sake of the children stop her. I am tired, I hope no company tonight. I am going to lie down now and rest. Its four o'clock. More later. No mail. I went over to Dee Dee's and discussed things with her. She has made up her bull headed mind so I am going to watch Marvin and Stevie James while she takes Ricky and Donnie.

August 27, 1965 Friday

Well it is nine o'clock, I slept real good. It is a nice sunny day. I take Marvin and Ricky to the dentist today. I am down to ten $10.00 cash and $10.00 in the bank and no money coming until Dec., unless Gwen sends the $90.00 she owes me, which isn't at all likely. More later you gator. It is now eight o'clock. I took Marvin and Ricky to the dentist. Marvin had one pulled and Ricky had one filled. I also took Marvin to the Dr. for his preschool examination, they were both real good. I ate supper at Dee Dee's. Little Stevie is real sick. They had a prowler last night. Pat was there. Dee Dee is having trouble with the car. I argued a lot with her today. She really gets me down. I've got to get out of this situation and start taking more concerns for my own future. Lord up in heaven, show me what I should do. No Mail. It's raining. Mom

August 28, 1965 Saturday

I woke up at eleven this morning, ate an egg and some toast. Got a letter from Peggy. Went to Dee Dee's and took Stevie for a long walk in the stroller and hung up the clothes. Then we took some things to the Renton Auction. I got out by the Big Bear and bought some milk—brisket and a onion, came home and put soup on to boil and phoned Buzz and Barb to come to supper. We done the dishes and walked around town. Then went for a ride up to Papa's grave, then to see the brick house that Peggy wants to buy, then to Bogues to see Vicki's new school clothes. Now it is eight thirty and I am home. Guess I will sew a while, then go to bed. Mom

August 29, 1965 Sunday

I got up at ten and ate my breakfast and at twelve, I was sitting and sewing and minding my own business when Dee Dee honked her horn and said; do you want to come over? I said O.K. got over there and Took Stevie James for a long ride in the stroller. She tried to get Yang up to go to work at two, she wouldn't get up so Dee Dee went and worked in her place and you guessed it, I baby sat. The kids were pretty good, except they have such poor eating habits and won't go to bed and go to sleep habits. I sure don't know how she is ever going to get Marvin up in time to catch a eight o'clock bus. I came home at eleven and slept real good. Well so goes another day, at least I earned my bread and butter today. Mom

August 30, 1965 Monday

I slept until 10, had coffee—banana and two doughnuts. The sun is shining. I am going to the dime store and get a marker pencil to mark Marvin's school clothes with. But first, I am going to finish my morning glory pillowcases. Oh dear Lord up in heaven what is in this days package.? Sissy & kids and Shirley Fitch—Snooks and Rodney came down, we had coffee—cookies and Kool-aid. Shirley has me on call to walk the picket line out at Country Cousins a hamburger joint. I sure hope I get on. I love my grandchildren but am really tired of babysitting. Well they left and Elaine came and sat a while. I hadn't seen hide or hair of Dee Dee or Yang Yang. But as Pop use to say: they will be around when they want something. I sewed a lot on the pillowcases today. No mail. It is six o'clock if anything else happens I will let you know, otherwise Amen. Mom

August 31, 1965 Tuesday

Woke up at six, fixed fried spuds & eggs. Walked over to Dee Dee's, nobody up so I came back. It is cold and damp today. I am sleepy, guess I'll sleep a while, more later. Well I slept until ten and felt much better. There was a letter in my mailbox. I got all excited but it was for Dee Dee from Gwen, so here we go again. Now she is really going on the bus. Dee Dee is selling everything for what she can get and paying my way down to help with the kids. We called Gwen, she said she would pay my way back. I dread the trip down, and I feel pretty shaky about all this but, I'll do anything once. No mail. Amelia was in to visit. Mom

September 1, 1965 Wednesday

Well diary another month is gone. I guess this one should turn out to be something else, with Dee Dee flying the coop. I woke up at nine, it is cool. Someone said it was going up to eighty today. I have my suitcase packed. I am dreading the trip down with four kids, but it will only be two days and a night and then it is over. I will try and visit Jim a week and maybe see Joe. I wish I had some money, my palm was sure itching last night, but it would have to be a muscle. More later you sneezy gator. Well Dee Dee stored quite a bit of her belongings with me, and I watched Donnie D and Stevie James most of the day. They both have bad colds and slept most of the time. Yang came by and lent me $15.00 that makes $50.00 I owe her. She is going to watch my apartment for me while I am gone. Dee Dee told me to call Trails way about their Deluxe fare down, it is $92.00 for all of us with food and all. It is $75.00 on Grey Hound, no convenience. I hope we go Trail Ways. I had supper with Slax and Elaine, had liver and watermelon. The package from Peggy came today, and George brought it up to me. Well that is about it for today. Mom

September 2, 1965 Thursday

Well I had lots of company today, Sissy—the twins—Shirley Fitch—Barbara and her sister in law—Elaine—and Mrs. Thatcher. I had Stevie James and little Donnie all day. My apartment looks like a cyclone hit it. I will sure be glad when this is all over so I can live in peace and quiet. I sure gotta sore stomach. The weather is cool. Yang slept all day. Mom

Fri. Sept 3-Sat Sept 4-Sun Sept 5 1965

Well these three days are a bit cloudy because I have been so busy helping Dee Dee getting ready to move to California. We left Seattle seven thirty Saturday morning. The kids traveled real well. Sunday morning they made us all get off the bus while they serviced it. We had a two-hour layover in Los Angeles. We got into San Diego at six in the evening. Tommy met us. Gwen had taken Debby to the hospital, she had got a hold of ant poison and got into convulsions. Well we are here. I called Jim and Joe, I am going to stay one week each place then home. Mom

Sept 6, 1965 Monday

I haven't been writing too much lately, to many handicaps. This afternoon Dee Dee and Georgia and I went to a beauty school and had our hair done. Dee Dee got hers cut real short, it looks nice. Gwen had a party last night, 3 navy wives with husbands overseas and their sailor boyfriends. They all got drunk, and in a fight. I stayed in the bedroom with Dee Dee's kids most of the time. Thank goodness, she acted like a lady. Now this is Wednesday and they went to register the kids for kindergarten, I am watching Kathy—Stevie James and Donnie. They are also going to bring home Debby from the hospital. Mom

September 7, 1965 Tuesday

Kathy was running a fever today and so was Kitten. I took Stevie James for a walk today. Gwen and Georgia went to the commissary today. They took Marvin—Ricky—Kitten and Freddie and Sherrill to the navy nursery. That was a new experience for Marvin and Ricky. Dee Dee and I watched Debbie—Stevie and Donnie. I am awful tired today and will be glad to get home if I ever do. Gwen worked tonight. Dee Dee and I babysat, pretty hectic. Georgia was expecting her sailor boy and her husband home unexpected like. Mom

September 8, 1965 Wednesday

The kids woke up at seven. Dee Dee got up at seven thirty, between us we got them dressed and fed. This is supposed to be my last day here. Joe and Dottie are supposed to come and get me tomorrow. Well it has been a long drug out day. Georgia and Marian were here drinking and fighting all day, and nobody got anything done. Gwen finally got the kids fed and went to work. It was sure a struggle getting the kids settled and to sleep. To many the same age in the same house. Tommy came about ten thirty. They left to bring Gwen from work. When they got home, Tommy—Dee Dee and I went to Mexico. We went to a wild basement nightclub and drank Mexican beer and tequila. There was two nude dancers. One a white girl and one a hot little Mexican number that had a complete sex act right on the dance floor. We left there and bought some souvenirs. We got home about three. Dee Dee and Tommy are having quite an affair. Mom

September 9, 1965 Thursday

Well the kids got up at seven. The house is a hell of a mess. Couldn't get Gwen or Dee Dee up. Fed the kids cereal and got Dee Dee's three dressed. Gwen finally got up and looked out the window and here was Joe and Dottie. She was embarrassed as the devil. I hated to walk out on my little boys, but I am awful worn out. Joes house is just plain nice. Four bedroom—two bathrooms and air condition. I laid down and had a nice rest. They are having steak and rib cook out tonight. It is very hot. More later. We had barbecued steaks—baked potatoes—green salad for supper. Afterwards we watched the Miss America pageant on T.V. I wrote a few post cards and went to bed by nine. I miss my little boys. Dear God up in heaven protect them. Mom

September 10, 1965

Got up at nine, we are going to church. I wonder who got up with the kids this morning. Well we went to church a Baptist one. They had a visiting Minister, he preached on the therefore in Romans. That we have sinned and should confess and ask forgiveness and lead a good life forward. It all made sense. We came home and had sandwiches and beans and milk. I took a long afternoon nap. Wrote to Jim and Dee Dee. Joe roasted a beef roast over charcoal. We also had potato salad—corn and lemon pie. We done the dishes and went for a ride to Apple Valley and seen the residence of Roy Rogers and George Air Force Base. Watched television for a bit and so to bed. I pray you dear God in heaven protect the little boys. I love them. Mom

September 11, 1965

Got up at nine, Sarah Jane and Patti started to school today. I wonder if little Marvin did. Today is Gwen's birthday and she is planning a wild party. Dear Lord up in heaven protects the little boys. We went to a variety store and got some embroidery work for me. I did hang up the clothes—dry the dishes and do a little ironing. This heat brothers me. We had roasted chicken—salad and baked potatoes. We went to Safeway this afternoon and a bakery. Joe worked from four this morning until seven tonight. He came home, and looked at his supper and said; what is this you are feeding me dead chicken. Well, so much for Joe and his jokes. My feet are swollen. Mom

September 12, 1965

Well this has been a slow day. I ironed for about two hours, hung the washing up and sewed. Took an afternoon nap and that is about it. Dottie took Fee Fee, the poodle to the poodle beauty parlor to be clipped and shampooed, it cost $8.00. They do it every six weeks, now I ask you ain't that something else? When I think of the times, $8.00 looked like a million to me and Dee Dee. Boy anyone say finances to me again I am just liable to say anything. We had rib steak—baked potatoes tonight. Sure am living high on the bush this week. I wonder how my little boys are. Dear Lord, again tonight I ask, I plead be good to them I love them. Mom

September 13, 1965

Got up at eight thirty. Dottie had taken Sarah Jane to the dentist so I sent Patti off to school. Dottie came back, I hung up clothes and ironed until one. Dottie went to get her hair done, I laid down and slept. Then I set my hair and sewed a while. We are going out to play Bingo tonight. I have never played for money. Wonder what kind of luck I will have. I also wonder what the little boys are doing. I sure do miss them. Well we will soon be eating. Ham—sweet potatoes—cottage cheese salad with pineapple. Sure am living it up this week. Wonder how my little apartment and Yang are getting along. It is five thirty, I will write more before I go to sleep. We went to the N.C.O. Club, had mixed drinks and played Bingo, but didn't win anything. Mom

September 14, 1965

Well this was mostly a last day. Didn't do anything but sew and watch T.V. Did finish the scarf with the lavender thistles on. Joe is going to Viet Nam quite soon. We had mashed potatoes—Spanish hamburger and spinach for supper. Watched Palident and the Twilight Zone. I thought about everything and everybody today. Didn't come to any real conclusions. So to bed, and God be with the little boys. Mom

September 15, 1965

Well I got a letter from Beverly today stating that they won't be able to come and get me. But they sent me bus fare so I am leaving for Oakland at 11:32 tonight. I have had a wonderful visit with Joe and Dottie. They have been very kind to me. I will however be glad to be on my way. I am getting anxious to get back to Kent. I don't really know why. I am getting farther away each day from the little ones I love, maybe there is a reason but I don't know what it is. Well I got on the bus at eleven thirty. Joe gave me a check for $20.00. Mom

September 16, 1965

I arrived at Oakland at one o'clock. Bev came and got me. We had to go back to the depot three times for my luggage. I thought a letter from Dee Dee would be here but no such luck. Mom

September 17, 1965

Well I woke up about ten. Jim was at church teaching his Sunday school class of boys. I heated up some coffee and took my pills. Bev got up and Jim came home, we had breakfast. I sewed and watched television. I wrote Dee Dee a letter which, she probably won't like but I felt duty bound to write it. We had roast beef—baked potatoes and green beans for dinner.

Bev and I went with another woman to the movies on the base. We seen What A Way to Go, it was real spicy and good. Well I wonder how the little boys are. I would appreciate a letter. Well tomorrow is another day. Mom

September 18, 1965

Well it's been a quiet day. I sewed a little, and ironed a little—watched T.V. and took a nap. I was disappointed I didn't hear from Dee Dee. Bev and I went to the show again tonight. We seen The Act of Making Love it was pretty good. Well I guess I'll soon be going back to Kent. I am going to find a job when I do get there. Mom

September 19, 1965

Well my day was a very nice one. I got a letter from Gwen & Dee Dee it speaks for its self and I answered it. Bev had to go to a meeting this morning so I vacuumed the house and washed the dishes, and put them in the dishwasher. She had to go to another one this afternoon, so I went to a shopping center and left me for three hours. I bought Bobby Joe a late birthday present and one for Angel. I bought some material to make a shift and a pair of slippers. We went to the show again tonight. Boy I haven't been to so many shows in my life. Today is Peggy's birthday. Mom

September 20, 1965

Well today was payday for Jim and Bev. They gave me $15.00. I checked my large suitcase home today. We went to Sears and the Goodwill. I bought a dress for .50 cents, it is lavender and white check. We went to the show again tonight Cinderella was on. I wrote Dee Dee a note and advised her to pay off Kent Hardware and Beneficial because she sold their stuff. I hope she listens to me and I hope her health holds up and I hope the little boys make the grade. I also hope I get a job when I get home. Mom

September 21, 1965

Well Bev and I went shopping this morning. She had to go to a meeting in the afternoon. I took a bath, and set my hair and took a long nap. We went to the movies and seen Murder Ahoy. Then came home and Jim took me to the depot and at 10:10 I got on the bus and started home. Mom

September 22, 23 1965

Rode the bus all day. Got into Seattle and got right on the Kent bus. Got home at seven. Yang had my apartment all cleaned up but the refrigerator won't work. Slax called the landlord and he said he would do something about it tomorrow. Sis and the kids were down a few minutes. Yang rented an apartment in the building across the parking lot from me. She came in at four in the morning with chicken chow mien. We yaked till six in the morning. I went back to bed and slept until nine. I shopped and went over to see Zelma about Dee Dee's mail but she wasn't home and new renters are in the house. Yang came over for lunch. We had clam chowder and strawberries with whipped cream. Dunc and Shirley stopped in. Damn landlord didn't come about the refrigerator and it is six o'clock. No mail. Mom

September 24, 1965

UGG, what a rainy gloomy day. Have been expecting Buzz and Barb up but it is noon and they haven't showed up. Yang goes to work at two. I have been reading—sewing—and writing letters. Hope I get some mail back. Well more later you hateful gator. Well its eight o'clock, what a BLAH day. I went to the Post Office, Buzz and Barb drove up and gave me back my iron and diary. They had been fighting and she was mad and wouldn't come in. Now I wonder what the hell is the matter there. I walked over to Zelma's to see if there was any mail for Dee Dee. Her and John sure acted funny. God, what's the matter with everybody. I went over to say hello to Arlene, she had two guys there drinking beer. I had one of them drive me up to Sissy's. They weren't fighting, they just weren't talking. Dunc and Shirley came and I rode down town with them. They were bickering too. I came home ate some soup and tomato sandwich, ironed—slept and sewed. Yang will be here at ten. Thank goodness, she ain't got nobody to fight with. Mom

September 25, 1965

Well I wrote a two-page letter to Dee Dee. I went to Safeway this morning. Yang and I started out at eleven, we coffee with Sissy and then went to Judy's and got most of Yangs stuff. Judy says Sugar is drinking all the time and giving her a rough time so she is taking off for California. Yang and I shopped in Renton and ate at Tonkins Cafeteria. Then we came home. I took a nap, and Mr. Hanson the landlord came and is coming back at seven with a different refrigerator. Well not much else to say. I seen Shortie today, he had been working east of the mountains, and got bit by a snake. He is a doll. I wish I could snare him, life wouldn't be so lonesome. Guess I haven't got what it takes anymore. Wonder how Dee Dee and the boys are, I miss them. Well I hope we get to go to the Drive In tonight, if the refrigerator comes in time I will. Sounds like Sissy is having a ball with Vicki and Robert. Well yes, life is jolly with teenage kids. NO MAIL.

September 29, 1965

Well I woke up at nine, someone banging on my door. It was Mr. Snow from the Parole Board looking for Dee Dee over Marvin. He had talked to Marvin last week and he had said he was coming home to Dee Dee and they were going to live together. Well I guess not, I called Dee Dee long distance and she said NO. Well I don't know, judging by the past I would say she is right but who knows the future, just can't be predicted. They claim a leopard can't change his spots but maybe he could dye them a little. Well not much else doing, been a weary day more or less. I cleaned up my new refrigerator sure is nice. I am making dishtowels for Dottie, got two done four more to go. I went to the Post Office and checked on Dee Dee's mail. They had held it ten days and sent it all back from where it came from. So I don't know what she got or didn't get. Well Yang is working. She will stop in at three in the morning with Chinese goodies. Sis—twins—Lorri were in about twenty minutes this afternoon. NO MAIL Mom

September 30, 1965

Well, not much doing today. I sewed a little—kinda walked the floor more or less. I can't help but worry about this mess Dee Dee is in. I worry about those little boys. I babysat Elaine's kids a couple of hours this evening. Amelia was in to visit. NO MAIL Mom

October 1, 1965

Thursday Shirley Fitch woke me up this morning and we had coffee. She said there may be some picket work in about 10 days. Well I sure hope so. Sissy came down at noon. We went to see Barbara but she wasn't home. So we came to my place and had toast and soup. Yang took me to Renton and we got our hair done and had dinner at the Beacon. I got a Thank You card from a baby shower. No word from Dee Dee. Mom

October 2, 1965

Friday Well I got a letter from Dee Dee and Gwen. They seem to be existing, of course, they won't get no welfare money this month. I went with Sissy to Judy Bealls toy party. She had eleven people but didn't make much, but they are fun. I went home with Aggie and had chicken supper. Got home at seven. Seen Yang a few minutes before she went to work. Boy there is a bunch of birthdays this month, I'll never make them all. Mom

End of the line. Have to start a new book.

Alex and Jim Kessack
Last picture taken of Jim

CHAPTER 7

VOLUME 3
OCT 2, 1965 TO NOV 26, 1965

October 2, 1965 Saturday

Well Oct is in. I woke up about ten, been a dull restless day. Yang came over about five and got two T-bone steaks. Buzz and Barb came about seven and visited about one hour, then Amelia came. It is twenty five till ten. I got my gas bill today it is $1.65. I will have to go to the bank Monday and draw $5.00 and pay it. Then I will only have $5.00 left and no relief in sight. I sure hope I get to walk the picket line. I wonder how the little boys are.

October 3, 1965

Well it was rather a dull day. I finished the dishtowels and started hot mats. I got bored in the afternoon so I went for a long walk down Meeker St to the Blinker and back. Then I went and woke Yang up. We went to Mayfair shopping center. Then we had supper together at her place. We had steak—salad and baked potatoes. I furnished the potatoes. We then started for the El Rancho Drive—In, and she locked her house and car keys in the Apt and had to call her landlord from Auburn to come and unlock her Apt. Well we finally got to the Drive In and seen I Want to Live and the Defiant Ones. We had a cheese pizza. Then home and to bed. Mom

October 4, 1965 Monday

Not much doing today. I went to the bank at ten and drew $6.00. That leaves me $4.00. I paid my gas bill that was $1.62, bought five—nickel stamps—a loaf of bread—some rolls and a ball of crochet thread. That about cooks me financially. It is a good thing my rent is paid. Elaine was in and visited, otherwise I am just working on hot mats. I have my heater on. Hope I get money enough to pay the gas bill next month. It is 2:10 will write more later. Judy Kessack came down with an Indian girl named Rose, they are coming to my toy party. Sissy and kids came at four and stayed a few minutes. Vicki bleached her hair. Jim had been to their place with Aggie and Al the night before and didn't stop to see me. Yang bought a scrabble board, we played two games, each won one. No mail, had supper together it's raining. Mom

October 5, 1965 Tuesday

Came home and washed out my clothes. She came and got me and we went to Renton. Ate at Newberry's, went to Mr. Lu's Beauty School and had our hair cut—shampooed and set. Then went through some stores and came home. Took a nap. Mrs. Thatcher was in a few minutes. Yang went to work at six.

It is seven o'clock, I am going to crochet a while and go to bed. Wonder how Dee Dee and the boys are. NO MAIL. Mom

October 6 1965 Wednesday

Got up at ten. Elaine came down and had coffee. I worked on the hot mats. Went for a long walk this afternoon, up one street and down another, about twenty blocks in all. Crocheted hot mats. Ate fried potatoes—eggs and toast. Heat up a can of beans for supper, had pineapple for dessert. It is eleven o'clock at night. Yang is at work, I can't sleep. Keep thinking about Dee Dee and the little boys. Guess I'll sew a while. Yang will come in at three in the morning and we will have some Chinese food. No, mail—no visitors—no nothing BLAH. Mom

October 7, 1965 Thursday

Well I got a letter from Dee Dee. Sounds like they are O.K. for which I am grateful. Woke Yang up at noon and we went to Patsy's, she gave me two pillows and three small cans of salmon. She gave Yang two ceramic donkeys. We came home and I walked to Lilly's and invited her and Becky to my toy party. I also invited Patsy and Harley and Leila and Janice. I hope I get my ten. Gold Finger was on at the Midway so Yang skipped work and we went. It was so fascinating we watched it twice. I sure did go to sleep easy tonight. Mom

October 8, 1965 Friday

Not much doing today. Elaine came down and sent me to the bakery for cream puffs. So we had cream puffs and coffee and talked. I went to a rummage sale but did not buy anything. I walked all over town and to the Goodwill. Spent ten pennies on two ashtrays. Came home and made pea soup. Laid down and took a nap. Pat came to see me. He was broke and hungry. I gave him hot soup—hot coffee and a roll. I gave him two nickels so he could make a phone call. His car is impounded with all his clothes in it. Woke Yang up at five, we visited about an hour. I came home and Amelia came in and left. Buzz and Barbara came and gave me $5.00. I sure was glad to get it. It is now ten minutes to nine. There was just a two-car wreck below my window. So I think to bed. No mail Yang went to work. Mom

October 9, 1965 Saturday

Well not much doing, Elaine came down and sat all morning. Pat came and wanted to leave his clothes here. I sure don't want to get mixed up with him, but I said yes. He took a shower and left. Elaine and I walked all over town. I seen Maybelle and Sonny. They verified the toy party, she is pregnant. I called Aggie and talked to her about Pat of course, she can't do anything. Pat came back at nine after his coat, he said he had some things to pick-up to sell tomorrow. It didn't sound good to me. I called his Dad of course he can't do anything either. Why in hell do people have kids they can't do anything about it beats me. I went to bed at nine. Yang came at four with chicken almond and fried rice. No mail. Mom

October 10, 1965 Sunday

Well not much doing. I got up at eleven., sat around until twelve thirty, went for a long walk. Came home by Tyson's damaged food store bought one can cocoa—two cans spaghetti—dropped a can of beans on my foot and bruised it. Came home and Aggie was pacing up and down in front of my place looking for Pat. He showed up, we had coffee and went up on the hill. I stayed at Sissy's while Aggie ran around from place to place with Pat. She finally came and got me. She said Pat was to go to Bud's at six o'clock with his belongings and stay there. I left them in the car fighting it out. Pat sat on my back porch until five o'clock and disappeared, his stuff is still here. Yang and I went to the Drive In and seen Alfred Hitchcock's The Birds and also Caretakers. Both of them, gruesome. Anyway to bed at midnight. Mom

October 11 1965 Monday

Well it is one o'clock. The sun is shining but the apartment is cold. So I got the gas heater going. Dunc was in for coffee, Elaine was too. No, mail nothing going on. It is Yang's day off but I guess she is asleep. More later you filthy gator. Well about four o'clock I woke Yang up and invited her over for supper. I boiled white and sweet potatoes—opened green beans—canned peas and fried ground round and made gravy. After we ate, we went to the Wigwam store and stopped at Snooks and borrowed her T.V. trays for my party. Elmer and Shirley were there and said they would come to my party.

Snooks said take Pat's clothes up to Bud's he is there so we did. He offered Yang $10.00 to pick something up after dark in Kent and take him to Seattle with it tomorrow. I told her she was crazy to do it, but she did. We went to Duwamish Drive In and seen Beach Ball and The Sea is Slow, got home at midnight. Mom

October 12, 1965 Tuesday

Aggie and Snooks woke me up at nine thirty. They were delivering the toys from Judy's party. We had coffee. Elaine came down when they left and we went to Tyson's and the bakery. It is raining. I got two dozen cup cakes and four dozen cookies. I am already for tonight. I have to borrow Elaine's table and chairs. Hope I have a crowd. My day is already ruin No Mail, my darling kids I love you too. More later, it is eleven o'clock. Well I set my hair and took a nap. Got up had a cheese sandwich. At seven, my guest began arriving. I had seventeen guests. Sold $66.00 of toys and got $9.00 of merchandise free. It is now two o'clock in the morning, my apartment is all cleaned up. At three Yang will come. In the meantime, I can't get to sleep. Oh well I will eventually I guess. Mom

October 13, 1965 Wednesday

Well its two o'clock in the morning, I can't sleep. Sissy is having a Tupperware party Oct 28. Judy is having a toy party Nov 8. So I guess Elaine and I will go. I sure wonder how Dee Dee and the kids are. More after while crocodile. Well it is now six thirty, Elaine was in for coffee about noon. I went for a long walk. I went with Yang at one o'clock to take Pat and some 70 lbs of copper to Seattle to sell. The she went and got the lights under the name of Susan Colby. Then she went to Safeway and got a $70.00 money order and mailed her rent. Sgt Foxley was at Safeway picking up some bad checks. I came home took a nap and heated a can of beans and made some toast. Done my dishes and am now going to sew a while. A letter from Dee Dee. Mom

October 14, 1965 Thursday

Well Elaine woke me up and we had coffee. I wrote to Joe and Sarah and went to the Post Office and mailed the letters. I came back and made a pot of vegetable soup. I took a nap and sewed and at one I went to Seattle with Yang and Pat. He was going to fourth and Pike Bldg to see about a job. We stopped at Andies Café. I had salad and milk. It is raining and cold. Came home and took another half hour nap. Elaine and Angel came down and I made coffee. Amelia came in with an apple pie she had made at work. So we all had some. At seven I went and woke Yang up to go to work. Now I am going to sew and read and go to bed. Mom

October 15, 1965

Friday Well I didn't get up until eleven, grouchy at that, cold and pouring rain. I am so damn broke and unhappy about it. I took a hunting knife down and asked Elaine to ask Slax if he would sell it for $5.00, well he did. Vicki—Cindy and Penny were down. They said Bogue got drunk last night and took off with Billy Joe. Sissy had to go after them five in the morning. I was going over to wake up Yang, I went out the door and left my keys inside. Took Elaine and I an hour to pry the lock off and put it back. Tonight Barbara and the kids came and Sugar dropped by. He gave me $5.00, he was sober but drinking whiskey. He said he would come and get me tomorrow for dinner. He also said Dee Dee pulled a dirty trick on Marvin and he thinks Marvin will get her. Mom

October 16, 1965 Saturday

Woke up late. Wrote Dottie a letter and mailed her the dishtowels and hot mats. Washed my clothes at the laundry mat and went to the store. Judy and Rose came and got me at one. I gave Judy the letter from Dee Dee, boy would Sugar boil if he knew Judy is going to leave and take up with Dee Dee. Well Judy fried chicken—mashed potatoes and frozen green peas. She brought me home at four. I slept an hour and lit the gas heater and sewed. I woke Yang up at eight and when I got back, Amelia came in and visited until ten. Yang came at five o'clock in the morning with egg fu young and fried rice. Mom

October 17, 1965 Sunday

It has been a lonely day. I mopped my floors and sewed a while. I walked across town and bought some thread. When

I got home, Yang came and I cooked dinner. We had fried Ham—yam—green beans—boiled potatoes and pineapple chunks. She went home, I read a while and took a nap. I went for a walk and mailed Sugar a birthday card. Now I am sewing on some pillowcases with horses on them. It is a cold grey day. I am supposed to wake Yang up at seven and go to a Drive—In movie. Mom

October 18, 1965 Monday

Not much doing today. Shirley Fitch and Snooks and Rodney woke me up, we had coffee and a nice visit. It rained all day so I stayed home and sewed all day. Yang went to work in someone else place tonight. No Mal. Mom

October 19, 1965 Tuesday

Went for a walk this morning, looked the new variety store over. Came home had a letter from the welfare trying to find Yang's adoption business over Jeffy. I took the letter to her. Came home and locked my apartment and went over to Lilly Hamilton's. Brenda and Ralph were there, they asked me to stay and have stew so I did. Leila Gifford came while I was there and brought me home. Elaine came down and we sewed for an hour. I woke Yang up then I went to the store. I am eating crackers and cheese. Mom

October 20, 1965 Wednesday

Well it's been an odd day, one way or another. Sissy came down with the twins this morning and Dunc came while she was here. I gave them vegetable soup and coffee. They left, Elaine came and gave me a pair of pink slippers she knit for me. At one, I woke Yang up but she didn't get up. I took a long walk and came home. Done a bit of sewing. Woke Yang up at five. Dunc and kids came in a while this evening. I can't get to sleep tonight. Some punk is squealing around screeching tires tonight. Reminds me of Geyman when he is drunk. Wish I could forget him. Wonder how Dee Dee and the little boys are. No Mail. Mom

October 21, 1965 Thursday

Well today, I kept on the go go. Went for a long walk, then to the bank and drew $3.00. When I got home, Aggie and Pat were here. I went with them to Auburn employment place then up to Shirley Fitches for lunch. Came home, took a nap. Elaine came down. Then at seven went over to Lilly Hamilton's and went with her—Linda and Barbara to Brenda's toy party in Auburn. When I got home at eleven, Pat was at the door wanting to know if he could sleep here overnight. So I let him. Yang came at three with hamburger deluxe. Finally to bed. Mom

October 22, 1965 Friday

Boy am I restless today. Geyman gets released today and I'm scared for Dee Dee. Just got a letter from her and Gwen. They seem to be O.K. hope it stays that way. More later. Well it is later now. About seven o'clock I have been so nervous today over Geyman and what he can do legally do to Dee Dee and the kids. My brother is dying and I didn't get to see him. I called Sissy and talked a long time to her. Also Barbara. Yang and Pat were just here, we had steaks. Yang brought them. Buzz and Barb might visit tonight, Amelia was in. Mom

October 23 1965 Saturday

Well I got up and Elaine came down. Sissy came, the kids and Shirley Kessack came. Well it seems Dee Dee had spent the night calling Geymans—Agnes and Bogues trying to get a hold of Marvin, to no avail. He finally got home Saturday night and called her. He is pretty pissed off at her. I don't know what is going to happen. Won't know until Monday. She wants back up here period. He says ; well get yourself back up the same way you got down period. Sarcastically. Sonny brought the toys in late afternoon, and Maybelle is in the hospital. Lilly and Linda were over for a while. I went home with Sissy and had supper, she brought me home at nine o'clock. No mail. Mom

P.S. I talked to Dee Dee on the phone, she sure is in a state of mind. WOW.

October 24, 1965 Sunday

Well it was a quiet day, but around evening, the percolator popped. First off, Geyman came for his clothes but only took three pair of jeans and a shirt or two. He said he was leaving to look for work. He was not sending for phoning or writing to Dee Dee. To hell with her. Well I wasn't long getting that information to her. I guess she called Peggy and more or less black mailed them over Tommy. They ain't gonna help her. Nope. She is in a real jam. Mrs. Geyman told her they had a lawyer investigating the whole situation. Welfare won't help her because he is able bodied. More Trouble. Mom

October 25 1965 Monday

Well I called Sissy this morning, had a long-winded conversation. I got a card letter and $5.00 from Peggy. I bought some squash—potatoes and Yang baked them. I looked at apartments for Dee Dee. Elaine and I walked to Spouse Ritz today. Yang and I went to Lewis and Clark Theater and seen Liz Taylor and Richard Burton in the Sand Piper. I wrote to Peggy. I wonder if she will ever get home with them, and what will happen if she does. Damn Geyman anyway. Hope he breaks his stupid neck. He sure is proving he don't give a damn about her or the kids. Mom P.S. Yang and I went to Lewis and Clark to see Liz Taylor in Sand piper.

October 26, 1965 Tuesday

Well I woke up late and ate some cream of wheat and went for a long walk. Seen Barbara taking Maybelle home. Said she might stop by but didn't. Done a lot of sewing, and wrote to Peggy. Seen Yang about five. She has bought a lot of stolen stuff from Pat. I told her she better watch her step. I went for another long walk and had a long telephone conversation with Aggie. It is about eight o'clock now. Guess I will go to the laundry mat and talk to Barbara on the phone and then come back and go to bed No answer so good night. Mom

October 27, 1965 Wednesday

Well it rain all day, so I sat at home and sewed. I made a big pot of stew and a big pot of coffee. I set up a small bed in case Dee Dee and the kids come in. Sure, do wonder what is going to happen to her and those little boys. No mail today. Elaine and Amelia were in this evening. Pat wandered in and is staying all night. Mom

October 28, 1965 Thursday

Well got up this morning just in time. Pat stayed overnight and Aggie came early this morning and took him to Renton to get his driver's license. Elaine and I went with Thelma Smith to Sissy's Tupperware party. I spent my last dollar on Tupperware. But I figured I ate enough so it was even Steven. Tonight Elaine and I walked around town. I spent thirty-six pennies on penny candy for trick or treats. After we came home, I walked home with Amelia. We got home about nine and I made hot chocolate. Yang stopped in at three and gave me $5.00 bill. No mail. Mom

October 29, 1965 Friday

Sissy and Shirley Fitch woke me up at ten. We had coffee and gabbed. When they left I went to the bakery and then to the store. I spent all but 20 cents of the $5.00 on food. Elaine came in when I got home. I mixed a batch of sugar cookies and she is going to bake them. I have one more dishtowel to make. Sure, wonder how Dee Dee and the kids are and what is going to happen to them.

Well diary this is November 6, 1965

I haven't told you anything for quite a while and this is why. The Salvation Army in San Diego gave Dee Dee a train ticket and $18.00 to get up here on and Geyman met the train and they have all six of them stayed with me for a week and I have just been too busy to write anything. They are now in an apartment over the cab—stand and on welfare. I really can't predict how they will get along. Her coil came out and she is quite apt to get pregnant. He is chasing as much as he dare with Pat, and Pat is out stealing so it don't look to good. I went to Judy Fitch's birthday party today. Then babysat for Geymans so they could go shop. Dunc and Shirley were in for a few minutes tonight, I am going to church with them in the morning. I am out of groceries and have 73 cents. I haven't any bread or coffee. Well that is all the breaks. Mom

November 7 1965 Sunday

Well last night at eleven, Dee Dee came and got me to babysit because Marvin and Pat had took off. I was there until two thirty then both of them came home. Elaine and I took off for Renton Long Acres Café and ate Chinese food and rode home with Yang at five in the morning. I got up at eight and got ready for church. I went and enjoyed it, he preached on the 24th psalms. I came home and slept until four. I went over to Dee Dee's and done her clothes at the laundry mat. Then took the three boys and Angel for a walk and penny candy. Elaine and Slax were at Dee Dee's. She looked awful tired. I don't know how long it dragged out. Snooks and Bud were down looking for Pat to go to court, he had taken off about an hour before they got here. Wish they would pick that kid up before the whole bunch get into trouble. Well not much else, I sold Shirley a set of dishtowels, I'm just broke period. It will buy some coffee and bread. Judy and Bobby were in to remind me of the toy party tomorrow. I can't buy anything. Mom

November 8 1965 Monday

Dear diary, Elaine and DeWanna—Angel—Marvin and Ricky all went to Judy's toy party. I won the door prize. A pair of Santa Clause slippers, for a small child. We stayed there until four and Yang picked us up. I ate supper with her. We had roast beef TV dinners and then went to Lewis and Clark show. We seen Joy In The Morning and Operation Crossbow, got home at eleven a big fire in a warehouse across from Virginia Tavern. Thus another day. I am broke, and I do mean Broke. Mom

November 9, 1965 Tuesday

Got up at six thirty, woke Dee Dee up at seven and got little Marvin on the school bus at eight. He has to go to O'Brien school. He looked so small on that big old bus. Well not much else doing. Don't get any letters and am just really not doing anything constructive or otherwise. Mom

November 10, 1965 Wednesday

Well just more of the same. Pat is out stealing, Geyman laying around drinking and bumming off Pat. No mail. Mom

A holiday, no school, no mail, no nothing. Life is a drag. Mom

November 12, 1965 Friday

Got little Marvin up and on the school bus. Elaine is down here all the time. Sugar came in one o'clock in the morning with Pat. Drunk as hell. He gave me $5.00. They went and got Geyman at three o'clock. They sat in my kitchen until six in the morning and all left. Dee Dee came at eight, we sent little

Ricky and Marvin to the 7th Day Adventist Sunday school. Marvin came home at eleven and conked out. So Dee Dee brought the kids over here and took off with Yang. Marvin came over mad as hell. About four thirty things calmed down. Sissy came and got me. I went up there for supper. Came home at seven and the building was jumping. Slax had a poker game going. Sugar and Geyman—Elaine and Dee Dee were in and out, finally a fight arose and all men scattered. So about one in the morning, everything settled down. I guess. Mom

November 14, 1965 Sunday

Got up at eight and got ready to go to church, but Shirley and Dunc didn't show up, looks like a dreary day ahead. Well ten o'clock, I get a telegram saying my brother died. Eleven o'clock Shirley came and sat, we didn't make church but her kids made Sunday school. She left and I walked to a phone booth and called Sissy. Her and the kids came down for coffee. She left and Elaine and Dee Dee and the boys came. When who knocks on my door but a Kent Cop looking for Pat. He finds him and arrests him. Seems he held up some people with a loaded revolver. Now Geyman and Yang are shaking in their shoes. Klecky Klack. Well that's enough for one day. Yang and I went to Lewis and Clark and seen Old Yeller and Glory Boys. Mom

November 15, 1965 Monday

Not much doing today. No mail. Shirley Fitch stopped by. Was back and forth to Geyman's. Her boxes came in from California. He worked for welfare today, big deal. Elaine and I walked to Spouse Ritz about eight o'clock. Yang bought a fantastic oil painting for $20.00. Well everyone to his own taste. Mom

November 16, 1965 Tuesday

Well just another ordinary day. No mail, no money, no visitors. Blah Blah Blah. Mom

November 17, 1965 Wednesday

Well I was back and forth to Dee Dee's—Yang and Elaine's all day. Sis—Lorri and the twins were in this afternoon. No mail. I got $2.00 from Yang and ate a bacon tomato sandwich at Meeker Café and bought a pumpkin pie at the bakery. I went with Thelma Smith to Snooks Tupperware party at night. Mom

November 18, 1965 Thursday

Well I slept most of the day. It has rained all day. Have been at Dee Dee's most of the day. Marvin is with old man

Fowler. She is going to work at long acres tonight. Marvin is supposed to come home and babysit but I bet he don't. The kids all have bad colds. I closed my bank acct today, a whole $1.70. I have enough pills for four days. Don't know exactly what I am going to do. Elaine has an awful hang over today. Her and Esther sure got drunk last night. Dee Dee wasn't far behind. Well no mail no money no nothing. Damn it anyway. Mom

Thanksgiving Day 1965

Well I haven't written much lately. I have been moody and upset. Marvin is drinking like a sun baked fish, and always takes it out on her. We all had it out last Saturday night. A lot of things came out. Since then things seem to take a slight turn for the better. All the kids are sick. Geymans are going to Geymans today. Yang and I are going to Dunc's and Shirley's. Thatcher had the day off. Elaine and Slax are having a house full of his relatives. Their kids are both sick. Joe and Dottie both wished me a Happy Day. The rest just plain didn't. Oh, well Ho Hum. More later you nasty gator. Mom

November 26, 1965

This is the day after Thanksgiving, it is pouring rain. I have eighty cents and a silver dollar. Two potatoes—one can beans—four eggs and a little coffee. My rent is paid until December 27. Big deal. There was lots of food at Dunc's yesterday but Shirley bitched and howled the whole day. Elaine woke me up at three in the morning. Slax had pawed her one on the mouth, she was drunk and crying. I looked out the window and seen Yang and a guy going up to her apartment. I am rather unhappy today. I have bad chest pains. I am almost certain the welfare won't help me and I hadn't guts enough to get a job. More later if anything happens.

Chapter 8
Aug 1, 1966 to Oct 4, 1966

I have decided to start a diary once more. It is nine thirty. I live in a downstairs apartment at 208 West Titus in Kent, by myself. I got up at eight and went to Meeker Café and had one hotcake and one egg and coffee. I stopped at Kent bakery on the way back and ordered a birthday cake for Dee Dee on Thursday, she lives in White Center with her four small sons. Her would be husband Marvin is back in Walla Walla. She will be 23 Thursday and some of us are getting together a picnic dinner at her place. I got a letter from my daughter Peggy, it is on the following page. I answered it the best I knew how. It is going to be hot today. At ten I am to phone Dee Dee and see if I am to babysit tonight and tomorrow, she works for Boeings. So until then I will say no more. Well I phoned and nobody answered so guess she is on her way out. Yang's here, more later. I went to Dee Dee's and babysat, she quit her job so now I won't have to babysit anymore soon. Mom

August 2, 1966 Tuesday

Some guy named Howard and a girl named Ray keeps calling Dee Dee. Patsy came over and mowed the lawn for Dee Dee. I stayed there until five o'clock and Dee Dee brought me home. I guess they are hiring a babysitter and taking her out tonight.

Don't like the sounds of it because they have been drinking all day. A letter from Dottie was here when I got home. Her and Joe are now expecting a child. I had to call up Sissy and tell her, she said she might come down later. I am supposed to call Dee Dee in the morning and get her out of bed. On Friday, I am going to get on a bus and go to Alameda and visit Jim and Bev and ride back up with her and the girls on the 12th. Well Buzz and Barb and the kids came calling. I gave them a quilt, we visited and had coffee. Sissy and the kids came and I went home and stayed overnight with her. Mom

August 3, 1966 Wednesday

Well I woke up at Sissy's, had pancakes and eggs. Had a good night's sleep. Aggie suppose to pick me—Penny—Robin and Cindy up at eleven, she didn't show up. So Sissy had Robert pick me a bouquet and took it to Papa's grave and then to my place. My check was here so I thought I better see Yang before I took off and darn that was a mistake, she got me for $5.00. I paid my rent and bought my ticket, have about $4.00 to spend. Ate at Moonlight Inn coffee shop. Had a Chef burger—green salad and French fries and ice tea. Roamed around town, spent about $2.00 and came home. Took a two-hour nap. A very disturbing letter from Peg, looks like Andy really beat her up. Thrasher came over. So after awhile to bed. Mom

August 4, 1966

Well Thrasher woke me up at eight. The Acme Apts were on fire, four o'clock this morning. Slax set his apt on fire. She is all shook up. Is going to try and find a place to move to. She was going to Dee Dee's birthday party with us, but isn't so sure now. She brought over a present anyway. My guess is she will be back to go. It is cool this morning even feels like rain. I am already to blast off. More later you nasty gator. P. S. It's eight in the morning. Well Thrasher went with us. The party turned out real nice. Sissy brought grandma Bogue. Sissy's brake went out on the way home. She got pretty shook up. We got home OK. I grabbed my suitcase and headed for the bus. On account of the airplane strike, the busses and bus depot's are really crowded. I am on my way. Mom

Aug 5, 1966

Well this morning was spent traveling. My digestive system is on the blink and I am running a temperature, but I brought my medicine along. Arrived at Oakland on time. Jim and Bev came right down and got me. I spent afternoon visiting and am retiring early. Mom

August 6, 1966

Well I woke up refreshed. Jimmie Jr. cooked my breakfast. Now we are watching Lucy Johnsons wedding on T.V. More later. Bev and I went to a big Goodwill store in Oakland while

Jim got new tires on the car. He gave us each $5.00 to spend. It was real hot, we were there four hours. I got a little bit sick. I bought a pair of thinning shears for 35 cents and a old fashion sugar bowl with lid for 20 cents and 3 large bags of quilt pieces for $1.50. We came home, had roast beef dinner. I took a hot bath and went to bed. Mom

August 7, 1966 Sunday

Got up early, sewed on quilts. Everybody else went to church. I feel a little better today. More later. Well we had a nice ham and egg breakfast and at eleven we went to the Penny fair, it is a drive inn movie where everybody brings stuff to sell. I bought an old fashion dish—two balls and two belts. It was quite hot and I got little faint. We came home, I rested a while then sewed and we had roast beef for supper. Gina made dessert a chocolate pudding cake served with ice cream. So to bed. Mom

August 8, 1966 Monday

Well we had a late breakfast. Bacon and eggs and fried spuds and cantaloupe. I finished my quilt and strip of eleven to go on Ricky's quilt. Jim and Jimmie are playing golf, Jim has night duty. Bev is giving Gina and Debby permanents. It is real hot today. I am resting quite a bit, although I feel pretty good. I got a letter from Thrasher today. More later. I spent the afternoon resting and sewing. We had stew and dumplings and salad for supper. Jim had the duty all night. Bev showed

Gina and I how to make a plastic trivet. Mine has a butterfly and seashells and leafs in it. Gina's has pictures of her—Debby and Jimmie Jr. in it, she is giving it to me. So to bed. Mom

August 9, 1966 Tuesday

Well slept in this morning. Had oatmeal with raisins in for breakfast. A friend of Bev's came and we went to see another friend. When I came home, I sewed and slept all afternoon. Then watched TV had fried chicken—coleslaw for supper, sure was delicious. It is quite warm. Expect to go to bed early. Mom

August 10, 1966 Wednesday.

Well not much doing today. Bev is very busy doing last minute things before our drive to Washington. I probably won't write anything tomorrow because we will be traveling. However if anything unusual happens I will be sure to write it down Mom P.S. Bev's friend gave us haircuts and hair do's. Jim is playing poker.

August 11, 1966 Thursday

Well I decided to write anyway. We left Alameda at five this morning and drove straight through in fifteen hours. So I am home. We had a very nice trip. Kids were good. I tried calling

Sissy twice but no answer. I called Shirley Fitch. I should call Dee Dee and the boys but it is eleven o'clock and I guess they would be in bed, and anyway I am scared to go out alone in the dark. Well tomorrow is another day. My stomach is sure kicking up a fuss. I left a note on Yang's door. Wonder if she will find it and come over. I'm going to leave a light on just in case. Mom

August 12, 1966 Friday

I got up around eight. Had some oatmeal and toast, fussed around. Went to the laundry mat and done my washing. Visited Amelia Thrasher, came home done my ironing and cleaned house. Stopped in on Yang, got back my $5.00 I lent her also sold her my radio for $5.00. Sissy and Marvin came. We went to Auburn and got my commodities, and then went to their place and spent the afternoon and I had supper. She gave me some fresh beets-fresh green beans—onions and cucumbers from her garden. I bought enough outing flannel to line one quilt. So to bed. Mom P.S. I talked to Dee Dee and the boys on the phone. She is working at Long Acres Café Fri & Sat night and already had a babysitter.

August 13, 1966 Saturday

Got up at eight, had two boiled eggs—toast—coffee and applesauce. Oh yes and my pills. Am going to sew a while, am suppose to call Dee Dee at ten so she will get up. More later darling. It's almost five o'clock now. I cooked a nice dinner, buttered fresh beets—fresh green beans—potatoes—one can B&M beans—jello—sliced cucumbers and had Amelia Thrasher over for dinner. We both enjoyed it. I also tied a quilt today. Two more to go for Peggy's order. Hope I get a nice one done for Patsy's birthday. I got Connie some paints and painting books for her birthday. Sissy and Marvin dropped in for coffee and while they were here, Shirley and Elmer came with my Tupperware. Then I went to Penney's and got material to line the other quilt. Unless somebody else comes this will be all for today. I am baking a spice cake. I seen Yang for a few minutes. No mail. Mom

August 14, 1966 Sunday

Today is Dunc's birthday. Amelia stopped over about nine and visited an hour. I called Dee Dee, she said Stevie James got hit by a car yesterday, however he was not seriously hurt. Shooked up and bruised. Aggie stopped in about noon, she had been babysitting at the Baptist church. She was in a foul mood. Well I tied a quilt and fussed around. I kinda figured Buzz or Dunc would show up, but they didn't. Yang came at eight. We went to Seattle to see Elizabeth Taylor and Richard Burton in The Virginia Wolf at the Blue Mouse. Got home around midnight. Mom

August 15, 1966 Monday

Well I am up early. Had cream of wheat and toast. Dee Dee is coming for me this morning. I will babysit tonight and come home tomorrow. Mom

August 16, 1966 Tuesday

Well I babysat the boys last night. They really are getting out of hand. Donnie is so damn spoiled. Well anyway, we managed. Dee Dee went out to breakfast with some guy after work and didn't get home until six. I got up at eight, fed and dressed the boys and cleaned up the house. Got her up at eleven. Her neighbor came over and gave me a bunch of scraps for quilts. We got up at Sissy's about one. We stopped and got the boys haircuts. I finally got home about three. Had chicken and dumplings—green peas—yams and applesauce for supper and milk to drink. Now I will mail Joe a birthday card, write Dottie and rest. Oh yes Peggy called Sis yesterday and said they had sold out and would be out here in four weeks. Oh Boy Sissle Pop. Mom

August 17, 1966 Wednesday

Well Shirley Kessack and kids came last night and brought me some meat. T-Bone steak—Beef Roast & Hamburger. We all went up to Sissy's, got home at eleven and went to bed. Aggie woke me up at nine, we went out and had breakfast and chased around. She bought me a big bouquet of Gladiolus. Mrs. Thrasher was here today, she was kind of snotty. Sis and kids and Shirley Fitch was here. I sold fifteen quilts today. I had T-bone steak—rolls—and applesauce for supper. I tried from eight fifteen to five minutes of nine to get Dee Dee on the phone. All I can get is a busy signal. I am going back and try once more and then give up. I'll let you know what happens. No mail today. Well I went to the phone booth and tried again with absolutely no luck. That woman on her line is impossible so to bed. Mom

August 18, 1966 Thursday

Well it's been sew—sew—sew today. Thrasher was here for breakfast, gave her applesauce—and a cupcake. Dunc was here for lunch, sure was glad to see him. He said he could scare me up a sewing machine. Well I mailed a letter to Dottie and just wrote one to Peggy. Well Sissy and the kids were just here. Now they are gone. Well no more news tonight I guess. No mail. Mom

August 19, 1966 Friday

Well Thrasher didn't show up today. I bet she went home and started making quilts. I started Peggy's three today. Aggie—Pat—and Robin took me to Seattle today. Pat had to get a felony card. We had refreshments in the Golden Goose on First Avenue. Sissy and the kids were down this morning. No mail, real hot today. Tonight I went and got a big square box for Donnie to sleep in tomorrow night. Looks like it might work out all right. Pat is looking good for coming out of a state pen, he said Geyman is worried whether Dee Dee will take him back or not. Frankly, I am curious. She sure isn't rushing that divorce any. Well one more block on Peggy's quilt, and the end of another day. Goodnight. Mom

August 20, 1966 Saturday

Well I better write early tonight. I babysit Dee Dee's kids. She works from nine to four and said she could bring them here. I have two boxes made up into cribs and a playpen so it should be easy enough. Sissy and kids were here today. Judy Grimes was here looking for Yang. Thrasher was here in the afternoon, her ex-husband is dying in South Dakota. Buzz and Barb and the kids were here last night. I get their davenport when they move. I hope I get it before Peggy comes. It would make an extra bed. Well I just shampooed and set my hair. Guess I will rest a while before the kids come. A letter from Peggy today. Mom P.S. Famous last words. They were here at four all wound up like klick klots.

August 21, 1966 Sunday

Well Patsy woke us up at seven. She wanted me to go to their tree farm and I sure would have liked to but had Dee Dee and the kids here. They sure are getting wilder as they get older. I fed them—Marvin oatmeal _ Ricky peaches—Stevie puffed wheat, toast and banana's for all of them. Dee Dee got up about ten thirty, her and the three older boys went to eleven o'clock mass. Donnie stayed with me. They all left for home at noon. I cleaned up the house. The people upstairs moved out. I got a nice dresser with a mirror from up stairs, he helped me move it down. I sewed all afternoon on Peggy's quilts. I have one ready to tie and two half done. Thrasher came over at seven. I told her the apartment upstairs was empty, she isn't interested. She is such a big phony. Well to bed. I baked a dark fudge cake. Mom

August 22, 1966 Monday

Well I didn't wake up until ten. At eleven I went to Penney's store and got a quilt lining. I ran into Aggie and Pat, they kinda gave me the brush off. I came home and sewed all day. Yang came over on her way to work, had coffee and jello. No mail no visitors, not even Thrasher wonder what she is up to. Guess I'll cut out some quilt blocks and go to bed. Mom

August 23, 1966 Tuesday

Well I got up late, I didn't sleep to well last night. Thrasher was here before I ate my breakfast. No mail or company today. I went to the laundry mat and done my washing, came home and ironed. Took a long walk in the sunshine. I finished the third quilt top for Peggy. I phoned Dee Dee, something is wrong with her car. She wants me to babysit at her house Friday night, I said I would. Shirley Kessack was here tonight, so was Sissy. I didn't see Yang today. No other news. Mom

August 24, 1966 Wednesday

Well just another day more or less. No company except Thrasher in the late afternoon. She is going to take a housekeeping job at Thomas for a couple of older people. She told me Mary Ramsey died at noon today. I baked three dozen oatmeal cookies. Made a pair of pajamas for Boofy and one strip on a quilt. I just went for a long walk. I am going to take a hot bath and go to bed. That's about all except I found an attic in this building and went through it. Somebody had stored some stuff in it some time. I got a few things. Mom

August 25, 1966 Thursday

I got up at nine. Baked an apple pie, made strawberry jello with peaches in. Spent the rest of the morning ironing and cutting out quilt pieces. At noon ate boiled potatoes—beans and sliced tomatoes. Thrasher came over at one, we had jello and cookies. Got a nice letter from Dottie. Aggie—Pat and Phillip Gifford came about three. We started up the hill to take them home, got hit in the rear by Kent Drug. Aggie is all shook up. Well now I am home waiting for Thelma Smith to pick me up to go to Shirley's for a Tupperware party. It is potluck so I am taking my apple pie. Will be getting home late so unless something unusual turns up for today this is all. A man just moved in upstairs. Mom

Aug 26 To Aug 29, 1966 Fri-Sat-Sun-Mon

Well Friday afternoon Dee Dee came and got me and I babysat Fri—Sat-Sun—nights. Aggie came and got me this morning. We had steak dinners at the Branding Iron and then she brought me home. It was cold so I lit the heater. No mail.

I went to Penney's and got some flannel and tied a quilt. Then I went to the laundry mat and done my washing. While the clothes were drying I went up to see Amelia, she is going to take a babysitting job on East Highway, $25.00 a week, two kids four and two. She will go home nights. It is raining. I have been sewing. Am going to have coffee and apple turnover, sew some more and go to bed. Mom

August 30, 1966 Tuesday

Well I waited all day for Shirley Fitch to come but she didn't show up. Mrs. Thrasher came over and stayed about two hours. We had cupcakes and milk. I sewed on little Marvies quilt today. Dee Dee and the kids came to visit tonight. They brought pop and cookies. They had been to clinic today. They stayed about two hours. Now I am going to write to Dottie and go to bed. No mail. Mom

August 31, 1966 Wednesday

Well got up at seven. Thrasher was here before nine, she is going into the social security office in Seattle and wanted me to go. But I am broke. Sissy and Shirley Fitch came down. Sissy brought me some quilt scraps. We had coffee, went to the Goodwill and they left. I made hamburger stew. I also went for a long walk. I finished little Marvin's quilt and started another. Thrasher came back at one. I gave her some stew-peaches and milk. Yang stopped in for ten minutes on her way to work. No mail. Well I am going to have some coffee. I baked a chocolate cake and a corn bread. I had forty cents so I bought a quart of milk and two stamps. I am going to mail Uncle a birthday card. Mom

September 1, 1966 Thursday

Well what a busy day. Thrasher came over early all shook up about social security. Sis and Shirley Fitch came and we went to Renton to Dodies Exchange. Shirley paid me for Darrell's quilt and I got a big box of quilt material and the woman gave me a sewing machine. We came home and I fixed chicken and dumplings—chocolate cake—peaches and we all had lunch. A letter from Peg and $15.00 for her three quilts. Shirley went home, I went to Penney's and bought two linings and two yards for little Donnie. I came home. I found a playpen in the storeroom. Shirley came back down with green beans and apples. She got the sewing machine so it will sew. I called Dee Dee, she is working tonight. She has a babysitter named Kathy. I finished Marvin's quilt and tied another one tonight. I have four done, have to have six by next week, also finished Darrell's. Well to bed. Mom

September 2, 1966 Friday

Well not much doing today. I made applesauce, baked an apple pie, tied two quilts. I used the machine today, worked real good until I broke a needle on a knot. Now I can't get it going again. Thrasher was here twice today. She was all up in the air, second time she came. Elaine had been over there raising hell over her stuff being gone. I think Thrasher was a little scared because she took Elaine's clothes over to the church. No Mail. I called Dee Dee, she wants me to babysit Sat. night and Sun. night. I told her to bring them out here and I would. Tomorrow is check day. Well it is ten o'clock, I should go to bed, but am going to sew a little while longer. Mom

September 3, 1966 Saturday

It is about three in the afternoon. I got my check today. Bought $18.00 groceries, mailed my rent and ate out. Expect a turbulous weekend. Dee Dee's babysitter went on a trip. So the boys will be babysat here. So I may not be able to write regular the next three days. I don't know how she is going to work it. More later you nasty Ole Gator. No other mail. Mom

September 4,-5th 1966 Sun & Mon.

Well the boys woke up 7:30 Sun. morning. I let Dee Dee sleep until 11:30. She was trying to get someone to work in her place Sun., nobody would. George came down from Enumclaw to get me to see their new house, be at Connie's birthday party and stay overnight. I went and Dee Dee lost five hours work over it because she couldn't get a babysitter. I hope she didn't lose her job and I guess she was plenty mad at me. We went for a long ride up past Carbonado and stopped at Grandpa and Grandma Kessack's graves. George and Barbara have a beautiful new $20.000 dollar home. Well I called Dee Dee, she said she was mad but needs me to babysit tonight and tomorrow so she is bringing the kids out pretty soon now. Amelia Thrasher was just here. Well more tomorrow when I am done babysitting. Mom

September 6, 1966 Tuesday

Kids woke up at seven. Dee Dee left at ten o'clock took Ricky with her. Kids were pretty good. Marvin kept bugging me to run to the store. We bought donuts three times and milk twice. She got home about 6:30, I was so tired I just rolled into bed and went to sleep. No mail, Sissy and Shirley Fitch were down a while. Mom P. S. Thrasher was over, she is taking graveyard shift at a living in home for retarded people where Wanda works.

September 7, 1966

Well I sewed all day, tied two quilts. Thrasher was over, she didn't take the job. We got in a money-spending dispute and she got mad and went home. Sis and Shirley were here a while and May Lyons. I called Dee Dee to see how they got along 1st day of school. Everything O.K. so far. She wants me to come in Friday on the bus and babysit until after clinic Tues. It's going to be quite a drag but I will try it. Buzz and Barb and the kids were down last night. She still can't make her mind on front room furniture. Well that's about all. Mom

September 8, 1966 Thursday

Sissy the twins and Shirley Fitch was down for a while today. She paid me for Judy's quilt and will pick it up tomorrow. I got a short letter from Dottie and the girls. I ate at Meeker today, had a French dip sandwich and salad. Haven't seen Thrasher, guess she got her feelings hurt. Well not much news. I am tired tonight, guess I better rest. Not much rest coming up over the weekend. Mom

September 9, 1966 Friday

I bought a bus ticket and went to White Center and babysat for Dee Dee. Also Saturday night. Aggie came in Saturday with a six-pack of beer, drunker than a skunk. Sunday morning she babysat at the Baptist church in Kent so I rode home with her. I went to Lewis and Clark Theater with Yang on Sunday night and we ate dinner out then too. Got home about one o'clock and slept until ten Monday morning. No mail, no visitors. Now four o'clock in the morning Dee Dee will be picking me up and I will babysit Tues and Wed and either gets home Wed night or Thurs morning. Wow, I wish this babysitting was over. I just ache from the strain. Well I could say no. Will write again Thurs or Fri. Mom

September 15, 1966 Thursday

WOW-was I sick Tues and Wed I just could hardly move. Her babysitter don't do any dishes or picking up. WOW was that house a mess. I cleaned it up Tuesday morning when Dee Dee left and Stevie and I slept for two hours. I watched Stevie and Donnie both Wed while Dee Dee went. Ricky came home at twelve thirty, wouldn't eat no soup or sandwich. He is badly anemic. He did eat some chocolate covered donuts. Dee Dee and I went to Patsy's Wed morning. I was so darn sick I had to lay down. Well when Marvin got out at three, she brought me home. I went right to bed and to sleep. Mom—No mail, I called Sissy today she has no car. Well I think I will sew a little more and go to bed.

Sept 16-17-18 1966 Fri-Sat-Sun

Well last three days were just days. I am feeling a little better but not exactly my ole chipper self. Fitches and Bogue's have been in and out. Thrasher was here this afternoon, she has been sick with a cold. Aggie had lunch with me today, fried ham—creamed peas—raisins and grated carrots was good. If I wasn't so lazy, I would go get a hamburger but no thanks. I have tied up two quilts and two baby quilts in the last three days. I wrote to Peggy and Dottie. I miss Dee Dee and the boys. I called her once. Well no mail and no news. So Sunday night and to bed soon. Mom

Sept 19, 1966 Monday-Tues-Wed-Thurs

Well last few days have been busy. Monday night Dee Dee and the boys stopped by and we went to the fair. Ricky got lost and found again. People have been in and out. The weather is good and I have been taking long walks and feel pretty good. Yesterday we went to Shirley Fitches and had a birthday lunch for Sissy. Shirley Kessack came with the Tupperware last night. Dee Dee and Patsy were out yesterday morning. I am still with the quilt making. No babysitting lately, maybe over the weekend. I haven't heard anything yet. Sissy got an odd letter from Joe in OKivinawa. Well we will see what happens today. Mom

Sept 23-24 1966 Fri and Sat

Well not much company on Friday. Dee Dee stopped in at seven o'clock and said she had stopped at Long Acres, somebody had turned her in to welfare. She had phoned Yang at Boeings and she was going to stop in on her way home from work and lend her $20.00. Well I'm glad somebody helped her out. I am down to $2.00 myself and another week to go. No mail. Saturday. Well I got hungry and made a chicken stew and a corn bread. Mrs. Thrasher came over and ate with me. Dee Dee and the boys came out, she is in a foul mood. She is going to try and get back on at Boeings. No mail. No other news, it is a dreary day like it's raining. Wish the T.V. worked but it don't. Well guess I'll nap a while then sew. Mom

September 26, 1966 Sun—Mon

Well this is Monday night going on nine o'clock. Amelia's Thrasher my very good friend was just here. Sunday I rode to Burien with Aggie, she fixed me steak and salad and took me to White Center to Dee Dee's about four o'clock. Aggie looked sick just absolutely beat. Yang came into Dee Dee's about eight Sunday night and took her to a show and eat. I watched the kids. This morning I watched Donnie and Stevie James while Dee Dee went to see if she could get on at Boeings. Not too much luck, she was terribly upset. They told her to go back to personnel Thursday and they might get her on swing shift. She wanted graveyard. She is so upset and hemorrhaging like mad. She brought me home about five. I called her at seven, she said she is alright and will come and get me Wednesday night is I can help her Thursday. No mail. Mom

September 27-28 1966 Tues-Wed

Well this is Wednesday morning. Yesterday was just another day. No mail-no visitor. I sewed all day. I went up and visited Yang about five minutes before she went to work. I went for a long walk-shampooed and set my hair, that's all. Now it's another day. I have had my breakfast. Dee Dee is going to come and get me tonight when Marvie gets out of school. She is going job-hunting tomorrow. That girl is going to get in a real mess yet. Well guess I'll go buy ten suckers and a paper. I have $1.00 and some change, don't get paid until Monday. Haven't sold any quilts this week and no money for babysitting. Dee Dee is broke too. Well if anything special happens, you will hear about it, otherwise fair ado. Mom

Sept 29-30 Thurs-Fri Oct 1-2-3-4th Sat-Sun Mon-Tues 1966

Well I have been having quite a time. I went in with Dee
Dee Wednesday night, she had spaghetti and garlic bread
and the house was clean. I watched kids while she went to
her church study. Thursday she went to Boeings and clinic.
Was gone till four o'clock. No results from either. Her old
supervisor called and told her to go back the next day. Well
not much more results but a little hope. She got a chance to
work Friday and Saturday night at the Swallow Tavern, so I
stayed over and babysat. I also watched Donnie while they
went to church, then I decided I wanted to come to Kent.
We stopped at my place, I had two letters, one from Dottie
and one from Hudocks. They will be here this weekend. Then
we went to Bogues and just missed Dunc and Sugar. So we
went to Dunc's, Sugar was passed out and his Indian friend
named George was there, Shirley was gone. We visited and
Dunc took us to Renton and bought hamburgers and fries.
Sugar woke up and him and George the Indian and I went
back up to Bogues. They drank a case of beer and ½ gal of
wine. We started back to Dunc's. Oh my God what a ride.
He stopped at a Mobil Station and went to the restroom. The
attendant took the keys and called the cops. I panic and called
Shirley to come and get me, she did and I left the scene. The
attendant lied and said I called the cops, so now I got two sons
and a Indian mad at me. Everybody hollers that I stick with
Dee Dee. Damn it I would have been better off if I had. Well
I stayed at Shirley's overnight and they are fighting like mad.
Dunc threw a iron skillet through the kitchen window. Shirley
took me to Dee Dee's and oh, my god what a mess that house
was. Well I got her up and between us, we got the two boys
off to school. I watched Stevie and Donnie while she went
back to Boeings. I got the laundry done and the house cleaned

up. We went to Patsy's for a ½ hour, came home and got her welfare check and she brought me home. For all this, I earn $8.00. Man I am home now and got my check, paid my rent, got some oil and groceries. I will end up with $20.00 to live on the month of October. Wonder what I will go through to make it to Nov. Mom

CHAPTER 9
NOV 3 TO DEC 7 1967

Dear diary. It has been a long time since I have wrote you and many things have gone under the bridge. Today I am a lonely widow of 61, feeling sorry for myself. I awoke at 10-2-7, called Dee Dee and Gwen at 10 after 7. You see I am their alarm clock. They live at 9431-18th S.W. White Center Seattle. Each has four kids and they live in a 2-bedroom house that Dee Dee lives in and pays for with welfare money. She has 4 small boys 2 in school—Marvin and Ricky. Gwen has 3 girls and one boy Freddie, he is in kindergarten. Kitten the oldest girl is in 1st grade. Dee Dee is divorced and lives on welfare and sneaks 2 days a week work at Long Acres in Renton. Welfare don't know Gwen is living with her. Gwen is suppose to get Navy child support and pay half the expenses, she also works. Boy is this a glorious mess. I done my laundry at the launder mat this morning while the clothes were drying I ate two hotcakes and two fried eggs at Meeker Café, cost .92 cents. After that, I walked over to Snooks house and sat a few minutes, she is my oldest granddaughter. She has 2 kids who of course are my great grandchildren. Their names are Rod and Tinky. Sharon Gifford was there and they were going to Fort Lewis so I didn't stay. Snooks house was messed up with laundry and some painting she was going to do. Yang called today, she is a mental patient in University Hospital she is also one of my daughters. Shirley Fitch was in for coffee on her way to work. Sissy another daughter and her twins, Candy and Billy Joe were here. She drove me to the 7-day Adventist church with a box of clothes I gave the Dorcas ladies. Then we went to St Vincent De Paul rummage store out on East Highway. I bought 4 books I thought I might read. I am reading a paperback book now named Little Me. It is 3 o'clock and I can't get Dee Dee or Gwen to answer the phone, darn girls. The little girl Lorri Young upstairs got into my garbage can twice today and I had to clean it up. I gave her mother Mary some flour and rice and a canister set today. I am cleaning out because in the near future I am going to move in one room at Buzzy's house and won't be cooking. He is one of my sons. He works on the state highway like his Dad use to do. He is married and has 3 children. They are very quiet and sensible people. Him and his wife Barbara have asked me, so for the rest of my old age guess that will be it. Hope I never get helpless and be a burden. My social security check came for $38.70 but my welfare check didn't come. I paid my phone and oil bill and I owed the bank $8.00 so paid that off and closed my account. It is now 8 after 3. Will finish writing this tonight. I ate a dinner steak at the Café where Shirley works for $1.29. An old lady from around the corner I think her name is Lawler just dropped in and invited me to a Stanley party next Monday night at seven thirty. It is now four thirty, it is very cold out. It isn't very warm in here. Peggy Hudock my second oldest daughter was just here on her way home from work. She lives in the country outside Auburn, she is legally separated from her husband Andy. She works at Boeings, she gets $150.00 a month child support for her three children at home. Charlie 14—April 11—Nancy 9. Well anyway, she took me to a lunch counter and bought me lemon pie and milk, she had coffee and doughnuts. It is her payday, she gave me $2.00 also. Now I think I will lay down and read. I feel all shaky inside. Well about 7 Peggy and the kids came again. I went with her to Penney's store, she bought a new purse for $5.00 then we went to Spouse Ritz variety store and she bought Susie a new skirt and some cards. Then we ate at Little Glens Café. I had clam chowder and milk. Then we went up to Bogues. Finally, about nine I got home. My apartment is very cold I went to bed. Mom

November 4, 1967

I woke up about 8:30. The apt is very cold. I ate a doughnut and coffee and took my 3 pills, I wonder if I still need all 3 pills. 'Am going to Dr. Shaw one day this week and find out. Nothing to do today, guess I'll go for a long walk and get a little colder than come home and wrap up in a warm quilt and read. Well I went for a walk and I am cold, I'm going to try reading a while. Peggy called and wanted Joes address, guess she is going to send Dottie a get-well card. Joe is my 3rd son. Dottie his wife is in the hospital with a slipped disc. He is babysitting his two little step daughters Patti and Sarah and his own little son James George. Joe is in the Air Force in Boston Massachusetts. It is now ten thirty, I am freezing. Larry from upstairs apartment just knocked on my door. In an hour, he is going to the dump and offered to take my garbage-good deal. It is eleven o'clock guess I will fry this steak I have. I don't know whether I'm cold—nervous or hungry, I'm shaking. Anne Burton stopped in and said hello on her way to work. I am constipated this morning so am drinking grape juice. Well its 15 to 12 and Larry just picked up the garbage and am I glad. I got rid of a lot of stuff I can't move and don't think I should leave it laying around. Well it is one 15 and I am eating some instant mashed potatoes with butter on and some canned spinach. Still cold. I tried to get the girls on the phone but no answer. I didn't get my welfare check today, in fact, I didn't even see the mailman. More later. Sissy the twins—Patti and Lorri were here for about ½ hour. Yang also dropped in, she has a 10 hour pass. She is over cleaning up her apartment. My check finally came. I paid my rent and sewing machine payment. It leaves me exactly $5.00 a week to live on which is better than nothing. It is 20 after 2 more later. I finally got warm and stopped shaking. Its 20 minutes to 5, I just had a piece of pumpkin pie and coffee. I spent the last hour reading. I can't get the girls on the phone. It is getting cold again. Well it is now 10 o'clock at night. Dee Dee and Gwen and all 8 kids were here, and Peggy and her 3. They took me home for late supper, we had baked salmon—shrimp salad—hash browns potatoes—peas and carrots and applesauce with milk to drink. Now if I can unwind I'll go to sleep. I brought home 3 books to read. Well goodnight ladies I'm going to leave you now. Mom

November 5, 1967 Sunday

It is 15 to 8 real cold outside not bad inside. I had the oil turned up all night. I just had a bowl of oatmeal and my pills. Guess I will have a cup of coffee too. Well I guess I will go for a cold walk. I went for my walk, the sun is shining and it is going to be a nice out. I wish I could go for a long car drive but no such luck. At 12 thirty Peggy and the kids picked me up, we went up to Bogues and then to Peggy's house. Susie and Nancy done quite a bit of fighting. For lunch we had tuna fish sandwiches and doughnuts and coffee. For 6 o'clock dinner we had steak and shrimp salad—kernel corn—mashed potatoes and milk. It is now seven 25. I go to bed about eight. So I will walk around ½ hour. So to bed. Mom

November 6, 1967 Monday

It is seven thirty and cold. Am having a hot butter horn for breakfast. It is 9 thirty, I have been for a long walk and to Snooks. Something tells me it is going to be a long day. I bought 2 papers back home to read. Hope they are interesting. Boy, it is cold. Well its 10 thirty, Mrs. Thrasher was here for an hour and yapped. I gave her hot cocoa and a cookie. I had coffee, she don't drink coffee it's against her religion. I think to kill time I will clean house. Well I got the front room done, it sure needed it. The mailman just came, a letter from Dottie. These are the 2 girls. Letter on next page. Well its 11 thirty, I mopped up the kitchen. Guess I'll go mail some letters and walk around a little bit. It's 12 o'clock noon, I am fixing myself some lunch. I boiled 1 potato with butter on, some smoked salmon and stewed tomatoes. It is 10 minutes to 2, I read and took a nap, it is cold. Guess I'll walk around a bit and exercise. The public health nurse was just here to talk about Yang Yang. It is 15 past 3. It is 20 minutes to six and who was here? Yang she had got $107.00 from Boeings, she is paying her phone bill—gas bill and gave me $10.00. It is now 9 thirty at night, Sissy and Marvin-Vicki-Robin and the twins were here and so was Shirley Fitch and Darrell. After they left I went to Mrs. Collars Stanley party. I ordered a man's pocket valet, figured it would be useful around Christmas. The girls won't answer the phone tonight. Well like Dad use to say, "when they want something you will hear from them" and he is so right. Well goodnight. Mom

November7 1967 Tuesday

It is seven thirty and another long blank day has began. I had
hot butter horn and coffee for breakfast. It is too early to walk
to Snooks yet so guess I'll walk around the apt and read. It is
15 to ten, I have been to Snooks and took the long way home.
It is raining. I got two birthday cards one for Shirley Fitch and
one for Yang. I will mail Yang's. Shirley said to come and have
coffee at 2 o'clock at the café, so I will take hers to her and a
pair of pillowcases. Well I really should get busy and finish
the silk quilt I am making. More later. Its 11 twenty, I got
the last 2 silk blocks put together, now for the fancy work. I
just talked to Gwen—Ricky has the pink eye. I am going to
have a raisin bread sandwich. It is now 5 after one, Sissy and
the twins were here. I went to the Goodwill with them. The
mailman brought a letter from Boeings to Yang, also closing
out papers for me from the bank. Guess I'll read a while. I
am suppose to go to the café and coffee with Shirley at 2 ten.
Think I will eat a dinner while I am at it. In the mean time
I'm going to walk around ½ hour and then read ½ hour, so be
it. Well it is 2 thirty, I went over and had a steak with mashed
potatoes—salad and 2 cups coffee. Shirley drank coffee and
kept me company. It is looking like rain, guess I'll go for a
walk before it does. It's 4 o'clock, Peggy was here and had
coffee, it is raining. It is 20 minutes to eight Peggy and the
kids were here with hamburgers and orange pop. I'm reading a
paperback book named Morans Woman. As soon as I tire out
I'll give up and get to sleep. Mom

November 8, 1967

It's 10 after 8 and raining, looks like a long dreary day ahead. It's 10 o'clock, I walked Over to Snooks and had tea and a doughnut. Rode back with Shirley Fitch. It is raining. Guess I'll sew on the silk quilt. It's 12 o'clock, I made a apple banana salad and am cooking some venison steak that Snooks gave me. It is raining and very gloomy. I tried to call the girls but their line is busy. Finally got Gwen her check didn't come. It is 2 twenty-five, just went over to the restaurant and had coffee and banana cream pie on Shirley. She invited me to go to Renton with her after work. It is 7 thirty and pouring rain. I have been chasing around with Shirley Fitch in her car since 4 o'clock. Just talked to Dee Dee on the phone, Gwen did not get her check. I am going to see them tomorrow. Well as soon as 8 o'clock comes, I am going to bed. Oh well another day under the bridge. Mom

November 9, 1967

It is 20 after 6 at night. I just got back from White Center. I started out at 7 fifteen this morning. They are doing O.K. I guess as far as possible with 8 kids. At least Gwen got her check today. It is pouring rain. I just got a light bill for $7.00. Mom

November 10, 1967

It is ten after 7, I have been up ½ hour. It is pouring rain and looks like a gloomy day ahead. It's 9 thirty, I took a walk around town and ordered some stove oil. I am sewing on the silk quilt, I can't seem to find anything to read that will hold my interest. Shirley Fitch was just here on her way to work. She left some of the Bee Line party clothes here. I guess Sissy is supposed to pick it up except mine and Peggy's. I finally found a story about an Indian catching a wild horse. It's 10 after 12, Sissy and the twins just spent about an hour here. The mailman just left. I got a nice card and letter from my sister Helen Grace. Well it's 5 minutes to 3. I went over to the restaurant and had clam chowder and fish and fries. Then walked to the doughnut shop and got 3 glazed doughnuts. Maybe Peggy will stop by on her way home from work. It stopped raining but the wind is sharp. Well its 4 fifteen, Peggy didn't come. But Sissy—Marvin and Robbi stopped. They just bought Robbi a pair of boots. Gwen called, Dee Dee is at the dentist getting her lower teeth pulled. Well guess I'll watch T.V. for an hour. Its 5-15 and Peggy was just here and had coffee. Aggie just called all in an up roar. Pat is sick and she don't know where he is. It is 8 o'clock. I just got home. Peggy and the kids took me to the Golden Steer to eat. I just called Dee Dee, her mouth is bad, her and Gwen are going out for a while. Well another day. Good night. Mom

November 11, 1967

It is eight o'clock, I have been up an hour, had a cup of coffee and a doughnut. Well another long day ahead, for what I don't know. It's 25 to 11, I have been for a walk and bought outing flannel to tie the silk quilt up, it's half way done. It's 5 minutes to 12, I finished the silk quilt, now I don't know what to do with it. I called the girls, Dee Dee says her jaw is all swollen from the teeth she had pulled. Well I guess I will read a while. It is 20 minutes to 2, Bogues were here. We rode out to Meeker's Landing to see if they had more films, they didn't. It is 20 minutes to 7. Looks like the day is done. Peggy—Charlie and Nancy came and we visited Bogues, got home at 9 and went to bed. Mom

November 12, 1967

It is 15 to 8 another useless gloomy day begins. Its 2 thirty Peggy and the kids stopped in after church. I rode up to Bogues with them. Then we took the kids to the Auburn show. Then bought hamburgers at the Arctic Circle and came over here and ate them. Guess I will go for a long walk. I did and bought some sleeping pills and a magazine. Came home and laid down and between 2 pills reading and television I went to sleep. Mom

November 13, 1967

It is 7 in the morning another long day facing me. It's 10 o'clock I went to see Snooks and had coffee. Then for a long walk. I guess I will go to the store and get some groceries. Maybe a piece of beef and a carrot—potato and onion. I can cook it in the electric fry pan. Not that I am hungry but just to be doing something. It is 15 after 11 I went to Safeway got a chuck steak and some vegetables to make a kinda stew. Stopped by and visited Thrasher a few minutes, guess I'll read some more. Its 10 minutes to 2. The visiting nurse was just here to discuss the release of Yang. I guess I will call Sissy and see what they done with Robbi. The police picked him up yesterday. Then I am going to go buy some pillowcases to embroidery, no end to this dull life. I called Sissy and they let Robbi come home. She said she would probably be down around 3 thirty so he can get a haircut. Well it is 5 thirty, Sissy and Shirley Fitch was here and their kids are really in a mess. Vandalism—1st degree burglary etc. Dee Dee called me and talked a long time. It is 20 minutes after 7. Yang was here, she is now out of the hospital. I heated up what stew I had and we had supper together. I hope I can get to sleep tonight, I have a real case of jitters. Mom

November 14, 1967

Its 15 to 9 and raining. I guess I will walk to Snooks and back. Its 10 thirty I have been to Snooks had coffee and rolls then went to Shop Rite bought 2 small steaks—some cookies—soup and toilet paper. Sure am in a sour don't want to live mood. Its 10 to 3. Sissy and the twins were here. She is all wound up over the trouble Cindy and Robert are in. I spent the day embroidering a pillowcase. Yang was here about noon, she said she would come back later. I told her fine we would have a steak and toast. A quiet lonesome evening and to bed. Mom

November 15, 1967

It is 8 o'clock and here goes another day. Sissy and the twins were here, we took Yang to Auburn to see her Doctor. Sis gave her bus fare back. I am cooking liver and onions, if she is hungry this afternoon she can eat. It is 15 to 4. Shirley Fitch stopped in after work and had a cup of coffee. It is raining. I ate some liver and onions, kept some hot thought Yang might drop in hungry. Guess I'll call the girls and see if I go visit tomorrow. Well I called, the answer is no. It is 5 o'clock, Peggy stopped in and had coffee. Tomorrow will be a long day, I will go buy some fancy work and something to read. Mom

November 16, 1967 Thurs.

Well its 8 thirty and another long day ahead. Its almost 10, I have been to Snooks and took a long walk. I didn't get the pajamas I ordered from the Bee Line party so they gave me a check for my money, now I have the problem of cashing it. Its 15 to 11. I cashed the check and bought Boofys Xmas pajamas and a pair of pillowcases to embroidery and 2 magazines to read. Its 2 thirty I went to the Café and had a steak dinner. Saw Shirley, she said she would pick me up in a few minutes and we would go up the hill. Its 20 minutes to 7. Shirley Fitch picked me up after work and took me home and I had fried chicken dinner. Mom

November 17, 1967

It is 15 past nine. I had a bowl of Total and a cup of coffee. Another day to kill. Its 10 minutes to 11, I have chased all over town. I went to a rummage sale but didn't buy anything. I wrapped the pajamas I had for Dee Dee's kids Xmas. I had one for Kitten but will have to get for Gwen's other 3 kids. Well I bought a pumpkin pie, wonder if anyone will show up to help me eat it. Guess I'll sew on the pillowcases now. It is 11 thirty, Thrasher was just here, we ate some pumpkin pie and said she heard that the government was going to cut welfare and social security. That sure would fix things up in fine shape. Well back to the pillowcases. It is 12 thirty, Snooks and her kids were here, I gave her tea and pumpkin pie and cookies to the kids. Back to the pillowcases. It's 2 o'clock, Sissy and the twins were here. I rode up the hill with them to the new 88-cent store when we came out Sissy's car wouldn't shift. I rode home with Leila Gifford and she had a slight collision. Well I just talk to Gwen on the phone. Its 15 after 6, Peggy was here and defiantly am having Thanksgiving with them. Well I can't see to sew any longer so guess I'll read. I'll phone Yang and see if she has eaten. It is 25 to 7, Yang just showed up hungry. I gave her $2.00 and sent her to Saipan for 2 deluxe hamburgers. Well we ate our hamburgers, she is convinced she is going to be a big movie star. It is now 7 fifteen. Peggy said they might be by later. Otherwise, I'm going to read. It is 9 thirty, Bogues were here. So to bed. Mom

November 18, 1967

Its 15 to 9 Sat. morning and a long useless day ahead. I guess I will sew on the pillowcases. Will have to buy some more today to kill this Sunday and all. Its 15 after 11, I have been chasing around town. I went just for a walk and then to Shoprite and bought some food, and then to the dime store and bought some sewing. I am making a stew. I guess maybe Yang will come sometime today hungry. Its 25 after one, I called Yang up to come over and have some stew. It is a gloomy day. It is clouding up to rain. I finished that pair of pillowcases. Will probably start another pair today. Well its 3 o'clock Yang was here and Bogues and Aggie. Bogues left for home and Yang left with Aggie. Now I'll do the dishes and sweep up the floors. Don't look like Peggy is coming today. It's 7 o'clock, Mrs. Thrasher was here, we had cocoa and doughnuts. Dee Dee called, Gwen is at work. Don't think anyone else will come now so I will read and go to bed. P. S. Its 10 minutes to 9, Peggy and the kids came and we went to Bogues. Now to bed. Mom

Sunday November 19, 1967

Its 15 to 10, another day to battle boredom. Guess I will walk to the store and get something to serve coffee with. Don't imagine there will be much company today. I have a pair of pillowcases to work on. Well it is 25 to 11, I went for a walk and went to Shoprite and bought 3 dozen cookies. So now to the pillowcases. I have a feeling it is going to be a long day. Well it is 9 o'clock at night, I spent the day at Dunc's and Shirley's sewing. I done a little ironing and a little sewing. Had roast pork dinner. So now, I am home and better unwind so I can go to sleep. I called the girls today. Gwen is working. Mom

Monday Nov 20, 1967

Its 20 after 8 and freezing cold. I am going to walk over to Snooks. Its 9 thirty I have been to Snooks and had coffee and rolls. It's very—very cold. It's 10 minutes to 11 Yang stopped in on her way to Auburn to see her Doctor. Its dam cold I am shaking. I called the girls, they are coming out tonight. I am going over to the doughnut shop and get some doughnuts. Gwen said to get chocolate ones. It is 12 thirty, the mailman left me a card and letter from Joe and family, also a nice letter from Jim with $5.00 in it. Guess I better get busy and write some letters. Its 20 minutes to 2, Sis—Robbi and the twins were here, then Yang and then her visiting nurse. It is 15 after 3. I wrote to Jim. Mrs. Thrasher was here, the day is slowly going by. I bought 1 dozen chocolate doughnuts the girls said they would be out tonight. Well it is 6 thirty the girls were here with all 8 kids. Yang and Judy came over, guess I will read a while and then to sleep. Have to wake the girls at 6 tomorrow. Mom

Tues Nov 21, 1967

It is 8 thirty, I ate ½ grapefruit and 1 cup coffee and 2 pieces of toast. It froze last night, I guess I will walk over to Snooks. It is 15 to 11, I have been to Snooks and Safeway store. I invited Mrs. Thrasher—Yang and Judy Grimes to supper at 5 o'clock. This should be jolly, guess I will sew a while. It is 1 thirty I did not get around to sewing. Sissy was here and gave me a check for $100.00. I cashed it and done some shopping. I paid my phone—lights and oil. So now, I guess I will sew on some pillowcases. Snooks wants 2 pair and Gwen wants 3 pair and I want some for Xmas Gifts so I better get busy. It is too early to start supper. Well my company all came and seem to enjoy themselves. Read and went to bed. Mom

Wed Nov 23, 1967

It is 25 to 9, I went over to Snooks. Now I am going to the store and buy 2 small steaks so if Yang comes over hungry I'll give her steak and toast. It is 15 after 10, I have done all the chasing I can think of so now I guess it's back to the pillowcases. Don't imagine I'll have any company today being the day before Thanksgiving and all. Mrs. Thrasher came over at noon, we had cocoa and cookies and we both sew on pillowcases. Dee Dee called and wanted a cookie recipe sure is a long day. It is 10 past 3 Yang was over and we had steak—toast and apricots. Back to pillowcases. It is 15 to 7. The 7 day Adventist church brought me a Thanksgiving box so now I'll lay down and read and finally to sleep I hope. Mom

Thanksgiving Day 1967

It is 9 o'clock I have been up for 1 hour sewing. Its 9 thirty Dee Dee just called and we had a nice talk. Wonder what time Peggy will come for me. In the mean time back to pillowcases. Its 20 minutes to 11, Buzz called and wished me a happy Thanksgiving, I could have gone to Renton with them but am waiting for Peggy. She will be here soon because Nancy called. It's 15 to 9 I had a very nice dinner. We went to Bogues tonight and visited. So now to unwind and go to bed. Mom

Nov 24, 1967

It's 15 to 9 I just got up. Wonder what will be today. Probably no company everybody has the day off work and all the school kids are home. Well I am having a cup of coffee and then to the pillowcases. It's 10 o'clock Sissy was here for a good half hour, she is going grocery shopping. Think I'll wake Dee Dee up evidently the kids were just tearing everything up. So I went for a walk around town. Guess it's back to pillowcases. It's 20 minutes to 11. Wonder when Yang will show up hungry. Guess I'll call Thrasher. Well she called me and came over, it is now 25 to 2. Yang is coming over at 4. It's 4 thirty Yang was here, we had supper she is gone and I done the dishes. Don't expect anybody else tonight but you never know. Its 6 thirty, Peggy and the kids were here. They are gone now so back to reading. It is 7 o'clock I think I will go to bed. Mom

Nov 25, 1967

It's 9 o'clock the sun is shining. Wonder what this day will be like. It's 10 after 10 I called Dee Dee. Beverly called and said they would be here in about ½ hour. I guess her sister Bonnie wants to buy a quilt. It's 10 after 11. Bev and Bonnie were here and bought the quilt. Peggy called and said they would be here soon. We are going to Benson Center to shop. It's 3 o'clock I have been shopping with Peggy and visited Bogues. Then I went to the dime store, I bought a small artificial Xmas tree. Run into Yang, she said she would be over for supper at 4 thirty. It's 20 minutes after 5 Yang and Thrasher and I had supper. It's real cold tonight. I've done the dishes, guess I'll read. It's 15 to 8 Bogues were here. To bed. Mom

Nov 26, 1967

It's Sunday morning 15 minutes after 9 and real cold, wonder what I will do today. It's 5 to 10 I went for a long walk it sure is cold. Guess I'll sew on pillowcases. It's 20 to 4 Peggy and the kids came after church. We took the kids to the show then went to Benson Center and had dinner at the Golden Steer. Then went to Bogues. Buzz and Barbara were here while I was gone so I called them. I told them I decided to stay here another year. Then I called Dee Dee, then I went to the dime store and drugstore and done some Xmas shopping and now I am home. It sure is cold. It's 20 minutes to 5 and very cold. It's 10 after 8 Sissy and Marvin were here. So now to bed. Mom

Nov 27, 1967

It is 10 minutes to 9, I guess I will go see Snooks. It's 15 after 10 I have been to Snooks and to Thrashers now I'm going to the store and get some rolls. Then try and settle down to sewing pillowcase. It's 3 o'clock and really cold. I just put scalloped potatoes in the oven and opened a can of carrots and salmon. I invited Yang and Thrasher over at 4. I made a pillowcase today and now I am reading a magazine. Its 5 thirty Peggy stopped after work. Thrasher—Yang and I had supper together again. Mom

Nov 28, 1967

I got up at 7 thirty and went to Seattle. In other words White Center to Dee Dee's. Her and Gwen had been out all night with Aggie, they didn't send the kids to school and I never seen such a mad house. I got on the bus and came home. Thrasher came over and had cocoa and cookies with me. It is now 20 after 5 and pouring rain. I bought 2 magazines in the bus depot so I have something to read. It's 20 after 7 I am laying down reading, will try to sleep at 8. Mom

Nov 29, 1967

Its 10 thirty I have been to the dime store and done some Christmas shopping. Now I am going to sew pillowcases. It's 5 minutes to 1 I went to Shoprite and got some potatoes—2 steaks and a pumpkin pie. I am going to eat a piece of pie then back to pillowcases, I guess no company today. It's 2 o'clock I finished the pillowcases. Thrasher called and said she would be over for pumpkin pie. Well its 5 after 3, Thrasher was here and had some pie. Dee Dee called she is bleaching her hair. It is 4 thirty Peggy was here took me out for pie and coffee. She put a $15.00 dress on lay-away at Penney's. I read and went to bed. Mom

Nov 30, 1967

It is 15 to 9 pouring rain. I am going over to coffee with Snooks then come home and sew on pillowcases. It's 10 to 10—I have been to Snooks, now for pillowcases. It's 25 to 12—I put some steak and sweet potato on to cook. Yang was here at one and had pie and coffee. It is now 10 after 4 and real cold. Peggy was here and had pie and coffee. I just went to Tyson's and got 1 qt milk. It is now 10 after 4 I am watching TV. Well no more company, I read and went to bed. Mom

Dec 1, 1967

It is 20 after 8 I am making oatmeal mush. It's 20 to 10—I have been to the laundry mat and done my washing. Guess I'll walk around and see if Thrasher is home etc. On second thought guess, I'll work on pillowcases. It's 25 to 12 I went shopping and got the Bogue girls each a comb and brush set. Its 2 thirty I was just over to the restaurant, Shirley Fitch treated me to clam chowder and coffee. Back to the pillowcases. Its 20 minutes to 5 cold and pouring rain. Peggy stopped by, I went to the bank with her, she gave me $5.00 then pie and coffee then to Penney's and picked up her new dress. She is going out tomorrow night and I will stay with her kids. Guess I'll read a while. Peggy came—we went to Bogues got home around 9, went to bed. Mom

Dec 2, 1967

It is 8 thirty and pouring rain. It's 10 to 12 my social security check came. I went to Shoprite and cashed my check. Sissy was here and had coffee and doughnuts. Peggy came I went home with her to spend the night. Mom

Dec 3, 1967

It is 11 thirty I just got home from Peggy's. I called Dee Dee.
Its 2 thirty I have been up to Bogues with Peggy. Gwen—Dee
Dee and all 8 kids came with Chinese dinners and Yang came
over and we all ate. Mom

Dec 4, 1967

It is 15 after 8 I gotta pile of dishes to do and clean house. I
am going to Snooks 1st and give her the pillowcases she paid
for. It's 10 o'clock I was over to Snooks and came home and
washed the dishes from last night, now to pillowcases. It's 10
after 12—Aggie was here we had clam chowder then went
to the restaurant for pie and coffee. Back to pillowcases. It's
5 after one, Yang was here and had coffee. Still with the
pillowcases. It's 10 after 2 I got my check and cashed it. Paid
my oil and ordered more. Stopped by to see Thrasher, came
home made out my rent, going now to mail it and come back
to pillowcases. It's 5 o'clock Peggy stopped in after work. I
tried to get Dee Dee on the phone but no answer. I hope
everything is ok. It's 5 to 6 I addressed Xmas cards, finally
heard from Dee Dee. Guess I'll read now. No company so to
bed. Mom

Dec 5, 1967

It is 5 minutes to 9. It is 15 after 3 I just was out doing a little shopping and stopped in to see Thrasher, she is sick with a cold. I gave her some oranges. I finished a pillowcase and mailed the pair to Beverly. Dee Dee called and said to come in tomorrow I will if it don't snow, it is real cold. It's 10 after 6—Sissy and Marvin was just here, they said everything on the hill is white with snow, guess I'll read a while. So to bed. Mom

Dec 6, 1967

I got up and caught 5 minutes to 8 bus to Seattle and went to Dee Dee's. Tom was there. I stayed all day. We went to Peggy's in the evening and they brought me home. Mom

Dec 7, 1967

It is 9 thirty, I just got up. It's 10 to 11—I went to Snooks and then around town. It's 5 to 12 I have managed to chase around all morning. I'm still on the go. It's 25 after 4—Yang was here about 2. Nobody else, I finished a pillowcase and now I am reading and having some hot cocoa. It's 25 to 6 Thelma was here and left material to make 2 baby blankets. Sissy and Marvin were here.

CHAPTER 10
DEC 8, 1967-TO-JAN19, 1968

Dec 8, 1967

It is 15 after 10—I have had a crazy morning. Yang was here at 5, Thrasher was here at 9. I am tying the little quilts for Thelma. I am real dizzy this morning. It's 10 after 4—I went to the Doctors and got my pills. Peggy stopped in after work. Well all kinds of company this evening. Bogues—Vicki and the twins—Shirley Fitch and Tommy—Charlie-Dee Dee and the four boys, and I had to pull a boo—boo and pass out. Mom

Dec 9, 1967

It is 9 thirty and raining. Guess I'll sew and read. Its 10 thirty—Sissy was here, had coffee and stayed ½ hour. It's 10 after 12—I finished a pillowcase, Peggy called. I am frying potatoes and eggs for lunch. It's 12 thirty—I ate my lunch and called Peggy. We get to go to Renton after awhile. It's 5 minutes to 4, Yang was here. It's 20 after 4—Buzz and Barbara were here, they gave me $10.00 for Xmas. Peggy came and we went to Renton. It is 15 after 7 so I guess I'll read myself to sleep. Mom

Sunday Dec 10, 1967

I didn't sleep well last night. It is 25 to 9—guess I'll tie the other baby quilt for Thelma. It's 15 to 5—I rode home with Peggy and Dee Dee brought me back. I walked to Harold's and got a hamburger now I am reading. Bogues came about 9 and stayed ½ hour, otherwise to bed.

Mon—Dec 11, 1967

It is 15 after 9—I just got up. Thrasher called and is baking cookies. Guess I'll go over and sample them. It's 15 to 11—I went to Thrashers then the store, I got another pair of pillowcases to do. Guess I better get at them. It's 3 o'clock—Yang was here and had coffee. Thrasher was here and had cocoa. I have been sewing and reading. It is getting cold. Peggy stopped in after work. I went to the store and got some rolls. It's 7 thirty—Bogues were here. To bed. Mom

Dec 12, 1967

It's 10 to 10-Snowed during the night. I have been to Snooks. Mike is out of work. Now I am going to sew. It's 25 to 1—Yang came over and I took her out to lunch. Now I am going to sew. Its 2 thirty I got 3 Christmas cards. Marvin and Sissy was here and the Shirley and Scottie came. So to bed. Mom

Dec 13, 14th 1967

I went to Dee Dee's and stayed overnight and watched little Donnie while she took Marvin and Stevie to clinic. Ricky went to school. Marvin is deaf in his right ear and partly deaf in his left ear. Gwennie left Dee Dee with $100.00 dollar phone bill. Mom

Dec 15, 1967

Got up at 8—received a Christmas package from Joe and family. Went over to Snooks. Came home, Thrasher came over and had cocoa. It is very cold am going to sew on pillowcases now. It's 20 after 12—Aggie was here and had coffee and paid me back the $10.00 she had borrowed. Peggy stopped in after work and had coffee and gave me $5.00. Then came back later with Charlie and Nancy, we went out and ate and then to Penney's and the Wigwam shopping. Mom

Dec 16, 1967

It is 10 o'clock.—It's 11 o'clock—I went and paid a $18.00 oil bill. Then went to Shoprite and got a few groceries. It is trying to snow. I got 4 Xmas cards in the mail. Nothing to do now but read. It's 10 after 2—Sissy the twins—Lorri and Patti were here. It's 5 to 5—Snooks was here and had tea. I just ate a TV dinner. Nobody here tonight so to bed. Mom

Dec 17, 1967

It is Sunday and 5 to 12. Thrasher brought some cookies over and I made cocoa. It's 20 after 5—I spent the afternoon with Peggy and her kids Xmas shopping. We went to Benson Center then to Bogues then to Newberry's in Renton. Now I am trying to settle down and read. Mom

Dec 18, 1967

It is 20 minutes to 11—Shirley Fitch was here and had coffee. Then we went to Snooks but she wasn't home. Then Thrasher came over and we had cocoa. It is very cold, I'm going to get under some covers and read. It's 10 to 1—I am going to fix something to eat. It is very cold. It's 20 after 4—Peggy was here. Bogues came around 5 otherwise Blah. Mom

Dec 19, 1967

It is 11 thirty—Thrasher was here and had cocoa. I walked to Safeway with her. Dee Dee called. It is very cold and looks like snow. It's 5 after one—Aggie stopped in and had coffee. It is snowing but not bad. It's15 to 3—Bogues were here with the twins. Peggy stopped at 4 thirty. Thrasher was here and we had chicken sandwiches and cocoa. Tom was here about 8 and picked up the tricycles and presents for Dee Dee's kids. I read and went to sleep about 11. Mom

Dec 20, 1967

It is 15 after 9—I just had coffee and doughnut. It is 11 o'clock—Thrasher was here, we had cocoa. I cleaned up the front room and washed the outside of the big window. Guess I'll read a while. It's 5 to 2—Tom, Dee Dee and the kids were here. Then I went for a walk. It's 15 to 6—Thrasher came over with chicken TV dinners and a fruit salad, sure was good. Snooks and her 2 were here, and then Bogues. Going to wrap up lay down and read, it's very cold. Mom

Dec 21, 1967

It is 15 after 9—there is one inch of snow and still coming down. It's 10 o'clock—Shirley Fitch was here and had coffee. It's 15 to 12—Thrasher was here and had cocoa and cake. Bogues were here and had coffee and cake and it's still snowing. I've got a pot of soup on. Its 1 thirty—Yang was here and had soup and cake. Its 5 thirty—Peggy was here after work. It is raining now.

Dec 22, 1967

It's 20 after 9 and Thrasher was here already. It is raining. It's 15 after one a Mr. Towne was here with a box of groceries for Xmas from the 7th Day Adventist church. Bogues and the twins were also here. Beverly called from Seattle and said she would be here tomorrow around one. It's 3 thirty—I walked around town and bought some books at the Goodwill. I came home and Peggy and Sissy—Vicki and Cindy were here. It's 10 o'clock—Peggy was here and took me home for supper and then we went up to Bogues and Elmer and Shirley were there. I'm wide awake so guess I'll read until I get sleepy. Mom

Dec 23, 1967

It is 15 after 11—I awoke at 9 this morning and got a great big Xmas box from the Kent Princess. Ham—spuds—all kinds of canned stuff. Bev and the girls came about 10 and gave me $10.00, it is raining. It's 10 after 1—Thrasher was here, she got a Xmas box, she is so excited. It's 20 after 4—Buzz and Barbara were here—Lois and Pam were here-Sissy and Marvin were here and Peggy—Susie and Nancy were here. When everybody left, I went for a walk. So to bed. Mom

Dec 24, 1967

I open my Xmas presents then went and fixed ham and eggs for breakfast. Thrasher was over. I am going home with Peggy after church. I went and had a very nice time. Sugar called me at 1 thirty, he is at Sissy's. Mom

Xmas Day 1967

It is 9 o'clock and raining. Dee Dee called and wished me a Merry Xmas. Dunc is suppose to pick me up at 10. I had a nice ham dinner at 2 and Sissy—Marvin and Sugar came about 3 and I went up there and had steak dinner. I got home about 8. Dee Dee and Tom left the 4 little boys with me about 10. I watched them until 2 in the morning. Mom

Day after Xmas 1967

It is 11 o'clock—I got up at 9 and put all Xmas things away and cleaned house and walked over to Snooks. It is now 11 and raining. I have some shopping to do. It's 15 after 4—Thrasher was here. Sissy—Vicki and Cindy were here and Peggy was here. Mom

Wed & Thurs.

Passed without much importance. Thurs I went to Seattle on the bus to Dee Dee's. She brought me home in her car. She is in a very disturbed mood. Mom

Last Friday in 1967

It is 9 thirty—I got up and cleaned my front room up, it really did need it. Now I am waiting for Yang Yang, she said she would come at 10 and we would go out for breakfast. I am watching TV. It's 10 o'clock—Shirley Fitch was here. It's 2 thirty—I have chased around all day with Dee Dee and her kids. She is trying to get new housing project on Benson Rd and it looks like she might make it. I walked over to Sprouse Ritz and got some embroidery work to do. It 4 thirty—Peggy was here and had hot clam chowder. Yang was here and had cocoa and is sure wound up. I am reading tonight. It's 10 after 10—Peggy and the kids came, we went out to eat and then to Benson Center and then to Bogues. To bed. Mom

Last Saturday in 1967

This is the last Saturday in 1967. It is 5 after 10—The weather is blank and chilly. It's 10 after 12—I chased all over town. I ordered oil, bought birthday cards and presents and doughnuts. I just got back and Sissy came and had coffee. Guess I'll do a little cooking now. It's getting colder. It's 10 to 6—Yang had lunch with me. Buzz and Barb was here. Peggy came and I went shopping with her. Then to Bogues. Now I am going to read. To bed. Mom

Sunday Dec-1967

This is the last Sunday and the last day of 1967. It is 5 minutes to 10. Peggy came and got me and I spent the day at her place. She brought me home and I read a while, and Shirley Fitch came and got me. I stayed at their place until The New Year rolled in. Mom

January 1, 1968

It is 10 to 11. I wrote some letters and went to mail them. While I was at it, I went for a long walk. Then Mrs. Lolled came for a visit. It is one o'clock-it is getting colder. Snooks is suppose to pick me up to go to Fitches for fried chicken supper. Snooks came we had a delicious dinner and played scrabble. Mom

Jan 2, 1968

It is 15 after 9—the ground is covered with frost. It is 10 to 11—I went to Snooks, came home and went to Thrashers. Now I am going store shopping. It is 15 to 3—Thrasher and Yang were here, it is getting very-very cold. Peggy was here and had coffee. Then I went over to Snooks and had supper. Meat loaf—green peas—baked potatoes—cottage cheese and pineapple. Then I came home and read and went to sleep. Mom

Jan 3, 1968

It is 10 to 11—the weather is blank. Judy Grimes was here twice. Yang stuck her head in and said hello. Thrasher came after that and had cocoa. Peggy came around 8 in the evening, so to bed. Mom

Jan 4, 1968

It is 20 after 10 quite cold. I walked over to Snooks and had coffee. Thrasher was here and had coffee. Dee Dee called and she is coming out to Auburn and rent her new house. It's 15 after one—Yang was here and borrowed $5.00 and some coffee. It's 5 o'clock and getting cold. Peggy was here, we went to the Hole in One and had coffee and pie. Then to Barneys and bought Susie a record. Now I am reading and waiting to hear from Dee Dee about the new house. Bogues came. I watched Dee Dee's kids from 5 to 8. So to bed. Mom

Jan 5,1968

It is 12 thirty the sun is shining. I walked to Snooks and had coffee, rode home with Shirley Fitch. Thrasher came and had coffee. Since then I have been chasing around town. It is now 12 thirty—am going to sew a bit on some pillowcases. Might take a walk. I went to Snooks for supper at 5. After I had been home a while about 7 Peggy—Charlie and Nancy came. Mom

Jan 6, 1965

It is 10-10, real cold, everything outdoors is froze. Sissy was here and had coffee, she had been grocery shopping. Marvin is gone Elk hunting. Sissy—Vicki—Cindy in fact all the girls were here again. I expecting Peggy before too long. It's 10 after 3—Dee Dee and Tom were here and invited me to Turkey dinner at 6. I went and had my dinner then we went to Peggy's and stayed until 15 to 12 and then to bed. Mom

Jan 7, 1968

It is Sunday 20 minutes to 9 and snowing. It's 5 to 11—It stopped snowing. Thrasher called, she is baking cinnamon rolls. Aggie and Pat were here, they are looking for a cheap apt to move into. I am waiting for Shirley Kessack to pick me up. I am going to spend the day at their place. They came after me, I spent the day there and had roast beef dinner. Wendy has a broken ankle. When I got home, I cooked supper for Yang and Pat. Then read and went to bed. Mom

Jan 8 1968

It is 15 to 9—I had coffee and toast. It looks cold out. 2 men were looking the building over, I hope I am not forced to move because I don't know where I would go. Dee Dee came and got me at noon. I babysat Stevie and Donnie until 3. She paid me $2.00 and brought me home. Peggy came we went to the Saipan, she had apple pie and coffee I had a steak. Bogues came in the evening. Mom

Jan 9, 1968

It is 20 to one. I done my washing at the laundry mat this morning. It is pouring rain. I went to see Thrasher while my clothes were drying. Dee Dee was here with Stevie and Donnie. They stayed with me while she went to the Saipan to get part time work. Aggie and Yang will be here soon. Well they came, we ate fried bread and hot dogs. Then Aggie and I went to Snooks. She was baking cookies, I bought 30 cents worth. I wonder if Peggy will stop in. I got 3 new magazines, looks like I will be reading tonight. Peggy stopped in. Mom

Jan 10, 1968

It's 15 after 2, I woke up to a snowstorm. I went to Snooks her kids are all sick with croup. Thrasher was over to have cocoa, my state visitor Kathryn Cooper was here. Dee Dee came with her kids, Stevie is ill—Marvin has the poops. Yang came over and had hot soup and borrowed $2.00. Peggy stopped in and had soup and coffee. Bogues were here later. Mom

Jan 11, 1968

Thrasher woke me up this morning at 9 and stayed until 11. At 11 thirty Thelma Smith came and stayed until 2. Dee Dee came with Stevie and Donnie about 1 and stayed until 2. Then I went to the Doctors office and got a prescription and went to the drug store and got it filled. Since then I have been reading

The Black Sun. Peggy did not stop today. I am going to the Saipan and eat, it is 10 after 6. Mom

Jan 12, 1968

Well it is 9 o'clock—I went out with Peggy and the girls last night and ate. This morning I am walking over to North Park to look at a house. I looked at the house but decided it was too far out. But there is an apartment on 2nd for $70.00 that I may take. I went to Snooks and had coffee, then to Yangs and got the $12.00 she owed me—then home. Thrasher came over and had cocoa. It is 15 after 12 and raining. I have hot soup on the heater. Peggy stopped on her way home, we went to the bank and then had pie and coffee. Bogues stopped in on their way to Leila Gifford's funeral. Peggy and Charlie came back at night and we went to the Golden Steer and ate. Mom

Jan 13, 1968

Got up this morning and went to Seattle on the bus. I went to a beauty school on 2nd Ave and got my haircut and a shampoo then went to Pike Place Market and ate dinner at a cafeteria that looks out over the waterfront. Then went 2 dime store, got some magazines and sewing and then home. Now I am waiting for Peggy and we are going grocery shopping. Mom

Jan 14, 1968

Thrasher woke me up at 8 thirty, made me irritated because I felt like sleeping. At noon Peggy and her 3 and 2 Bogues were here—Shirley Kessack—Wendy—Scot and Linda were here. I went to Dee Dee's with Peggy, came home cooked steak with vegetables and invited Yang over. We ate and went to Renton and then Seattle to see Valley Of The Dolls. It is now 8 thirty and I will read a while and then sleep I hope. Mom

Jan 15, 1968

It is 5 to 11—I walked to Snooks today, had coffee and rode home with Shirley Fitch. She says Dee Dee is having a bad time with her kids especially Boofy. It is raining, I just walked around town bought a scrabble game and some Valentines. Thrasher called. I am sewing on some pillowcases. No mail just advertisements. It's 12 noon. A man from immigrations office was here over Sugar. A nurse from Public Health was here over Yang. I have the TV going, but am sewing on pillowcases. I rode at 6 with Shirley Fitch up to Dee Dee's, we played scrabble and visited. Bogues came and brought me home. Mom

Jan 16, 1968

It's 9 thirty—It has been raining but now the sun is trying to shine. I went to see Snooks, stopped in at Thrashers asked her over to lunch. I sewed on pillowcases. Peggy stopped in after work. Thrasher came again at night for cocoa. Bogues came. I settled down for night, and Yang came with super hamburgers. So to Sleep. Mom

Jan 17, 1968

It is 20 minutes to 12—The weather is blank. I went to see Snooks this morning. I think I will put on some soup and go for a long walk. I feel shaky this morning. Well Took 2 or 3 long walks, got a letter from Joe. Bogues were here in the evening. Can't make up my mind whether to more or not, still reading crazy magazines. Mom

Jan 18, 1968

It is 11 o'clock—got a letter from Patsy with $5.00 in it. Thrasher came over for cocoa, stayed 1 ½ hr. I am sewing on pillowcases. Guess I'll go for a walk, better call Sissy first see if she is coming down. Can't go see Snooks this morning, she's tied up with bible study people. The weather is mild. See you later Alligator. It's 25 to 4 and raining. Yang was here. Dee Dee and Tom were here. I took a 2nd long walk and ordered oil. I got some paperback books at the Goodwill. Wonder if Peggy will stop tonight. Well it's 15 after 4—Peggy was here, we had coffee and rolls and Thrasher was here again. Am going to wash up some dishes, have a chicken sandwich-write a letter to Joe and spend the evening reading. Bogues stopped in. Mom

Jan 19, 1968

It is 20 after 12 and raining. I went to see Snooks then
went to pay my phone bill. Went to Safeway got some clam
chowder and rolls. Then went to the dime store, got some
new tennis shoes and sox. Came home and ate. Guess I'll sew
on the pillowcases. It's now 15 to 4—still raining, I finished
the pillowcases, read some and watched TV. Peggy just parked
across the street and headed for the bank. Hope she comes
in. Bogues came down and Peggy and kids all landed here the
same time. Bogues left first then Peggy and the girls and I went
to the Wigwam and ate at the Golden Steer. It was almost 10
when I got home, so to bed. Mom

CHAPTER 11
JANUARY 1 TO MARCH 10, 1971

Volume 1 1971

Year 1971—I spent New Year's Eve with Dee Dee and her boys. Donnie and Steve, got one sleepy and went to bed. The rest of us of us watched TV, the Big Valley was on. New Years day we were pretty much out of groceries. We had scrambled eggs and toast for breakfast—Deviled egg sandwiches for lunch and fried potatoes and eggs for supper. Jim and Bev and Peggy came and got me after that. We stopped at Jim & Bev's and had ham sandwiches and root beer floats. Then Peggy brought me home. Next day I took down the Christmas tree. I went to the store and bought a steak—cottage cheese and bread. Jim and Bev came that evening, they had been to the Navy commissary. They brought me a box of groceries. Then we went up to Bogues and played Michigan Rummy. Aggie and Jimmie came up. Aggie told me I should call Peggy and tell her that Andy had hired somebody to kill her and the girls. Sunday was rather a long day. Hamilton's came in late afternoon and Peggy and the girls. Geri and Leroy came around noon. Leroy says mom I am in love with your daughter, I said well anybody that is crazy enough to fall in love with one of my daughters takes their own chances. Well Monday I went to the drug store and cashed my social security check and my welfare check. I bought money orders for my rent and little bills I owe. I bought Palmolive dish soap-1 potato to bake and 1 tomato slice. Spent the rest of the day crocheting a hat for Scott's birthday, and making out money orders. Well now, it is Tuesday morning Jan 5th. Patsy called she is going to pick me up between 9 thirty and ten. I am going to buy food stamps and we are going to shop. More tonight. Patsy came at 15-2-10, we went to White Center Light Co., I bought my food stamps and then went across the street to Kremlins and bought 5 skeins of yarn, then to St Vincent De Paul and bought 5 lbs of nylons and a pillow. Then went to Safeway and bought some groceries. Then to Westward Village Bank where she collected $12.00 for a Xmas tree. Then the car wouldn't go, the gears froze. We had to call a yellow cab and go to her house. I stayed for supper, we had fried chicken—baked potatoes—green salad and corn—meal muffins with milk to drink. Harley got the car home and said it was OK, we started for my place got on the other side of the project the car conked out. She called Jim, he came and got us. Took her home and then me. They are having lots of trouble with Duke age 12. He set 2 mattresses on fire, smoking and don't get along at school. Patsy and Harley are not getting along. Annette don't seem too happy but very restless. Wow-what a mixed up world. I got a nice letter from Dee Dee today with a check for $20.00. I don't want that money, I really don't. It is 2 o'clock in the morning and I can't sleep, so decided to get up and write. I called Snooks tonight, she said her and the neighbor girl had a Ouija board. I called Peggy to see if she's OK. Well guess that is about all. The weather looks like snow. Guess I'll write to Dee Dee and if I am still not sleepy, I will crochet. I am going to make scarves one for PG and one for Nancy, the color is bisque. Ta To C-U-Later Mom

Jan 6, 1971

Finally went to bed at 3 thirty last night and fell asleep, woke up at 10 this morning. Well another day. It is—thirty, got a letter from Helen Bailey, one from Patsy. I am cooking a beef pot roast with onion and carrots. 3 o'clock—I had a nap, some hot tea and a cupcake. Just wrote a letter to Gwen, so back to sewing and crocheting. It's 15 to 4 Margret came in to visit. I am getting hungry. The flying nun will soon be on. It is 7 o'clock—Viola was just here to visit. North West Travelers is on TV. It's 9 o'clock the Jonny Cash show is on, I'm ready for bed, going to have 2 boiled eggs and tea first. So another day. My legs feel odd tonight, like they aren't circulating right. Cold tonight. Bye Now

Jan 7, 1971

It's 8 o'clock, time for Len Samson on TV. It is 10 o'clock just called downstairs, Cliff says Sally was sick all night, this really upsets me. I am burning a spice candle, sure smells good. It's 15 to 10 and little green monster called phone has not rang today. I should pay 10 a month to look at the stupid thing. It's 15 after 11 and the monster rang. Gerri is on her way out-woo pee. It's 10 after 3 I have been to sewing circle really enjoyed it. Called for Sally, she is still sick. Bev came over at six thirty and went thru the 2 boxes of clothes Gerri left here. Then we went to the Giant T and shopped. I bought a scrabble game for DD and a pair of pillowcases to embroider-2 skeins of white yarn—some glue and color crayons. TV is terrible tonight. My legs are full of pins and needles, awe misery. Its 10-2-9. Tood a loo

Jan 8th 1971

It's 10 after 8 raining. I just put a handmade scarf in the mail for PG and a hat for Scottie. I wonder if the little green monster will ring today. Its 11-25 just talked to Patsy on the little green monster, said she now has a 62 Chevy and might be out this afternoon. Also talked to Aggie seems the Great Andy Hudock put himself in the Vets Hospital this morning. I am cooking some chicken in the oven. Talked to Sally on the phone, she is feeling a little bit better. Margaret was in for 5 minutes, says she feels awful nervous—she has emphysema and has had a nervous breakdown. Poor soul she is pitiful. It's 20 after 1—Patsy was here to visit, stayed about 1 hour. I am now eating chicken and rice a roni yum yum. It's 6-10 nothing going on. 5 after 11—Goodnight All.

Jan 9, 1971

Its 8:30, wind blowing and raining. It's 11 o'clock, pouring rain. The little green monster is awful quiet today. It is 11-30, got nice letter from Dee Dee, and also got free sample Vaseline hand lotion. I would go to the store but the rain is so wet and cold. 15 after 2—Margaret was here. I was key watcher for 1 hour. Was just talking to Peggy her and Nancy and 2 little girlfriends may stop in later. Guess I will bake a small cake for tea. Tee Hee. Well it's 10-20-5 and nobody showed up yet. I baked honey-date muffins. I also cooked a hamburger steak smothered in onions and ate it and fell asleep in my chair. The little green monster rang once today, guess it has ho hum mouth. Well it is 6 o'clock little green monster rang, it was Sally she sounds like her good little old self again. Its 7—Peggy—Nancy and her 2 girlfriends were here. Peggy brought me some pillowcase patterns.11 o'clock it's a day.

Jan 10, 1971

It's 9 o'clock—all is calm and quiet. It's 10 o'clock, Dee Dee called and she is hemorrhaging, sure, hope nothing serious is wrong. Dr. gave her a hormone shot. It is snowing up there, and raining here. It's 1-20—Margaret was here, she seems so restless and unhappy—unsettled or something. I'm getting hungry, so am cooking spuds—carrots—sloppy Joe hamburger. Quit raining and sun is shining. Little green monster is awful quiet. It is 20-2-3 and snowing like mad. Talked to Bev, Jim is out on the highway running a snowplow in the north end. Sounds bad. Burr. It is 3 thirty—there is a good inch of snow and still coming down. I am going to have tea—a muffin and the sew a while. It's 10 o'clock. What a dull day, even television is blah. I inch snow outside. No company—no little green monster chatter. I'm going to find something to eat and go 2 bed.

Jan 11, 1971

It's 4 in the morning and I can't sleep, so got up and had a cup of coffee and baby its cold outside and snowing. It is 15-2-9 I am watching the Len Sampson show. Patsy called this morning. At 10 o'clock I will go to the drug store and will get some embroidery thread and then to the grocery store. It's

10-2-2—went down 2 see Sally, she is better but Viola is sick. It is 3-15 was just over to Rebecca's, she taught me how to ripple crochet, now I can make those pretty round pillows and afghans. Whoo—pee. Stopped snowing, now it is freezing. Got sleepy at 8-30, laid down—went to sleep. Didn't wake up till 3 in the morning.

Jan 12, 1971

Got up at 4—it is very cold outside. It's 20 after 7—I finished the white scarf-braided the arms and legs for Humpty Dumpty and took a hot bubble bath-washed out my underclothes. Now I'm ready for my second cup of coffee. Len Samson will be on at 8. It is snowing. It is 20 after 4—just talked to Yang she is coming to take me to clinic tomorrow. Thank God for small mercies and wonderful daughters. Going to eat now. It is 9 o'clock—a stupid ball game on TV instead of the program—darn. I talked to Dee Dee, she is snowed in but feeling better, the hormone shot helped her. Got 3 letters today all from granddaughters. Bless the little darlings. Am working on my rug tonight. I made macaroni salad. Margaret visited me today. I gave her spiced tea and cookies. Going to bed soon.

Jan 13, 1971

Its 10 after 9—I got up at 7, watched Len Samson. Had prunes and raisin bread for breakfast. Am going to clinic today if Yang and Leroy show up. It snowed last night. Well Leroy and Yang came at 11 and had hot-spiced tea and their fortunes told. Then we went to the hospital got there at 12 so went to the cafeteria and had lunch. Then upstairs to the clinic. I didn't see the Dr. until 3. Then had a blood test and waited for medicine, got home at 5. Snowing like mad. They went straight home. I had a hot beef sandwich, laid down and went to sleep. Patsy called and said they were going to the church of Philadelphia tonight. Sounds like Quakers or something. Got my phone bill it was $16.25. Well no other news, so to bed.

Jan 14, 1971

It's 10 o'clock—I just got up. Margaret was here and wants me to help Elizabeth serve at the sewing circle today because she has to go to the Dr. It is 12 noon—I received 3 letters. One from De De one from my sister Helen and one from Patti my granddaughter in Colorado. At 1 one I go to sewing circle. It is five o'clock—I have been to sewing circle, we stuffed monkeys. They served gingerbread with whipped cream. I came home at 3 and took a nap. I am going to have a hot Tamale for supper. I went to bed at 7 o'clock. Sweet oblivion.

Jan 15, 1971

Got up at 7:30—it is now 12 noon. The little green monster has not rang today. The blasted little idiot. I am key keeper this morning. The mail truck is next door and will soon be here. When Eva comes back and takes the key, I am going to the drug store and grocery store. Eva came back, it is 20 to 1. I will leave for the store about 2. Am cooking a beef pot roast. It is 2 thirty—I have been to the store and a good thing because a big rainstorm just came up. No rings from little green monster and here I am sending 16 dollars and 18 cents to the phone company, nuts I say nuts. It's 10 after 3—I went downstairs to give Viola some ric—rac and watched her and Eva shoot a game of Pool. Viola gave me some yarn. It's 15 after 6. Little monster hasn't even yipped. Well one more day.

Jan 16,1971

It's 10 o'clock—I just got up and am having sweet Roll and coffee. Well I just got the mail a cute picture from Donnie Geyman a $5.00 check from Peggy and a receipt paid in full from the magazine co. It isn't raining or anything, this morning just blah. I go to Jim Jr. going away party tonight. Well guess I will clean up the apartment and sew a while. Little green monster rang, it's Patsy. I was talking to Bev—Jim will pick me up today and I can buy yarn on my way over to their place and be there for the party tonight. It's 1 o'clock Sally was just up. I just finished my January pillowcases. Buzz and Barbara were here and Jim and Jimmy Jr. Then I went to Jim's for supper and the party. Played Michigan rummy till 1 in the morning. Then home. Jim is taking me to Monroe Tuesday.

Jan 17, 1971

It is 20 to 11—I just got up. The weather looks calm, we had a big windstorm last night. It is 1 Thirty—my clothes are in a dryer. Dee Dee called she is trying to get her friend Maurice lined up with Yang and Leroy for an apartment. I told her he might have better luck going to 2nd Ave center. I also told her Jim was bringing me up Tuesday. I am making a pair of pillowcases out of pink Hawaiian cloth to take to Dee Dee's—it is a blah day, outside of Dee Dee calling little green monster is very quiet. It is 20 after 2—I have done my ironing, now am having my lunch. Cold sliced beef—sliced tomato—roman meal bread and milk. It's 10 after 5, Margaret was in a few minutes, she sure is restless. Little green monster sure is quiet. It's 11 o'clock and I am going to bed.

Jan 18, 1971

It's 10 after 6—I just can't sleep any longer, so I got up. I hear the elevator running so someone else is up too. It is 20-2-10 I got welfare papers to fill out and mail, have done so now I am going to the drug store. Little green monster hasn't even yipped. Well it is 3 o'clock—Peggy was here, we went to Giant-T and Value Village. Dee Dee just called and her lawyer told her he had the parole officer's report and they are asking probation. She also asked me to call Mrs. Geyman and have her Avon delivered here for me to take up there. I have been trying to get her but no answer. It's 25 after 5—Patsy called and wished me God speed. It's 10 to 11—I watched Cat Ballou tonight sure was a good movie. So to bed.

Jan 19, 1971

It is 15 after 8—I have had a hot bubble bath. Little green monster rang, Sissy wanted Yangs phone number. Vicki has to go to court today and hasn't a way home until Robert gets out of school. So she was going to call Yang 2 C if Vicki can stay there. It seems Vicki was picked up stoned in the submarine room, which is a drinking joint. Well I'm ready 2 go 2 Monroe as soon as I hear from Jim. So will write more up there later. Well Jim and Bev came at 10 and we went to their house. Mrs. Geyman—Keith and Eda came with Dee Dee's Avon. Then Jim and I took the bed and away we went. In the excitement, I forgot and left my bags in Jim's car. Jim and Bev had to come back up with them tonight. Kathy got home about 4-10 and cooked supper. She says, she is writing Marvin a letter and breaking it all off. Well I don't know but I guess that is that. I had a very bad gas attack today.

Jan 20 1971

I am writing this a day late. Dee Dee took Donnie to Orthopedic Hospital and I stayed home alone. I had supper ready when she got home. I had baked a cake mix and made jello. We had Roast-potatoes and diced carrots. We played 2 games of scrabble and I lost both of them. We talk a lot. Marvin called but it wasn't a very happy conversation. Ricky was crying over his homework and never did get it done.

Jan 21, 1971

Got up at 7—had oatmeal mush and toast. Ricky didn't want to go to school. Donnie slept until 10. Kathy is gone to court. Georgia Lee took her. I am sitting here mighty jumpy. I wrote a letter to Margaret. Rose was over, she is on 2 years probation and can't have anything to do with people that have been in trouble with the law. That takes care of Sugar—Steve—and Marvin. The neighbors came in and sat until we were ready to scream. Dee Dee took the boys to Pak meat at the school. I took Donnie and went to the church and watched slides on Indonesia. Home at 9:30.

Jan 22, 971

A gloomy rainy let down draggy day. Sally called, anyway that made me feel good. Marvin called at 7 thirty, Dee Dee gave him the low down and they both said good-bye. To bed at 9 thirty.

Jan 23, 1971

Well this is Saturday. It is still raining. Dee Dee and Donnie still asleep, the others are up watching T.V. cartoons. Marvin is supposed to go to a birthday party today. Ricky and Steve to basketball and also this is clean up day and shopping day. We shall C. Well we landed up taking a taxi to Safeway—walking to Candy—Cane Drive In, having deluxe hamburgers and then shopping at Safeway. Came home had spaghetti and spinach. Linda and Maurice was over. Well, early to bed.

Jan 24, 1971

Got up at 7:30—made the coffee and the bed and put the roast in the oven, woke Dee Dee up. We went to Sunday School and Marvin-Ricky and I stayed for church. Stevie's teacher took us home and had dinner with us and brought me home. She seems to be very nice. A letter was here from welfare stating they are not sending a welfare check. Boy am I shook. Yang and Leroy are taking me to the welfare 9 in the morning to find out why. Called Peggy, Susie is very sick. Called Sally, Cliff is very sick. Eva came in 2 C me. It is 10 after 8, I am tired and going to bed.

Jan 25, 1971

It is pouring rain and 8 o'clock. Yang and Leroy are coming at 9 to take me to welfare. Aggie called me at 11 last night slightly drunk. Pat is coming home today, oh boy now the fun begins. It is 9 o'clock. Yang called and said the car broke down. I got welfare on the phone they said they never got the papers back, the dirty liars. They are sending out more papers. I am mailing them back registered special delivery this time. Then they can think of something else the Jack Asses. Its 10-2-10 raining. I talked to Patsy on the phone at 10, I am going to the store. I have been to the store, it is now 25 after 12. I received in the mail 2 birthday cards, each with $5.00 in and a nice letter from Patti Kessack, also letter from her mother Dottie. It's 9 o'clock—I shall soon be in bed.

Jan 26, 1971

It is 20 after 9—I just got up and had a hot bubble bath. It's 20 to 11—I am key watcher. I vacuumed the apt this morning, it looks nice. Little green monster is awful quiet this morning. Weather calm. Received new welfare papers, also talked to Robert Hart on phone, those Jack Asses better straighten things out, I'm at the end of my rope. Well I walked to the drug store, came home. Sally said I could ride with them to the welfare tomorrow morning so boy here I go with my horns out. Its 6 thirty—Pat Beall called he got home last night. Its 10 after midnight, I have been to bed but can't go to sleep. Guess I will sew for a while. Went to bed at 3:15.

Jan 27, 1971

It's 5 to 11—Cliff and Sally took me to the welfare, I had my little paw-wow there. Yang and Leroy picked me up at 10, we came home and had coffee and rolls. Now the day ahead of me is open. It's 1-30—little green monster rang, it was Patsy. I have some scallop potatoes ready to eat, guess I will cook some hamburger and I have pickled beets. C.U. later. Sally just got back from welfare and they won't help her and Cliff because they have an insurance policy. Boy. It's 20-2-7—I am so ho ho tired I am going to bed. Yang and Leroy are going to bring Kathy and the Boys to the party Saturday. AU REVOIR

Jan 28, 1971

It s 9 o'clock-foggy an rainy. I talked to Patsy on the little green monster. Today is sewing circle.10 o'clock—Sally called. Went to sewing circle, we stuffed monkeys. Eleanor played the piano. We had fun. It's 8 o'clock—at night, going to bed pretty soon.

Jan 29, 1971

It is 8 o'clock—Len Samson is on. Dee Dee and the boys are supposed to come today. I better go to the store and get fresh milk—cereal and sweet rolls. It's 15 after eleven and little green monster hasn't even yipped. Well I had a half-thawed hot tamale and a cold biscuit, and believe it or not little green monster rang—it was Barbara. It is 2:30—I have been to the store, I got ½ gallon fresh milk—a package of puffed rice and 6 cinnamon rolls and a quart of orange juice. Dee Dee and the kids will be here at 8 to stay the weekend. I just had a Japanese noodle dinner it was quite good. They are 7 for $1.00. Patsy called and said she is frying 10 lbs of chicken and making potato salad. Bev says she is baking the cake and making coleslaw. Aggie is bringing spaghetti and Yang a ham. I'm making jello, Snooks is bringing noodles and tuna. Wow guess I'll make parker house rolls. Well I'm going to sew a while. It's 4 thirty—my mind is in circles. Its 20 minutes to 8—Peggy called, her and the girls will come tomorrow, now I am waiting for Dee Dee and the boys to arrive. They arrived at 8 and all is well.

Jan 30, 1971

Well we had puff rice for breakfast. Went downstairs and set the tables and put the chairs around and Viola made the coffee in the big urn for us. Came upstairs had ham sandwiches and potato chips. At one thirty, the guest began to arrive. By 3 we were eating. We had 40 guest and 8lbs ham—10lbs chicken—4 salads—coleslaw—baked beans—spaghetti—tuna fish noodles—relish tray—sandwiches—hot rolls—cake—ice cream—jello—coffee—punch—beer. I received so many gifts a radio—electric can opener—relish tray—trivet—$10.00—a pants outfit—a blouse—a sweater—material—stationary—necklace—2 plants—sauce pan set—photo album. So now I am 65, a good time was had by all.

Jan 31, 1971

Got up at 7—fed the kids. Elvira picked them up at 9. I cleaned the apartment, bought a monkey and now ready to relax. It is 11 o'clock—little green monster hasn't rang. Eva was in and had birthday cake and coffee and a nice visit. She complimented me on little Marvin, what a clean cut little gentleman he is. My heart burst with pride. Little monster rang and it was Bev. Sugar called and he had his jury trial and was found guilty. In spite of it all, he wished me a happy birthday. It's 20 to 1—Patsy called and Holt is very ill with allergies. It's 2 o'clock—Jim and Bev were here we had a bite of lunch. It's 10 to 5—Margaret was in and had tea and cake and a little visit. I am going to bed early tonight. I am very tired. I am now 65.

Feb 1st 1971

It is 9 o'clock—I just had toast and coffee and my usual pills. I am listening to the news on my new radio. It is 11—little green monster hasn't even squawked this morning. I am key keeper. I have beef dinner on boiling, weather seems to be nice not raining. It is 12 thirty—Bev called and said she got three letters from Jim Jr. I didn't get any mail. I just had lunch. Went to bed at 7. Amen

Feb 2, 1971

Got up at 8 thirty, am having coffee and 2 cold biscuits. Guess I'll go to the store an spend my dollar bill and change today. It's 12 thirty—I have been to the store, bought a Chinese noodle dinner—1 qt milk—1 box jello and 1 can peaches—and 1 qt orange juice. The mail has come, I received a letter from Jim Jr., he is in the Navy training at San Diego. It's 2 o'clock—Sally was up to visit. Went to bed at 8. The ground hog seen his shadow.

Feb 3, 1971

Got up at 9 thirty am—having oatmeal and coffee, mailed Cindy's earring. The wind is blowing and it looks like rain. How now brown cow—what happens today? It is 20 to 11 and little green monster hasn't even yipped. It is 10 to 12 my social security check came but not my welfare and I can't get them on the phone, don't know what to do now. It's 20 to one—I called welfare, they said to call a food bank. Sally was up, gave me a red sweater for Kathy. It's 25 to 2—little green monster rang and it was Patsy, both her boys are home sick, oh happy day. It's 20 to 3—Cora came in to visit and I was also key keeper for a while. It's 15 to 10—They had a meeting downstairs tonight, then we played cards. I played Kings Corner.

Feb 4, 1971

It's 8 o'clock—I have been up for ½ hour trying to get welfare on the phone, all I get is a busy signal. Rats. It's raining, I have to go to the store at 10. I had coffee and peaches. Am watching Len Samson. It is 10 after 12—I went to the drug store and cashed my social security check, and got money orders and bought pillowcases and thread for Feb. Went to the grocery store bought cookies for sewing circle and kipper salmon& rye bread to eat. Who should I meet at the checkout stand but Frances. Then who came along but Peggy, she is laid off at Boeings, We came home, had a nice visit and she is taking me to welfare tomorrow 2 C about my check I didn't get. I served at sewing circle today. Aggie called and said Andy went berserk, she didn't know Peggy was here, what a Ha Ha surprise. C U later. Well I have been to sewing club, came home, got welfare on the phone, my check is there will pick it up tomorrow. It is 4 thirty. It's 10-2-8—Lois called, Pammie goes to surgery in the morning, talked to Thelma and Butch.

Feb 5, 1971

It's 15 to 7—am having coffee—rye bread and butter, watching 2 men from Apollo 14 walking on the moon. It is 25 to 10 and Peggy isn't here yet to take me to welfare to get my check. I have more handi caps than Apollo 14. It's 5-2-10 and I am boiling. It's 20 to 2—we have been to welfare, it took 2 hrs, and I signed my name 5 times but finally got my check. We went to Value Village—then to the bank and bought food stamps—then to QFC and shopped—then home and had turkey TV dinners. Now I am ready to settle down. It is 5-15, I am having sliced tomato—kipper salmon—buttermilk and raisin bread with butter. Patsy called and Margaret was in. I am at peace with the world. Its 6:30, Bev called. I'm sewing on Donnie's quilt and watching T.V. To bed at 9:30.

Feb 6, 1971

Sat. morning 15 to 8—It frosted last night, well a new day I wonder what is going 2 B today. It is 10 after 11—Little green monster is awful quiet today. No mail yet. I have been making Valentines and writing letters. Shampooed my hair with Palmolive dish soap, set it in curlers. It is a nice spring day. Guess I'll cook a steak. More later you nasty gator. It's

15 to 2—Yang and Leroy were here, we had a nice visit, tea and cookies. Little green monster still hasn't yipped. It's 10 to 6—I'm tying a quilt. Julia and Margaret invited me downstairs tonight at 7:30 to play Kings Corners. I don't know yet, and I don't know why I am paying 10 to 15 a month for little green monster. He certainly isn't cute and dumb as all get out. It's 25 to 8—I am pooped so am going to go to bed. Lois call at 8:30 last night. Pam is getting along OK but they have to operate again.

Feb 7, 1971

It is 20 minutes to 9—It froze last night, but sun is shining this morning. It's 10-2-11—no calls no company. Its 10-2-1—Little green monster rang—it was Thelma Smith, we gabbed for 20 minutes. It's 15-2-3—Jim and Bev were here with 2 big bags of groceries. I taught them how to play Kings Corners. We had fun. It's 15 after 5—Margaret was in and wanted me to sit in the lobby with her. I don't like to sit in the lobby so I didn't. I ate noodles and chicken for supper, now I'm going to watch TV and sew. I talked to Dee Dee on the phone, Ricky has a bad cold otherwise, they are OK. It is 20 to 11—am going to eat some grape nuts and go to bed.

Feb 8, 1971

It is 20 after 8—I am having coffee and grape nuts and watching Len Sampson. It's 15 after 12—I have been to the store, bought glue-envelopes-4 pair shorts for Geyman boys and stamps at the drug store. Then went to the grocery store bought package of frozen stew vegetables, am cooking a beef pot roast to put them in with. Mailed out bunch of Valentines, still got 3 bunches to make. It's 10 after 3—finished the pajama's for Marvin, guess I better make the 8 Valentine I have to make yet. It is 10 to 9—I am getting sleepy. Aggie called about 7 to see if I got my check. So, too—doo—loo for another day.

Feb 9, 1971

It is 8 o'clock, Len Sampson is on. It's 11 o'clock-Eva was in and had coffee with me and gave me some fresh eggs, someone had given Alberta and she don't eat eggs. Patsy called, she is down with the flu. There was a big earthquake in Los Angeles at 6 this morning, the news is full of it. Apollo 14 is supposed to splash down from the moon at 1 o'clock and there is suppose to be a lunar eclipse tonight. Crazy things going on. It is raining. I seen the mail truck at El Toro apartments, that means we will get our mail in about 30 minutes. Got a letter from Patti Kessack in Colorado, and a Valentine from Hudocks. It's 15 after 1 Yang just called, she wants to go back to Bill. The astronauts just returned to earth. I got Stevie's quilt laid out to tie. It is 4 o'clock—Margaret was in for a few minutes. It's 10 o'clock—TV was good tonight.

Feb 10, 1971

It is 20 minutes to 9 and raining. Peggy just called confirming my clinic date. It is 15 after 9—Patsy just called and is on her way over, I just climb out of a hot bubble bath. Well Patsy came at 9:30, we had coffee, played 2 games of Kings Corners, went over to visit Bev and then to Patsy's and had lunch. Yang and Leroy came and we visited then they brought me home and stayed for supper. We had pork chops—mashed potatoes—buttered carrots—pickled beets—tossed salad—canned pears—French bread and milk to drink. Buzz and Barb had been here and left me 4 skeins of red heart yarn. I received notice from welfare, I will get $63.25 a month, that is fine. I got some pussy willows today.

Feb 11, 1971

It is 9:30—all ready little green monster has rang twice. 1st Barbara and then Patsy, looks like a going day. Sugar goes to court for sentencing today. Tonight at 6 thirty we have pot luck dinner downstairs. It is almost 10, I have had my breakfast now I am going to finish tying Stevie's quilt. Hope to finish it today. Sally just called and she is sending Cliff up with the sewing machine. It is 11 o'clock. I guess Eva and Loretta have been tormenting Margaret. It is 10-2-1—I got a Valentine from Dottie and Joe. Patsy called twice today. Duke has played truant from school for 4 days. The police picked him up on his bike on the freeway and took him to Juvenile, so now maybe something will be done for him. It's 2 o'clock—I finished Stevie's quilt. It is 3-thirty—Georgia Lee and Howard Gering were here. Then I called Peggy she is coming for lunch tomorrow. I sent Donnie and Stevie's quilt to Monroe with Gering and Marvin's pajamas.

Feb 12, 1971

It's 9 o'clock—Peggy is coming for lunch, so I better get on my high horse and gallop around and get things done. It's 10 after 10—I talked to Patsy over little green monster. Duke is at Grandma Hamilton's. They go to Juvenile court Tues. with him. Harley reacted like a typical man, took Patsy car and $5.00 a week allowance away from her and said if she went to group, he would go out with a girl. It's 11-15—called Peggy 2 C what time to bake the potatoes, she said she would be here at 1. Called Sissy. No answer, called Bev and Jim is home, said they might drop over this afternoon. Peggy was here, we had lunch, baked potato—Hawaiian chicken—buttered carrots—French bread—and canned peaches. Jim and Bev came, they brought me a beef pot roast and 2 pkgs. Hamburger. Kriss and Karen were here with them. We had a nice visit. Now it is 2:30 and I'm alone again. Received heart box full of chocolates and pretty Valentine in the mail from Dee Dee and the boys. It's 15 after 4—pouring rain. Debby called, she liked her Valentine. Margaret was in. Little green monster rang at 9, a man wanted to buy a bass guitar. I had a good laugh at that. Wrong number.

Feb 13, 1971

It is 9-10 it has rained all night. Looks like it might rain some more. A new day a new adventure, who knows. It's 5-2-10—I have chatter box on that I might hear the news at 10, so far nothing but ya ya music. It is almost 11—little green monster must be ill, it has even yipped. Guess everybody went to group last night and crawled off and died somewhere. I am cutting out quilt blocks for Ricky's quilt. It's 12 o'clock—I see the mail truck next door at the Manhattan Apts. Our place is next. Well guess I will wander out into the lobby and C if I got any mail. Well surprise, nice letter from Helen Grace my sister, she broke her arm. My phone bill I expected it 2 B about $15.00 but was only $9.80, guess I'll keep little green monster around after all. It is 15 after 3—Sally was here and Margaret. Little green monster is awful quiet today. I thought Sissy was coming but I should know better. It is 5 o'clock—I am going to fix Chinese noodles and go to bed early. It's 20 after 8—Lois and Pam were here, brought me a beautiful Valentine flower arrangement.

Feb 14th 1971

Valentine Day, and where oh where is my sweet heart? It is 25 after 8 and Sunday. I am invited out to chicken and dumplings dinner at 2 if Thelma and Al Smith pick me up. Lois is having us over. It is 10 after 10-little green monster is silent, the whole bldg sounds dead. Turned on chatterbox a few minutes to news, nothing really new. Am cutting out quilt pieces. Little green monster rang and it was Dee Dee, everything is fine there, and she seemed real happy. It's 20 after 11. Little green monster rang again it was Holly wishing me a happy Valentine's Day. Wow the world is full of joy. It is 5 o'clock—just got home from Lois's, had chicken and dumplings—coleslaw—mashed potatoes—baked squash—peas—noodles. MMMM good had a nice time. Jim and Bev were here, brought a beautiful heart box of chocolates for Valentine's Day. We plan on going to Enumclaw tomorrow.

Feb 15, 1971

It is 9 o'clock and raining. At 11 we are suppose to go to Olga's and Alex's in Enumclaw, by we I mean Jim and Bev and I. Well it's 10-20 they said 11 but knowing Bev we will be lucky to get going at 12 in the first place, she don't want to go and man can she putter, well we will C. Little green monster hasn't rang. I just turned chatterbox on 2 C if I could hear some news. It is 15-2-4—we have been to Auntie and had stew—potato salad and prunes, she gave me $2.00 for my birthday and some yarn to make her a afghan. Then we stopped at the dime store in Des Moines and I got three wallets for the boy's birthdays. Then went to Burien and got outing flannel for .22 cents a yd, I've got 15 yards and almost 4 yards print at .11 cents a yd. Then home. Then I walked to the drug store and got 2 skeins black yarn and a money order to pay for little green monster. Now I'm home and tired. Its 10-2-6 I have had supper—ground round steak—green beans—sliced tomato and plums. Now I will crochet and watch TV. It is 9 o'clock,—I finished the white shawl for Lois. Am getting tired, will go to bed pretty quick. Amen

Feb 16, 1971

It is 20 to 10, am just going to have breakfast. It is 20 to 11—my dishes are done, my bed is made, my garbage is dumped, not a word out of little green monster. I tried to call Peggy but no answer. It is 6-15. Peggy came at 11-30 we had lunch and went up to Sissy's, had a nice visit. Shopped in Kent and went to Peggy's and had supper. Came home and bought 1 monkey. Am going to clinic tomorrow, Peggy is going to take me. She said we would lunch out. I am going to do my lunch dishes and sew and watch TV until I get tired.

Feb 17, 1971

It is 8 thirty—Patsy just called, she brought Duke home yesterday and now he is broke out with measles. Poor girl. Its 5 after 10—I wrote a letter to D.D. I finished the one afghan now I am going to tie on Ricky's quilt. It is 4:30, Peggy and the girls took me to clinic, we had lunch in the cafeteria. I had a stuffed pepper and tapioca pudding. Peggy said Charlie left Sedanar. Dee Dee called it is 6 o'clock, she wants me to come up next Tues. with Yang and Leroy and babysit while she goes to group. She also said Sugar and Steve each got 15 years. It is 11 o'clock—I am almost done with the gold shawl. Am going to tie a row on Marvin's quilt and go to bed. Had a good time today. Love Peace and Too-doo-loo.

Feb 18, 1971

It is 15 after 9—just got up and it is raining. Well wouldn't you know. It is 10 o'clock—talked to Patsy on the little green monster. Duke has very bad measles. Annette is sick with her back or flu or something. Well gotta go 2 the store. C U later alligator. It is 12-20—been to drug store and grocery store. Frances walked home with me. Got a letter from Patti Kessack. Sally was up, sold her one of my monkeys, am going to put

$1.00 in Xmas bank buy 2 autograph hounds at the drug store with the other $2.00. They are .99 cents each and have a pen with them. Make nice gift for Patti and Sarah on their birthdays. Might get 2 more for Lorri and an extra. Am going to sewing circle at one. After while crocodile so smile. It is 10-2-5 been to sewing circle and went to dime store shopping with Sally and Cliff, also stopped at Pacific Iron and bought some rose colored material to line a quilt. Am going to have steak—toast and sliced tomato for dinner. A letter from Patti today.

Feb 19, 1971

It is 10-2-10 I just got up. It is 10 after 11—talked to Patsy on little green monster. Duke is very sick with measles, Annette is sick too. Harley is home making Tamales. I can C that kitchen. I am tying Marvin's quilt. The sun is shining. I see the mail truck at El Toro Apts, will be here in 30 minutes. Wonder if I will get any mail. It isn't likely. 20-2-12—no mail rats. It is 5 o'clock—I am having chicken rice a roni and V8 juice. Went to bed at 11.

Feb 20, 1971

It is 10 o'clock—just got up and turn chatterbox on to hear the news. The sun is shining. Its 12-30, I have been to the drug store, bought stamps—scotch tape and an autograph humpty dumpty for my gift box. Came home and robbed all my banks to raise $5.00 for Leo the lion for Dee Dee's birthday. I was afraid they would sell it. I am getting hungry will eat pretty soon. 1st am going to wrap the 3 wallets for the boy's birthdays. It is 3-15—little green monster is awful quiet. It is 10-2-6—Thelma and Lois were here, we had honey date muffins—butter and jelly and coffee and a nice visit. I showed them Leo the lion, I just love him. Well 8 o'clock Yang-Leroy-Dee Dee and the 4 boys came, they wanted me to babysit Marvin-Ricky-Stevie, while they took Donnie and went to open house at Se Der Nar 2 C Tommy. Well I did. I don't know what is behind it all but the man upstairs keeps their books and some day we will all look toward heavens and say" here comes da judge" and it will be everybody for themselves. Amen.

Feb 21, 1971

It is 10-25—they have been here and picked up the boys and left. I cleaned things up and am waiting for Snooks to pick me up to go to Tinky's birthday. Told Leroy and Dee Dee tea cups, they were quite similar, each had a grave and a capital M, no tears, can't imagine. It is 7:30—I have been to Tinky's birthday party and Bud took us all out to dinner at Rubentino's in Renton where Merle, Robin's husband works. Their baby is adorable. I had a real nice day. Sure can't help but wonder about DD and her motives. I think it would almost have been better if she had been sentenced. I'm very-very upset. Talked to Peggy and Charlie on the phone about the situation, they are just as upset as I am. But what can any of us do? Maybe the man upstairs will take a hand. Time will tell. It's 10 o'clock my mind is in a turmoil, but my body is tired—so I think I will go to bed.

Feb 22, 1971

It is 20 after 10—I just woke up, it is raining. It is 11-30—Peggy and Charlie were just here, we had sweet rolls and coffee. Charlie is preparing to go into the Navy. Talked to Patsy and Sis on the little green monster, Duke ran away again, and Vicki aint doin as good. It is 20 after 3—I have done my washing and ironing. Little green monster has not yipped today. I wonder how long it will be before I hear from Dee Dee or Yang, bet they both have guilty conscious. Well it is 10 after 9—Elizabeth was up to visit tonight, she is having trouble with her eyes. It is pouring rain. Guess little green monster isn't going to ring. Thought that maybe Aggie would call, but guess that is wishful thinking. I wonder if they found Duke. So uncertain about her and what she is doing to her kids. I love those little boys, bet they grow up and tell her off. All I can do is pray for their well being and hope for the best. Amen

Feb 23, 1971

It is 8 thirty I just got up, am going to eat and then a hot bubble bath and shampoo my hair. It is 9-30 I had my bath and shampooed and set my hair. Little green monster rang, it was Peggy. She ran into Yang at the Pied Piper last night and she was drinking and drunk. She had broke up with Leroy. Which I'm sorry to hear, I really liked the guy. Oh boy what next? Talked to Patsy and Duke is in youth center. Talked to Sissy she is having her fun too. The school called and said

Cindy wasn't in school. Sally called, we will get together before the day is done. I am cooking ground round steaks—boiled potatoes—and tomatoes. I have raspberry jello and iced tea in the refrigerator. It's 10 after 12 I had a good dinner, now to sew. It is 15 to 2—Sally was up to visit. I didn't get any mail, Blah. It is 20 after 3—just had a glass of iced tea and a dish of jello, am tying a small quilt. It is 9 o'clock am watching a movie on TV, soon to bed.

Feb 24, 1971

It is 9 o'clock—Patsy just called and said she is coming over. The wind is blowing and I do mean blowing. It is 10 after 11—Patsy was here, we had coffee and visited and played Kings Corners. I got some mail, a chain letter, a pretty card from Lorri and a magazine. I am ordering Ladies Home Journal—New York Magazine—McCalls—American Home magazine. You are suppose 2 B in a prize pool, my lucky numbers are D-484-G-027-E603-K862, I never win but who knows I might. Patsy said Yang and Leroy visited her yesterday, and that Tommy rejected D D. I don't know. Time will tell. It is 15 after 12—I had a fried egg sandwich and jello & hot tea for lunch. Sent the chain letter on its way. It is 2 thirty—I have been to sewing and thinking, and I suddenly decided to bake a coffee cake. Sissy was suppose to call today, but I had a feeling she wouldn't. I get vibrations that DD has had so much rejection lately it is hard to tell what she will do next. It' 15-24—just had coffeecake-jello and coffee. It is 20minutes to 7—I just ate supper, warmed up hamburger-potatoes & tomatoes. Another day. Amen

Feb 25, 1971

It is 9 thirty—I just woke up, the weather looks calm. It is
10 thirty—I happened to look the window and would you
believe it, it's snowing. Little green monster just rang, it was
my pal Sal. She is sick, today is sewing circle. I'm going to
slide her birthday card under her door today, although her
birthday is tomorrow. Well back to sewing and thoughts. If I
was paid by the hour for meditation, I would be wealthy, as
it is, I just worry and wonder. It is 11 thirty—I see the mail
truck at El Toro apts, in about 30 minutes it will be here. I am
having Bean with bacon soup today. The sun is shining. Well
it is 3-30—I had coffee and doughnut with Viola, she gave
me a nice pink knit suit, then went to sewing circle. Phoebe
& Martha served today, they had lemon cheese cake-Cherry
and Blackberry pie. Now I am home going to relax a while. It
is 4 o'clock—I took a notion to go to store and bought a cube
of butter—a can of peaches and a package of slice turkey and
gravy. I only had a $1.00 food stamp, came home and divided
my change, amongst my 4 banks. Am now baking a potato
for my supper, it is real cold outside. Now for a quiet evening
of sewing & TV. It is 6—DD called and felt real bad at her
rejection by Tom, but I guess she will get over it.

Feb 26, 1971

It is 9 o'clock—it froze last night. Well another day is on its
way. It is 20 after 10—Viola and Eva gave me a box of scraps
for my quilts. It is 11-30—I am cutting out quilt blocks.

Little green monster is very quiet, guess it is going to B a quiet weekend. I seen 1 flake of snow. It is 12 o'clock and snowing, mail hasn't come yet. I don't expect any anyway. No ding a ling on green monster either. Little green monster rang at 15-2-1—it was Bev, she had a letter from Sugar, he is blaming DD for his predicament. I got an advertisement in the mail. It really is snowing now. It is 10-2-3—Yang & Leroy were here, we had coffee & gabbed. They are moving into the El Toro apts. It is 7 o'clock—I think the day is done, am watching TV and sewing. Going to have a bowl of Clam Chowder. It's 10 o'clock, I am tired so am going to bed.

Feb 27, 1971

It is 10 o'clock—I just woke up, it is snowing and has been. It is 11-30—I am key watcher, am baking Parker House rolls and cinnamon rolls. The mail has been here. I got my Feb. food stamps Thank God for that. It is 12 thirty, I am having a bowl of clam chowder. The little kids in the Manhattan Apts have a big water puddle in the driveway. One little boy got his mothers washing soap and put it in it. Now the kids have big sticks whipping up bubbles, aw the joy of childhood. I was just sitting here thinking Pegs says it is Dee Dee's fault Tommy is where he is, and Sugar says it is her fault he is where he is. I think they are all full of shit, it's their own faults they are where they are. Hers included, and anyway as I said before the man upstairs is keeping the books. Oh, well back to my rocking chair, my sewing and knitting and the blues. It is 2 thirty, gloomy as a dungeon and snowing. Little green monster is sure quiet. I had chatterbox on once, but it had so much static I turned it off. Am baking a potato. Gloomsville-blah. At 3 thirty I am going to Gov-Mart with Jim and Bev. It is now 5-30 very cold. I have been shopping, am now eating supper. It's 20 after 8—I have been downstairs playing Kings Corners. Dear Sugar-Dee Dee & all the rest you kids—stop a minute and remember Gods got his peepers on you.

Feb 28, 1971

It is 8 thirty—cold and the ground is covered with snow, bout 2 inches. I didn't sleep well last night. Well up & at em. Sewing today, don't expect no company, and there is no mail on Sunday. It is 11-30 the sun is shining. I called Sissy on the little green monster. Andy woke them up at 7 this morning, he is on weekend leave from the hospital. Vicki will be 19 tomorrow and she got a job driving a car for a cement company at $2.00 an hr. Am going to have sauerkraut and pork chop for dinner. It is 15 after 2—Little green monster has not yipped, my doorbell has not rang, I got the poops. The sun came out and melted the snow. It is 6-15—haven't talked to anyone today except Sissy this morning, haven't seen anyone—little green monster has not rang. I had baked potato and pork chops for supper. Am going to watch channel 5 tonight.

March 1, 1971

It is 10-30—I just woke up, the sun is shining, looks like March is coming in like a lamb, so we can expect it to go out like a lion. Today is Aggie's birthday, little did I dream years ago where I would be today. She is 46 and a alcoholic.

Well—well, water under the bridge. Wonder what will happen today. It is 20 after 12—did I ever get the wind knocked out of my sails. I only got $47.25 on my check when I was expecting $63.00. Went down and cried on Sally's shoulder, had chocolate cake and coffee. Well I will just have to make the most of it, no use crying, think if they raise social security. I will find a beach shack somewhere and move into that. It is 3-30—Yang & Leroy were here, I showed her how to crochet, gave her 9 hook and some yarn. Showed him how to play Kings Corners, gave them coffee & rolls. Now to sew. It is 9 thirty—Yang was over 2 C how to crochet her corners. Leroy had gone 2 a AA meeting. I am going 2 cut some pieces 4 the quilt and go 2 bed.

March 2, 1971

It is 10-2-9—Leroy was here and had coffee with me, he is upset over Yang, she is going into one of her depressions. It was snowing when I got up, but is now raining. Peggy is supposed to come and we are going shopping. I hope she will take me to Sissy's first. It is 15-2-10—Leroy was just here again to tell me he just left Yang, she lost a damn good guy. I just hope she don't buzz the hell out of me. It is 15-2-3—Peggy came, we had a bowl of hot soup, took the material up to Sissy for Billy Joes and Donnie's suits. Had coffee—grocery shopped in Kent Safeway, went to Benjamin Franklins, I bought rug yarn she bought a new turtle bowl and home. Is blowing and raining. I have a sore throat, am having hot spiced tea and raisin bread for supper. It is 8 thirty, Joe Frazier is boxing on TV. Amelia Thrasher called me on little green monster. Patsy called this morning, and Sally was up this afternoon. My throat sure is sore, gotta doctor up and go to bed pretty quick.

March 3, 1971

It is 8-15—Dee Dee just called, everything is fine there. My throat is very sore and I have a fever. It is snowing. It is 2 o'clock—I received my social security check in the mail, went to the drug store—got a money order for my rent—my march pillowcases—some envelopes and glue. Stopped in at El Toro apts to see Yang, had coffee and came home. My throat sure hurts. I am drinking pink lemonade, am going to sew now. So sick, just gave up and went to bed.

March 4, 1971

It is 9 o'clock—everything outside is covered with snow. I feel a little better this morning, but I still ache all over, going to take it easy a couple of days. It is 10 o'clock—Patsy called on the little green monster. Holt and Duke are both home sick. Harley must not be working, he went to the tree farm. The back of my neck sure does ache. Ugh I feel awful. It is snowing. It is 10 after 6—Patsy was here and gave me some quilt material. Yang brought a beef roast, we cooked it and had supper. Jim and Bev came and brought me 2 boxes of groceries. I got a letter from Sugar it speaks for itself. I am feverish, the back of my neck hurts. It is 8 o'clock—I wrote to Sugar and Barbara just called.

March 5, 1971

It is 7 thirty—it snowed last night, this morning the sun is shining. It is 15 after 10—a lady called and wanted a baby sitter tonight, I told her I had the flu but I would ask Yang Yang. The sun is shining. It is 20 after 12. Amelia Thrasher just called on little green monster for a gab session. All the mail I got was a sears sales catalog, wonder if Yang is going to come over. It is 3 thirty—I am tying Dee Dee's quilt. The lady called and said she got a babysitter. It is good because it don't look like Yang is going to come today. Hope she isn't sick. It is 15-2-5—Mike Douglas show is on. Bev called 2 C how I was feeling. It feels like it is getting cold. It is 20 minutes to 9—Yang was here for about an hour. TV is bum tonight, so I think I'll call it a day.

March 6, 1971

It is 9 thirty and trying to snow. This morning I have an earache. I also bought Leo in from the lobby, they have another lion now they can use it for display. I want Leo in here where he is safe. This is Saturday, wonder what will happen today, probably nothing. I have to go downstairs and dump my garbage. It is 20-2-12—I got .70 cents change from the package I mailed. 2 quarters for laundry and 2 dimes for sewing circle, also received the paper clippings from Thrasher about the April welfare cut—Wow. Cora—Frances-Viola stopped by 2 C how I was feeling. I put some chicken in the oven 2 cook. It is 1-30 my right ear is aching. It is raining. I had my dinner—chicken—baked potato—baked apple—pickled beets. Little green monster is sure quiet. I'm sewing. It is 4-15 I am having chicken and noodles and iced tea. Cora was here and borrowed Leo, she had an argument with Viola over his mane, he is back home safe again. It is 10-2-11—Yang came over, we watched Doris Day in the Glass Bottom Boat. On the news there is no more welfare in Nevada.

March 7, 1971

It is 10 o'clock—I am listening to chatter box, things sure sound wild, welfare cuts, labor trouble with the farm labor. It is 12 o'clock—pouring rain, haven't heard from anyone, anywhere. Just one of those days. I am busy though sewing and thinking. It is I o'clock—Francis and Viola were here, we had quite a discussion on government welfare and what have you. It is 15-2-3—Buzz and Barbara—Connie—Caroline and Ronnie were here. They gave me $8.00 and said after this they would send me $10.00 every month. I hate to take it, but it will help out. I am making Yang a bank to save a down payment for a car in. It is snowing, really snowing. I have a stuffed chicken in the oven roasting. It is 10 o'clock—Yang came over, she bought some bear claws for evening coffee. We watched Walt Disney and Bonanza.

March 8, 1971

It is 9 o'clock—the sun is shining. Patsy just called, her and Harley had been out to C Sissy and also had gone dancing.

John Christi's mother died with cancer. Little green monster just rang, it is 10 thirty, it was Bev she said Peggy took Vic to the airport and will come by and pick me up and we will go to Bev's for banana bread and coffee. It is 10-2-3 Peg was here, we went to Bev's had a nice visit. I shopped at the drug store and grocery store on the way home. I have had my lunch—fresh bread and buttered cold sliced roast chicken and milk to drink. Will have jello and cool whip soon. Now I'm going to sew. It is 8-30—guess Yang isn't coming over tonight. Maybe she made contact with the painter. I seen him over there this morning. My throat hurts tonight.

March 9, 1971

It is 9 thirty—I just got up and had breakfast. It is raining. My head is stuffed up with a cold. It is 15 after 12—Thelma Smith called from Carol's and we gabbed. It is still raining. All I got in the mail was a Tandy Leather catalog. Sally was in earlier. I have a big pot of chicken soup on cooking. My throat hurts. I am knitting. It is 11 o'clock—Yang came over with 2 little boysenberry pies. We had them with coffee and watched River Of Gold and Dr. Welby. So to bed.

March 10, 1971

It is 10 o'clock—I just ate breakfast. Little green monster rang twice today. Aggie called and Patsy called. It's pouring rain. I am all congested up this morning. It is 11-30 pouring rain. The mail truck is at the El Toro apts, it will be noon before it gets here, probably won't get anything anyway. I put some stew beef and onions on to cook and made orange jello with fruit cocktail in, I do love to eat. A letter from Sugar, that speaks for itself. It is 11 o'clock—Aggie—Penny & Jim were here and Yang. I am tired, so going to bed.

Kessack Children Grown

CHAPTER 12

MARCH 11, 1971 TO MAY 18, 1971

Final Journal Novella Died August 2, 1971

March 11, 1971

It is 20-2-10—I just woke up. It is 5-2-12—Viola was in 2 C how I was. I talked to Patsy on little green monster, she sure is having troubles with Duke. I received a 3 page letter from Gwen, everything seems to be in apple pie order with them. It is raining. I baked a pumpkin pie. Today is sewing circle, I am going for a while at least. They are playing Bingo downstairs tonight, but I don't feel well enough for that. It is 10-2-4—I have been to sewing circle, I enjoyed it but I sure don't feel good. Am cooking some rice—warming up some meat and peas for supper. It is raining. It is 5-25—Mrs. Doherty brought me some rice and milk for supper. Sally stopped by, Dee Dee just called she is going to school 2 B a 1st grade teacher. It is 11—Yang came over with angel food cake-fresh strawberries and whipping cream. I am tired so to bed.

March 12, 1971

It is 15-2-8—I woke up and got up. It is 5 after 10, Patsy called on little green monster, we yakked for 20 minutes. It is

12 o'clock—I got Photoplay in the mail and the boys Tuffy Tooth sets, wrapped them up to mail tomorrow. I am key watcher. My stomach hurts. Patsy called the 2nd time to C which boys are having birthdays, she is mailing them cards. The sun is shining. It is 8-30—Sally called to C if I was OK. Yang didn't come over today. Maybe she went out, wouldn't blame her she is young. The Partridge Family is on. Went to bed at 11.

March 13, 1971

It is 10 o'clock—The sun is shining, I'm listening to chatter box the news is on. It is 11-15—Viola invited me and Eva down for coffee and toast, so we had a good visit. It is 2-15—I got my phone bill in the mail, went to drug store to get money order to pay it. Then to grocery store got two baking potatoes—1 tomato, .49 cents. Stopped in to C Yang, she is getting a car Monday. Leroy got drunk, got in a fight and thrown in jail. I am baking a potato and a slice of halibut. Cutting out quilt pieces. Margaret was in to visit. Sally was up a few minutes, said she might come back. It is raining. I paid $11.28 for little green monster today and it hasn't rang once. I am miserable, I got the poops. Its 5 after 1, I watched the late show, so to bed.

March 14, 1971

It is 10 o'clock—The weather looks calm, I am going to have my breakfast—a bubble bath and shampoo. A brand new day, a new adventure on the path of life. It is 5 after 11—I had my bath—my shampoo—and set my hair, now I will knit and sew and meditate. It is pouring rain. I do mean pouring. It is 12-30—Little green monster rang. Peggy called and will be here at 3 to take me to her house for dinner. Charlie is leaving for the Navy. Peggy came, we had a good time visiting and a good dinner. Steak—Shrimp salad—baked potato—asparagus—pumpkin pie and whipped cream—hot tea and fortunes. We talked about super natural things, took pictures. It is 10 o'clock—I am, tired but want to hear the news, so am going to get comfortable, then to bed.

March 15, 1971

It is 20 after 9—The sun is shining, oh what a beautiful day, what hast thou hidden to surprise me with? It is 12 thirty—Sally was in a minute, Kathy called seems an investigator was at her place from Olympia over welfare but everything is OK. Bev called and said they might be over tonight. Viola is sick. It is 15-2-3—Leroy was here just wanted to gab I guess. I gave him hot-spiced tea. Patsy called on the little green monster. Well so far it is a lot of little surprises, what next oh fate what next? It is 6 o'clock—Sally was here and borrowed some flowers for decorations for tomorrow night. Snooks called and said she had a box of thread and yarn that used to B grandma Bealls that Bud was going to throw out. I seen Yang leave with George to go to Renton to get her car. It is 15-2-11—Jim and Bev were here, left me $2.00 cash. I put it in my Xmas bank. They enjoyed themselves reading my old diaries. Guess I'll be going beddy by pretty P.D.Q.

March 16, 1971

It is 20-2-10—The sun is shining. A new day, a new adventure, I am ready and willing. I done my dishes—made my bed—swept the apartment. Mailed the money order for some magazines. Hope I win the April 15th sweepstakes-Ha I should be so lucky. I would rent me a small house for 5 years—plant a garden and some flowers—buy me an adult tricycle and live it up man, live it up. As I say Ha, I should be so lucky. I brushed my hair back in a tiny little ponytail and put a ribbon on it. Cora said I looked cute, like a little gypsy. It is 5-2-1 I went out to get the mail, I got my change from the package and an advertisement. I ran into Julia she said Maude Van Winkle fell last night and broke her hip. I haven't heard from Yang wonder if she got her car last night. She probably did and that is why I haven't heard. Put em on wheels and pow the fun begins. It is 15 after 1—A beautiful day, sun is shining. I opened all my windows, let some fresh air in. I just had lunch boiled potato—sliced buttered carrots a can of sardines—applesauce and a glass of milk. No phone calls, no visitors. It is 20-2-7—I looked out the window it is snowing, am going downstairs to the St Patrick celebration. 9 o'clock, Bev called. Jim Jr. is in the hospital with ruptured appendixes.

March 18, 1971

It is 7 o'clock, everything covered in white frost. I am watching early morning news. Charlie leaves for the Navy this morning. It is 10 after 9—Little green monster rang, it was Bev, they are going to a funeral tomorrow. Peggy came, we went to Kent got 3 turkey TV dinners and went and had lunch with Sissy. Came home had nice letter and card and $5.00 from Dee Dee. Walked to Yangs and to store, she came home with me and had dinner. I am sending to Sears for 6 yards flannel and sending card to Dee Dee. Am going to sew and watch TV, also have some dishes to do yep. It's 20 after 8—TV is good tonight. 20-2-11—I am sleepy, day is done. To bed I go.

March 19, 1971

It is 15-2-10—the sun is shining, Patsy called. It is one o'clock no mail. Margaret was in to visit, she brought us each a banana and cookies. She is going to the Dr. at 1 thirty. I am going to have a cup of hot-spiced tea and nap in my rocking chair. I made macaroni—tomato hamburger casserole for food today. The sun is shining. Dee Dee just called she has the flu, it is 2 thirty. I'm going over to see Yang. I went to see Yang, she came home with me and had dinner. I let her talk to DD on the phone. I wish I could find a way up there to help her. I am scared to ask anyone for fear of refusal. Guess I'll talk to the man upstairs. It is 20 minutes to 7—Jim is going to take me to Monroe tomorrow at 11. My suitcase is packed, and all the little goodies I am taking along. I have phoned everyone and gave Sally my key to take care of my mail.

March 20, 1971

Got up at 7 o'clock, ate a piece of bread and butter and coffee. Talked to Peggy, Andy was out there terrorizing them she called the cops. Jim called at 10 and said he would pick Joe up at Mc Cord Air force field and then take me to Monroe. I went over to see Yang and we went to Dairy Queen. I bought a deluxe hamburger, she bought a vanilla ice cream cone. We went to my apartment and visited. Then I sat out in the lobby and visited. Then Margaret came in and visited. Jim—Joe and Mack came at 3-15—we went over and visited Yang then came up to Dee Dee's. We had Sloppy Joes and milk for supper. Linda and Dale are here we are all visiting.

March 21, 1971

Got up at 7 made coffee. Ricky got up at 7 thirty, by 8 all was up. Marvin. Ricky, and I went to Sunday school. They held it in Georgia Lee's house because the church had run out of oil, and when they filled the barrel, the pipeline had a bubble in it. Came home and cooked dinner. Roast beef—mashed potatoes—kernel corn—jello and cake. Watched the kids in the afternoon while Dee Dee worked. Took Stevie and Donnie and went to church. Nellie Foster was there, haven't seen her for 10 years. Now the boys are all in bed. Linda—Steve and Casey are here, they have killed two bottles of wine. These guys are Viet Nam vets and college graduates. Linda and Dee Dee are both stuck on Casey, personally I would pick Steve if either. Just being men cook their goose with me. Well another day. So goes the world. Casey stayed all night, some kinda deal going on between him and Dee Dee. 1st day of Spring beautiful day.

March 22, 1971

Ricky, Marvin and I got up at 7:30. Steve came and got Casey 2 go 2 work. I took Ricky to the dentist and spent my bus fare home like a doo—doo bird. I wrote some letters and cards. Dee Dee made meatloaf-kernel corn and potatoes for supper, also slice peaches. Casey stayed again, Linda is after him but seems DD has him for the time being. Steve lives with his Grandparents. Went to bed early, it rained today.

March 23, 1971

I got up at 7, made pancakes for Marvin, Ricky, and Stevie. Played Kings Corners and sent them to school. Steve came and woke DD and Casey up, they had fried potatoes and peas, it was all there was. DD had nicotine fit so I went to Linda's and borrowed cigarettes. Casey and Steve left to go to work. DD and Linda hitched hiked to Seattle. A Mrs. Brown comes to do house work on Tuesday, so she watched Donnie and I went to Vince's Café picked up DD's pay and done her shopping, it is now 1 o'clock and raining. Carol the girl next door took her little boy and Donnie to school. I am going to sew and rest a while. I will cook supper tonight. Hard telling when them gals will get home. Well Casey came from work and he, the kids and I had supper. DD got home about 8, Linda came over for a while. About 9 thirty DD fixed scrambled eggs-fried potatoes-toast and tea. The kids were in bed we had fun gabbing. P.S. they were picked up for hitch hiking.

March 24, 1971

It is 8 o'clock—I got up with the boys, we had cheerio's for breakfast. Marvin and I had a game of fish and Kings Corners. Steve was having fits because he couldn't take his bike to school. Now Donnie and I are here at the kitchen table, he's amusing himself with a deck of cards. I made the beds and done the dishes. DD and Casey are still asleep. Well they finally got up and who came over and stays and stays and stays Linda. Well finally, I went to bed to take a rest and fell asleep, when I woke up everybody was gone. The kids finally came home, and then Kathy came home and cooked supper. She kind of had her dander up, I guess Linda was getting to her. Rose's youngest boy came over and I told his tealeaves. I went to bed early. Linda and Steve were here, they were playing records and drinking wine, and visiting.

March 25, 1971

Got up at 7, got the kids up, made cream of wheat and toast and coffee. Steve has a bad ear—Ricky a sore throat—Marvin and I played 3 rousing games of Kings Corners, he won 2. It is 9 now, DD and Casey are up. It is 5-2-4—Georgia Lee called and invited me to supper and church. I went to the little store and got bread—peanut butter and spray starch. DD cleaned house today, we went to Rose's and had coffee this afternoon.

I went to Georgia Lee's, we had a dinner salad which consisted of shredded lettuce a mound of cottage cheese to which grated carrots had been added and generous chunks of cold baked salmon—green onions—watermelon pickles—bread and butter—cookies—pineapple walnut ice cream—hot tea. We also had quartered fresh limes to squeeze on our salmon. We visited and then went to Thursday night church. Then back to DD's. Casey and Linda were there when I got home. I went to bed after a very few minutes.

March 26, 1971

Got up at 7 fixed scrambled eggs and coffee and toast. Had breakfast with the boys, played 2 games Kings Corners with Marvin. DD and Casey got up at 8 thirty. Steve came and got Casey, they went to Seattle to look for a place to live and go to school. The weather is bad, high wind and rain, it is very cold this morning. Guess I'll sew. Well not much going on today, lots of rain and wind. Rose came over in the afternoon for coffee and gab, and I assure you we had both. For supper we had chicken legs—hamburger patties—potatoes—kernel corn—left over macaroni casserole and raspberry jello. Linda came over at night with paperback book dealing with reincarnation—ESP—prophesying—past life etc. I finally got tired and went to bed. Little Marvin stayed overnight with Kevin a neighbor boy. Ricky—Stevie and Donnie camped out in the front room. Casey came in during the night. Sally called and she had contacted lock jaw, sure was good 2 hear from her and home.

March 27, 1971

Woke up at 7 to the Partridge Family screaming on the record player. Casey was up cooking his breakfast. Poached eggs on toast—leftover potatoes. I made coffee. Steve picked him up, they both went to work. I made oatmeal for the boys and I. It is 10 o'clock—Kathy is not up yet. Makes me wonder who feeds and takes care of the kids when I'm not here. Which is going to be quite sudden, because I figured out how to get home, I am going. Can't stand the noise. Am sewing. Linda came over with a book on reincarnation-prophesying mystic etc and stayed put till Casey and Steve came. The battle of see was on. This is a verse Steve wrote. Life is but a short trip in which man try to understand and comprehend the wonder and simplicity of nothingness. Casey told DD she was trying to scramble up his head

March 28, 1971

Up at 7, boy was Casey glum. He left with Steve, I fed the boys oatmeal and toast. Got DD up and went to Sunday school with the boys. Came home, baked a coffee cake—made split pea soup—mashed potatoes—kernel corn—creamed tuna fish and cherry jello. It is pouring rain, DD is at work. I see Linda is over at Norma's. The TV is on, the kids all have full tummies, but are a bit on the wild side. I really am beginning to wonder how I'm going to get home. Well it looks like a long dull afternoon. But one never knows what's going to happen so we shall C. Rose and Linda came for coffee, Norma is moving and the kids are playing. It is 25-2-8—Casey came home, I fixed him something to eat. DD came home, he bathed—ate and now he's gone. I called Jim he is coming to take me home tomorrow at 7. It rained all day.

March 29, 1971

It is 10 to 2—I got up at 10-2-7, got the boys up, gave them scramble eggs and toast and sent them to school, tried in vain to get DD up. Her and Donnie did not get up until 9 thirty. He didn't get any breakfast. He borrowed mayonnaise from the neighbor Carol and we had lettuce tomato salad at noon, he has gone to school. It is pouring rain. DD and I played scrabble 2 games, she won both. I laid down ½ hr. She went back to bed. I made up 2 boxes chocolate pudding and put in refrigerator. I don't see anything else to cook, there is some white beans but it wouldn't do any good to cook them, the kids won't eat them. I just couldn't live like this and it makes me wonder what goes on when I am not here. I have got up every morning with the boys. I just don't dig it all. I am going home tonight. Jim said he would be here about 7, I will be glad to get there but will be wondering how the boys are. Well I got home about 8-15. Sally came up, seems Viola and Cora are fighting. We are going to play Bingo Thursday night for prizes. Everybody brings a wrapped gift worth $1.00 or under. Talked to Snooks it seems Butchies had a large tumor with 2 feelers removed from his back.

March 30, 1971

It's 8-30—I have had coffee-toast and marmalade and a hot bubble bath. Talked to Patsy on little green monster. The weather looks blah, I will soon go over and see Yang. It is 5 after 9-I could not get Yang 2 answer the door. I stopped in to say hi to Margaret. I am going downstairs 2 see if Cliff will cash my $5.00 sears check today. Well no answer so I came upstairs made a new Sears order and mailed it. Also wrote to Patti Sue she wants me to make booties for Keiko's baby, so I am, also hat night and quilt. It is 15 after 3—I went over to visit Yang, she came home with me. She went to the store for me. Got 1 potato—2 little steaks—1 tomato—and some whit bias tape. She has gone home now, it is raining. I am cooking chili and sewing. It is 7 after 4—I wrote to Charlie and I wrote 2 DD. I also wrote a note to Yang, just to see if she would get it. I am eating chili—steak—toast—sliced tomato and spiced tea. It is 20-2-6—Little green monster rang, some guy asked for Kathy, I asked him who he was, he said his name was Lee. I can't imagine unless it was a sneaky bill collector.

March 31, 1971

It is 5-2-9 Patsy just called, she is coming over. The sun is shining, guess March is going out like a lamb. It is 20-2-10—Patsy was here and we were going to Sissy's but she called the school and Duke was not there, so she had to go home. I got another chain letter. It is 5-2-12—Aggie and her house pet Jim were here. She is house hunting. I just ate a bowl of chili. Received the cute verses from millionaires club, they want donations. I thought about sending them a dollar, but decided to send it to the Geyman boys for Easter. I am going to make cards and glue a quarter on each one. Am going to make DD a book of verses. It is 1-30—I am having early afternoon tea, hot spiced—bread and butter—and marmalade. Wonder if Yang will be over today, hope so. It is 4 o'clock—went downstairs with Margaret and had coffee and cookies with Viola. Am now doing laundry, baking a potato and green beans. It is 10-2-7—no sign of Yang, I wonder why? I am sewing, done my ironing. It is 9 thirty Johnny Cash is on. I'm getting tired and going to retire.

April 1, 1971

It is 20 after 7 a sun shining day. Should also be payday. What other surprise it has who knows? But I am ready. It is 15 after 8—Yang is here and done her welfare phoning, are checks will be a day late. Patsy called, she will be here at 9 we are going to Sissy's. Well the surprises are rolling in. It is 20-2-4—I went to Kent with Patsy and Yang. We stopped and got cinnamon rolls. I bought an ashtray for a prize for tonight's Bingo. My welfare check and food stamps were here, so I went to the drug store and grocery store, then to sewing circle. Now I am home trying to sort out my affairs. Got a letter from Dottie today. It is 6 o'clock, I talked to Bev on the phone, they are going to the commissary tonight, to a wedding tomorrow and will come to C me Saturday. I have 1 hr before I go downstairs to play Bingo. Am going to wear my new green muu muu, and pink sweater. Sally brought me some macaroni salad, it has shrimp and olives in MMM good. It is 20-2-10—I had a very pleasant evening. Playing Bingo I won I won 2 prizes. 1 apothecary jar and a Kleenex box with a mirror. I really enjoyed it.

April 2, 1971

It is 15-2-9 The breeze do softly blow—The sun does brightly shine—Birds flitting to and fro—This spring day is mine. Am having cereal and coffee and listening to chatter box. It is 20 after 11—my material came from Sears. I got $1.35 change, will send for something Monday. Got Ladies Home Journal in mail too. Talked to Patsy on little green monster. Well guess I'll boil a sweet potato, cook a steak and slice a .30 cent tomato, nothing like being pampered. It is 10 after 12—I had my deluxe dinner—talked to Peggy on little green monster. Now I am going to sew and rest. It is 3 thirty—Yang was here for coffee and visit. Julia was here for a minute. It is 20-2-6—I just had supper—baked potato—oven fried bacon—sliced pickled beets—banana—orange salad. Am listening to evening news and sewing. It is 7-30—Thrasher called on little green monster. Her check was cut $4.00. It is 9, Peggy was here and had tea, she paid for her Tupperware. I am tired am going to bed.

April 3, 1971

It is 7-30. The sun is shining brightly. I should get my social security check today. Jim and Bev said they would be here today. It is 15 after 10—I have been making Easter cards, now I am, it seems Eva and Loretta had a bad fight, they used 2 B the best of friends. Wow. It is 4 o'clock I have had company all afternoon. 1st I got my social security check, went and cashed it and got some groceries. Came home and Viola came. I made coffee and Eva came. We visited all afternoon, and Margaret came, when she left, I had dinner, new potatoes boiled with butter on—a slice of baked halibut—pickled beets, then Sally came. She has a new wig, which looks terrific. 6 o'clock Jim called this morning and said Bev is sick so he has to do the house work today, don't know why Debbie and Gina can't do it but I did not ask. It is 15 after 8—TV is very dull tonight and I am tired so think I will go 2 bed. Wonder how the little boys are tonight, also wonder if they are alone or if their mother is with them and if she is there, is she drinking wine? I can only worry and wonder.

April 4, 1971

Sunday morning 20 after 8. The sun is shining, what happens today? I do not know. But I am ready, so come what may. It is 15-2-12—I am having lunch—polish sausage—fried potatoes—buttered carrots—pickled beets—milk to drink. Finished Yang's quilt and pillow. Am listening to chatter box. It is 5-2-3 Yang was over and had coffee and cookies. She gave me some things for my gift box and I gave her a quilt and a pillow. The sun is shining. How now brown cow? It is 15 after 8—I had deviled egg sandwiches for supper. Jim was suppose to bring over my quilt scraps, but he didn't come, well that's life. I wonder why I haven't heard from Dee Dee, wonder if the boys R—OK. Well TV is good tonight anyway. Guess one can't have everything.

April 5, 1971

The kiss of the sun for pardon. The song of the birds for mirth. One is nearer God heart in a garden than anywhere else on earth. 5-2-9—Sun is shining. Monday morning a new day—a new week, so here we go. 10 after 10 the mail has been here and gone but I did not get any. I expected Peggy today but she didn't show. Looks like a blue Monday. Aw shit I'll just sew. It is 11—little green monster rang and Bev said they have 2 blankets I can use for quilt fillers and they will try and get those scraps 2 me tonight. Good deal. I am cooking chicken thighs from Idaho in my oven. 12 noon, am listening to news on chatterbox. Am having deviled egg sandwich—tea cookies and jello for lunch. Am also making the April pillowcases. Putting Mexican motifs on them. Little green monster just rang, it was Peggy, she said she was picking me up in 45 minutes. She didn't say where we was going. Whoopiee, now what is cooking. Tell you later alligator. It is 5-2-6—Gwen just called from Virginia. I have been 2 Kent and out to Peggy's had fun. It is 9—Bev was here, I am tired Goodnight.

April 6, 1971

It is 10-8—looks like a nice day. It is 9 o'clock, Patsy just called and said she would be over after a bit. There is a wet-cold-drizzly rain today. April showers I presume. Today is little Donnie's birthday. I sent his package last Friday. Peggy bought him 2 pair's shoes and a package of socks they are going in today's mail. He is her grandson and her nephew and Gods child. Sometime when you want a brain twister, figure that one out. He is my grandson also, my great grandson, some kid huh. It is 20-2-12—Viola was here and gave me pillowcases to do for sewing circle. The mail sure is late today. Wonder when Patsy will come. It is 4 thirty—Patsy-Annette and Holt were here. So was Yang, she stayed for supper, we had fried chicken—boiled new potatoes—peas and carrots—beets pickles—peaches. Well I expect Beverly and her company tonight so I better get busy. 20-2-8—Bev called and said we are on our way over. Yang was here and got her phone message about her check being at the other apartment. They were here with big box of groceries. I have been invited to Dunc's for Easter dinner. Amen. Tried to call DD line is busy.

April 7, 1971

It is 20 after 9—I am eating breakfast—bacon and eggs—toast and coffee and of course my 4 pills. The sun is shining. What Ho beautiful April day, what do you bring? 20 after 10—Dee Dee called she and the boys are fine. She got cut $14.00 on her check. She is going to start school. It is 11-20—The mail has been here. I received letter from Charlie—and Easter card with $1.00 in from Peggy & family. It is 15 after 2. Margaret was in. Talked to Snooks on green monster, Pat is back in jail. It is 6 thirty—Yang had supper with me. We had—breaded veal—small new potatoes—green beans—sweet pickles—jello with cool whip. She hasn't received her check yet. Eva was in, she don't look well. Barbara called, her and Buzz are bringing Auntie & Uncle down tonight. I whipped up a chocolate cake to serve. It is 10 o'clock my company has come and gone, we had a very pleasant evening. I sent Buzz over 2 get Yang so she could visit too. Boy now to bed. Buzz gave me $10.00, now my phone bill is taken care of. Auntie brought a cake—oranges—bananas—bread—cheese—eggs. Happy Easter.

April 8, 1971

It is 15-2-9-raining. Today is my turn to treat the sewing club, tra la la dear ladies. Wonder if I'll get any mail. It is 15 after 11—I talked to Sissy on little green monster, Penny went back home to Bud. Eva and I went down to the kitchen of the rec—room and prepared for the luncheon this afternoon. It is rainy and gloomy. I C the mail truck at Manhattan Apts. It will be here next. I wonder if I got any. It is 15-2-12 the mail has been here, I received 2 Easter cards and a letter. Now I'm fixing lunch as it will soon be time to go to sewing circle. It is 20 after 12—Patsy and Annette were just here with a pretty Easter card an orange and a banana. It is 15 past 4—sewing circle is over, it all went very well. I am tired, almost passed out, wonder if Yang got her check—hope so. Hope to get my haircut tomorrow. I told Cora to send the gal in. It is 15 after 6, Sissy—Marvin and the twins were here. It is 10 thirty—TV has been good tonight. I am tired am going to bed.

April 9, 1971

It is 10 to 9—and pouring rain. I hope Cora tells the barber lady I want my hair-cut. It is 20-2-10—Elizabeth Richards was here trying to sell used dresses to cut up for quilts. No dice, still raining—am knitting on my rug. 5-2-11—Eva was in and insisted on me taking $1.00 on yesterdays serving at sewing circle, still raining. Phoebe knocked on my door but seen Eva and wouldn't come in. 20 after 11—Mail has come I received Easter card from Yang—a Tandy Leather catalog—a Sears sale special. 25 after 2—Margaret was in, so was the lady 2 cut my hair, she done a good job. Patsy called on little green monster, Holly is sick in the Burien Hospital. It is 7 o'clock—I am extremely drowsy. Television ain't so hot tonight, still raining. Think I'll rest a while. Big joke, I went to sleep period.

April 10, 1971

It is 9 o'clock—The sun is shining. It is 11 o'clock—Cora was in for a visit and later on Margaret. I received nice Easter card from Linda Le Feet at Monroe, no word from DD which is unusual. I am doing my laundry. It is 12 noon—I am going to fix some lunch. I talked to Freda Geyman on little green monster, she is hard luck, Jenny as usual is going to deliver the Tupperware next Friday. Richard was left partially blind from his wreck. Eda is pregnant, no word of the high and mighty Marvin. I am having lunch-baked ham—green beans—and special tea. We had a flash snowstorm but the sun is shining again. Cliff was here we are having potluck dinner next Thursday night. It is 1-30—Rebecca was in for a visit, she is a very nice friendly person. It is 2 thirty—Yang was here, she didn't get her check yet. I sent her to the store for me. Gave her one or 2 items in the eat line. It is 15-2-5—Pouring rain. I just gave myself a shampoo and set my hair. I have a potato baking. It is 20 after 8—Thrasher called on little green monster, we discussed the whys and where for's. I am about ready to call it a day. Sally just called and then she came up.

April 11, 1971

It is 8 o'clock—Dee Dee just called, the kids are hunting their eggs and are going to Sunday school. Then have a ham dinner and go to a Eagle Easter egg hunt. Well I am going to have breakfast and then a bubble bath. It is 15-2-9—Just had said bath, all dressed up for Easter wearing the pretty pastel dress Bonnie gave me—lavender beads—panty hose—and dress up shoes. It has clouded over, looks like rain. Well Easter Bunny, looks like you're going to get your paddy's wet. It is 15-2-11—Bev and Jim called to wish me Happy Easter, they are having Roast Turkey. Gina is sick with cold. We had a flash rainstorm, now the sun is shining again. It is 12-15—Jim was here and Sissy called. Jim stopped at the El Toro to take Yang home 2 dinner, but nobody answered the door. Safe 2 bet she is either asleep or out shop lifting. Either is a hell of a way to spend Easter. People here in the building are coming home from Church so Shirley should be after me soon. The sun is shining, Amen. It is 15-27—I had a good dinner and a nice day, I also have a new plant.

April 12, 1971

It is 15 after 7—My phone rang twice and I jumped out of bed to answer it and nobody answered. Ha Ha. The sun is shining. It is 15-2-10—According to little green monster I will have lots of company about noon. Like Peggy and Snooks. Yippee. It is 10-30—Sun is shining brightly, mailman is at Manhattan apts. I C it is a new one, should be here soon. I received a late cute Easter card from DD and the boys. I have baked honey date muffins—chicken in the oven—sliced beets and Chinese noodles on top and tea and coffee, yum-yum. It is 20 minutes to 9, I just got home and done my dishes and called Sally. We all had lunch and then I went to Kent with Peggy and shopped for canned vegetables at Safeway. Spent $6.50 food stamps and $1.00 bill in cash. Got ball of string—2 pictures and some picture hangers. Wonder if Yang got her check today. I am tired and will go to bed early. I got 2 cans of meatballs for casserole for Potluck dinner Thursday night. Ah Revoir—Adios—Goodnight.

April 13, 1971

It is 8 o'clock—The weather seems to be clear. I am listening to the news on chatter—box and eating breakfast, a bowl of cereal called pebbles—coffee and my everlasting pills. It is 20-2-11—I have visited with Viola this morning and went over 2 C Yang. She hasn't her check yet but expects it today. Loretta is in the hospital. The sun is shining. I mailed a letter to Dee Dee. Wonder if I will get any mail. Little green monster is awful quite. It is 11-30—I have a new potato in the oven baking for lunch. Just talked to Patsy on little green monster. Am waiting for the mailman to come, not that I will get any. But I can dream can't I? It is 2 o'clock—No mail 4 me, but Yang got her check. Patsy and Holly were here, we all went XL Sooper—Yang got her food stamps and I got 2 cans fruit—2 envelope soup-some bear claws—and apple turnovers. Phoebe was in for me to sign a card for Letha Smith. I sent cards by Sally 2 Maude & Loretta. Sally was in and borrowed some foil. Viola invited me down to sew and I am going pretty quick.

10-2-4-Margaret came in and gave me a big red apple, I am going to bake it. Took Margaret and 3 butter horns and went down and had coffee with Viola. It is 10 o'clock I am tired. I have had a happy go lucky day. So long.

April 14, 1971

It is 5-2-8—The weather looks clear, oh brand new day—you are on your way. I had a mixed up dream last night about Dad-Dee Dee—Tom, old houses and horses. I would say it is an omen of another—how. Little green monster is quiet., the building is quiet—the weather is deadly quiet seems like lull before the storm. Any way I am busy like a bee sewing. 5-2-10—Dee Dee just called everything OK there. It is 12 noon, just got my phone bill, it is $9.96. I have $5.00 to the good, time I pay for money order. Guess I will send for Ricky's gun and pay for monkey. Guess I'll go to drug store. Sally was in for a few minutes. It is 4 o'clock—Viola and Eva were here. Vicki just called she is home for the week. It is 20 after 6, Sally just brought up 5 passes to the flea market Sunday. Peggy & Nancy were here, I am tired think I will call it a day. PG is coming out in May. Menu suggested for Welfare Families, cost .83 cents per person a day= Breakfast Grape fruit—fresh cream of wheat—toast& margarine coffee. Lunch—Cheese& bologna sandwich—tomato soup—cottage cheese with canned peaches as a salad—rye crisp cookie. Dinner Ham—hash browns—peas & carrots canned—oatmeal muffins—tapioca pudding—cookie—coffee.

April 15, 1971

It is 7 o'clock the sun is shining. This is sewing circle day and pot luck dinner tonight. So it sounds like a busy schedule. It is 9 o'clock—Amelia Thrasher called me, she had gone to prayer meeting last night and missed the deal on TV last night about welfare so she called me to C what it was all about. I am sewing. It is 20-2-1—just sold $1.00 of cards 2 Mr. Lester. I C the mailman at El Toro Apts. Wonder if I'll get any mail. It is 4 o'clock—have been 2 sewing circle, came home and rested—went back down and helped Sally and Cliff set tables. Now will sew until 6 and then go to Pot Luck dinner. Got a magazine in the mail. It looks like rain. Dinner turned out wonderful. We all joined the Inquisitors Club. We voted a check of $25.00 be paid from the Bazaar fund and that paid 1 yrs. Benefits for everyone in the building. Whoopee.

April 16, 1971

It is 4 o'clock in the morning, I can't sleep. I decided to just get up. It is 10 after 2. Mrs. Geyman was here with my Tupperware. His Majesty Marvin gets out this month. Peggy came and had lunch with me. I called social security, we get our raise in June. I called Dee Dee she is fine. It looks like rain. I gave Peggy some things to sell at the flea market Sunday. Wonder if Yang will be over. Talked to Patsy this morning on little green monster. It is 15 after 3—Margaret was in 2 visit. It is 10-2-9—Yang was here, brought steak-salad-cheese cake 4 dinner and visited. Also gave me 10 yards material. Sally was here, seems Eva & Byron are on the warpath. It's raining. Will crochet a while and go to bed. I love you true—I love you mighty—I love your pajama's right next to my nighty—Don't get excited now don't dread—I mean on the clothes line not in bed. John Hauge gave this poem to Aggie.

April 17, 1971

It is 6-30 and raining. It is 10 after 9—I have done my morning chores, had bacon and eggs and hash browns, now sewing and crocheting. What oh mysterious day do you have for me. It is 15 after 11—Just got a magazine in the mail. The sun is trying to shine. It is 15 after 3—Yang was here she had been up all night with her new boyfriend Eric. We had coffee and a nice visit. The sun is shining. It is 20-2-7—I just ate a hot tamale that Harley made, my mouth is on fire. It just occurred 2 me that little green monster hasn't rang all day. In the news, there was 2 marches in Seattle today. One 2000 people marching for peace—the other 200 Jesus people. Unless something unexpected shows up I guess it is a day. 10 O'clock Adios

April 18, 1971

Sunday It is 8-30 weather looks calm, am suppose 2 go 2 the flea market with Jim & Bev this morning. It opens at 9, wonder what time we will actually get there. Bonnie and Ray are going too. Peggy is going to have a selling stall. Well at 9-20—Jim & Bev picked me up and away we went to the flea market at Midway Drive In. Jim bought me a hot dog. I had a ball. Sally & Cliff were there. Peggy had a stall, didn't do bad. I bought myself a vase—a picture for Yang & 3 blouses for Dee

Dee. At noon we went to Jims had a sandwich and coffee and went to South Center. Bev wanted material. I bought 2 skeins of rug yarn. Then went back to Jims. I took a nap, Bev cooked dinner, we had roast pork—spuds—gravy—coleslaw—apple sauce—corn and milk to drink. It is 20 after 7—Peggy, Susie & Nancy are coming over to visit and give me my loot from the flea market. Dee Dee called me this morning. Seems 2 B OK.

April 19, 1971

It is 15 to 9. Just got up, the sun is shining. It is 15 after 10—the mail has been here but not for me. I got nothing. I mailed a manuscript to Mc Fadden Editors. Wish I would get a few cents out of it. Am going 2 sew a while then go 2 the store and will stop at Yang's. It is 3 thirty. Margaret & Sally has been here to visit. Yang was here and went to the store for me. A beautiful day. It is 25-2-9—I am sleepy, they ruined TV tonight with a stupid basketball game. Guess I will just go to bed and dreamland. Adios old world

April 20, 1971

It is 25 after 7—We all have 2 B in the lobby at 9 and get new keys to the bldg. It is 20 after 10—we got our new keys, R they big. {she outlined the key, and they are big} Julia was here and brought me scraps for stuffing. Margaret was here to visit. The mail truck is at Manhattan Apts, should be here soon. I am mailing a package to Dee Dee. Elizabeth Richardson is quite ill. Neither rain or sun today, just a quiet blah. Patsy called me on the little green monster and said Holly is missing since 4 o'clock last night. Police have been notified. It is 2 o'clock—Patsy called and said they had picked Holly and Mary up in Bellingham. So they are in Juvenile Hall up there. It is 20-2-5—Sally was here, had coffee and cinnamon roll. Margaret came and Yang. Now I am alone watching TV and fixing supper. It is 20 after 7—Sissy-Marvin-Lorri and the twins were here. Still raining. It is 11 o'clock—Yang was over around 10, wanted D Dee's address, she also had coffee. I bid you adieu.

April 21, 1971

It is 15to 8—Just woke up. It is 1-15—The mail came, I received a letter from Charlie-my cookware from Fingerhut, also the free watch. I am going to give Yang. Hope she comes over pretty soon. Eva was in to visit. She knows that Byron is going around with a petition but she isn't worried. Little green monster hasn't yipped today. Well wonder if this day has anything interesting in hiding. It is 15-2-5—This ole building is in an uproar. Eva found out that Esther is taking up a petition to get her fired and things are humming. Yang just called from grocery store and invited me over to dinner. So in 15 minutes I shall go. It is 7 thirty—it seems, I am a rat because I answered Eva's questions truthfully. Well 2 HELL with these old biddies. I went down 2 C Julia, she still loves me. It is 8 o'clock—I went down to Frances apartment—Viola and Cora was there, I got things straightened out.

April 22, 1971

It is 10-2-8—Mrs. Doherty was in and asked me about the rumpus, she ran into it in the laundry room last night. We both decided to ignore it and go on as usual. It is 20 after 12—Thelma called, Marty is back in jail again involved in an armed robbery. It is raining. I C the mail truck at Manhattan Apts., wonder if it will get here before one. Wonder if I will get any. 20-2-4—I have been to sewing circle, everyone was polite enough except Margaret, she looks like an old sour puss. I feel exhausted, going to sit in the old rocking chair and rest. It is 9 o'clock—Yang was here and gave me some material and a little suit for JJ. Got tired and went to bed.

April 23, 1971

It is 15-2-10—Had my breakfast-peaches-toast and coffee. The sun is shining. Guess I will go to the store. It is 25-2-11—The mail truck is at the Manhattan Apts. I wonder if I will get any mail today, goodness knows I haven't sent out enough bait. My heart is pounding badly today. It is 15-2-12—No mail. Boo hoo, talked to Peggy on phone no news really. Talked to Patsy she is going through hell with Duke. Sound 2 me like he might be on drugs. Peggy just called and said it came over the news, that the 2 missing 6 year old boys had been found stabbed and strangled. The world is going 2 B a horrible place 2 B. It is 8 thirty—I went to the store, got a fried chicken TV dinner—1 potato—1 bunch green onions—1 qt milk—1 loaf raisin bread—1 cube butter—1 dozen eggs. Today I felt like I just can't face things here, but then I realize the biggest fear is fear itself. Guess time will take care of things. Will go to bed early. There is so much good in the worst of us, and so much bad in the best of us, that it does not become any of us to talk about the rest of us.

April 24, 1971

It is 5-2-10—Am having breakfast—applesauce—raisin bread and butter—coffee and my evitable 4 pills. Wonder what happens today? God give me the strength 2 C it thru. 25 after 10—The mail truck is at Manhattan apartments, will be next. I wonder if I got anything. I am going to take a hot bubble bath right now. The weather is blah. It is 20 after 11—I received a Thank You card from Vicki. Mrs. Doherty invited me in and gave me some nylon for stuffing. If Margaret looks would kill, I would be dead. Ho Ho Ho. It is 10-2-12—Viola was in for a few minutes, friendly enough. I am eating lunch—2 poached eggs—raisin bread and butter. Am listening to chatter box. Thousands of demonstrators all over U.S. against the Viet Nam War. It is 12-30—I made a macaroni salad, will bake a corn bread later. Little green monster hasn't even shivered today. It is 20 after 4—I had a month end smorgasbord for supper—macaroni salad—corn bread—kernel corn—polish sausage—and brownies with milk to drink. Am tying a quilt. There is deadly silence over the building. Everybody has crawled away to feel sorry for themselves. Boo Hoo

April 25, 1971

It is 10-2-9—Bev just called and said they would be here 15-2-10—to go to the flea market, 2 B ready. The sun is shining. Bev—Jim—Bonnie & Ray picked me up at 10 o'clock. We went to the flea market at Midway. I bought a typewriter for $3.00—3 pictures for Yang—and a little suit jacket 4 Donnie. I had a hamburger and lots of fun. Now I am going to type some letters. It is 5 o'clock I took a nap now I am fixing hot scones and a fried chicken TV dinner. Lorri called she said they got to go to the flea market and they all enjoyed it. I know one thing I have to have, a new ribbon on my typewriter. It is 9 o'clock—Yang was here. By phoning around we found out that Jack Sullivan is on the loose. Am tired, will go to bed soon.

April 26, 1971

It is 10 o'clock—The sun is shining. I had a cold scone with apricot jam and coffee for breakfast. Have talked to patsy on little green monster this morning. It is 10-2-10 at night, it has been a beautiful day. Peggy came at 10 this morning. We went 2 her house and got her mail then 2 Kent. I left my typewriter to get a new ribbon. We went up to C Sissy but she wasn't home, so we went 2 C Snooks. Then 2 Peggy's, she mowed her lawn till the kids came home, then we took Susie & her girlfriend to swim at Sumner. Then we went 2 Kent and got the typewriter then back 2 Peggy's and had supper. Back to get Susie then home. I went and got Yang, we both had letters from Dee Dee and also she called me tonight so we both talked 2 her.

April 27, 1971

It is 20 after 9—Weather looks blah. Am having coffee and doughnuts for breakfast. It is 11 o'clock—I have chatterbox on for the news. The mail truck is at Manhattan Apts., wonder if I get anything today. Talked to Sissy on green monster today. She had a big argument with Shirley Kessack. Also talked to Peggy. Weather is windy & cool. Guess Patsy & Harley are at Orthopedic Mental Clinic with Duke today. Just had a bowl of Clam Chowder. Believe it or not, Margaret spoke 2 me today. The panic button rang on F floor 3 wonder what is up now. It is 4 thirty—I had a long afternoon nap in my rocking chair, now for supper and an evening of TV. Yang did not come over today, maybe later. It is 7 o'clock—no visitors, no mail, no phone calls, boy I really am black balled. Looks gloomy like rain.

April 28, 1971

It is 10 0'clock—It is also my wedding anniversary. The wind is blowing, I have chatterbox on 2 C what is going on in the world. Am eating instant oatmeal & coffee. It is 25-2-11—The mail truck is at Manhattan apartments, soon to be here. Wish I would get some mail. It is 11-15—No mail & I just cannot understand it. I am always mailing out but nothing comes back. Guess I will sit and pout a while. The sun is trying to shine. It is 12 o'clock—I am done pouting, just had a homemade TV dinner now am going to enjoy a pot of spiced tea. The noon chimes are playing, they are always soothing to the nerves. It is trying to rain. Little green monster is very quiet. I looked into old records, it is 20-2-4—I would have been married 46 years today. I felt lonely today. Have the last picture taken of Dad. It is 25-2-5—Rebecca Doherty was in to visit, she gave me some quilt pieces. It is now 9 o'clock—Yang was here and went to the store for me. She is writing a story, so is Dee Dee so am I. Which one of us will meet with publication and success first. Who knows?

April 29, 1971

It is 15 after 8—The sun is shining. This is sewing day. It is 20 after 10—I am doing my laundry, the clothes are in the dryer. I seen Viola in the hall, she said be sure to come to sewing circle. I said OK. It is 12 thirty—Eva was in, she sure is shook up over this petition to get her fired. I don't blame her. Everyone seen her in here, I suppose I am in for it now. Well it is always darkest just before dawn and every cloud has a silver lining. I had deviled egg sandwich on raisin bread for lunch with a cup of tea. It is 15 after 3—Have been to sewing circle, had a good time, was made to feel welcome. Went to bed at 10.

April 30, 1971

It is 9 o'clock—Dee Dee just called, her and the kids are coming down by bus next weekend. I am having peaches & coffee for breakfast. The sun is trying to shine. 25-2-10—Little green monster just rang, Patsy is coming over, yippee. Patsy came, we drank a cup of coffee then went and had lunch with Sissy.

Then I went home with Patsy and stayed for supper-MMM baked potato—hamburger—salad—corn on the cob and milk. Brought me home a big bouquet of dogwood. Got a letter and some paper clippings on social security from Amelia. Nice day, sunshine. It 5 thirty I have a headache.

May 1, 1971

It is 20 after 11—I have had coffee, pills—2 fried eggs—2 slices of toast. The sun is shining. Yang is here. Am waiting for the mail to get my welfare check and food stamps. I am key keeper, Eva went to drive Stan's car from the hospital. It is 5 o'clock—My food stamps and check came. Yang & I went to the drug store and grocery store then home. I went to Frances apartment to get the recipe for oatmeal cake. We had steak—tossed green salad—baked potato and frozen raspberries for dinner. I baked the cake, Yang has gone to the store for a small can of milk to make the glaze. Yang is writing a story, I listen to it and we talked about it. I got a letter from P.G. It is 10-2-10—Yang and I had a swell day together, visiting, working etc. I will be going 2 bed P.D.Q.

May 2, 1971

It is 15 after 9—I am listening to chatter box, a discussion is on between a minster, a priest, a rabbi about helping criminals when they get out of prison. Geyman gets out tomorrow, wonder what he will be doing? Bev just called and invited me to go to the flea market with them. So I am ready. I have a irritating gland soreness in front of my right ear. The sun is shining. It is 10 after 7—I have been to the flea market. I bought a tea pot—two pictures frames—1 shirt & sweater for Stevie. We took Cindy home because she didn't feel good. We went 2 C Auntie & Uncle, gave her the shawl, then went to Dunc's and Shirley's. Gave her a quilt and pillowcases for her birthday. Then home, had a steak—2 fried eggs—salad—and 2 rolls—buttermilk. Talked to Peggy & Tom on little green monster, invited them over for evening tea. Was going to call Dee Dee but changed my mind. It is 20 after 9—Peggy—Nancy & Tom were here. They brought a pair of dress shoes for Donnie. Don't look to me like Tom is going 2 C or talk to Dee Dee. Well personally, I think she could do much better, like it was any of my business.

May 3, 1971

It is 20 after 9—The sun is shining. I have 2 chicken halves on to cook. Have put Dottie's birthday package in the mail and been down and had coffee with Viola. Now waiting for the mail and my social security check. It is 4—Have flittered away the day. Had chicken and cabbage rolls for dinner. My social security check came. I went and got Yang, her lights are turned off. She is spending the day with me. Eva came in and spent the afternoon with us. We called Dee Dee and got her going over Tom. She said Marvin called her. We had salad—cold chicken for supper. It is now 9 o'clock—Yang has gone home to her dark apartment, they turned her lights off today. I am sleepy and will go to bed early. Dee Dee and Ricky got to ride in an airplane with his scout troop today. She also said her ex—husband Marvin had called her and asked if he could see the kids. I asked her if Casey—Tom and Marvin all showed up one Friday night what would she do. She said Wow that would be an orgy, guess she would go with the parole officer.

May 4, 1971

It is 20-2-3 in the morning, I woke up and can't go back to sleep so decided to get up. I had coffee and a piece of oatmeal cake and sewed until 5. Went back to bed, fell asleep and slept until 9. Now I have had 2 fried eggs—2 pieces of toast—coffee & pills. Also talked to Bev & Bonnie on little green monster. It looks like rain. I put the package for Gwen & family out to be mailed, now guess I'll clean up my pad and either sew or write or both. It is 12-30—Peggy called and said she would take me shopping, so I went over and told Yang. She is in a sleeping mood. The mail came they took my package. I got some more paper clippings on social security from Thrasher. I talked to Sissy this morning. We discussed whether Vicki would see the Queen of England as they are both in Vancouver B.C. It is 10-2-4—Have been to Kent with Peggy, done some Safeway shopping. Came home had coffee, Peggy is very upset over Tom. I ate my boiled dinner, am making rhubarb pie. It is raining. It is 10-2-9—Jim Jr. called, he is home on leave. Good Tuesday night movie on, so another day.

May 5, 1971

It is 20-2-8—Just got up. More later alligator. It is 10-2-9—I ate rhubarb pie and coffee for breakfast. Patsy just called on little green monster, she is coming over. It is 7 after 11—Patsy—Holly and their neighbor Lee was here. They had tea, I told Lee's fortune. Patsy brought my dish soap I ordered from Annette and a big dish full of lilac's and blue bells, a container shaped like this.{ shows picture of rectangle shape} I have them on my TV between my daisy plant and bouquet of dogwood. I wonder where Yang is, and is she going 2 come over. Well back to sewing. The mail is late today. I just got my mail, lots of hanky panky advertisements, 15 cents change from the package I mailed to Gwen, and a Mother's Day card from Joe & Dottie with $5.00 bill in it. I put the $5.00 up in my phone envelope so I will have enough to pay my bill. I am now going to have lunch. It is 20 after 2—Dee Dee just called on little green monster. Her and the kids can't come this weekend because she has 2 work 2 shifts, 1 Sat—1 Sun. It's 10 after 9—Little green monster rang and it was Fred Norman, drunk as a skunk calling from Virginia. Well goodnight.

May 6, 1971

It is 5-2-9—Had 2 boiled eggs—raisin bread toast and coffee for breakfast. Now going into a hot bubble bath. Weather looks blah. It is now 11—Today is sewing circle day. Wonder how that will turn out. Just listened to morning news. Lotsa protest going on. Wonder if I will get any mail, seems 2 B a day of wonder. 12 Thirty—I received no mail, the sun is shining. I have had lunch, warmed up leftovers, will go to sewing circle at one. Oh, well what the hell. I went to sewing circle, stuffed one lion and Bev & Jim Jr. came and got me. We had coffee, Jim had tea I told his fortune, then I went back to sewing circle and had refreshments and stuck my neck out to serve next week. Yang came for supper, we are making sample napkins for a baby shower. Bev is going to give in June. It is 10-2-1—I have been to bed but can't get to sleep, so will stay up a while.

May 7, 1971

It is 25-2-10—Sun is shining. Woke up at 6 thirty. Yang came at 20-2-8. Dee Dee just called 2 C what bus Yang would come in on. She is taking Yang and the boys to the Rodeo this weekend, lucky people. It is 20-2-1—Yang is on her way. I received a beautiful tapestry from Dee Dee and boys for Mother's Day. It has a deer on it, I love it. 10 after 2—Bev & Bonnie were here, ordered 30 napkins for baby shower, 15 stork pattern-15 bootie & teddy bear pattern. They had spiced tea, our conversation was also spiced. It is 15-2-7—I had an afternoon nap in my rocking chair. I had chicken and noodles with sliced tomato for supper. Don't expect any company, but you never know. Little green monster sure is quiet. It is 15 after 10 and I believe today is done. Adios Amigos

May 8, 1971

It is 15 after 5—I woke up and that seems to be that. There is a pink sky this morning and the old saying is Red sky in the morning is sailors warning. So Ho Ho Ho away we go. It is 20 after 9—I have spent the morning writing and typing. Holly just called and said they would be over about 12. Gloomy weather. Barbara called this morning and invited me to go on a picnic with them tomorrow, I sure go for that. Patsy—Holly—Eve and Holt came 2 C me and brought me a nice set of china dishes. I got a nice card in the mail from Gwen & Fred with money order 4—$5.00. I am writing on my life story, really getting into it now, I just got started. It is 3 o'clock—Bev called and said she is getting me a dictionary for Mother's Day, but won't get it until next week when she goes to the commissary. Peggy will be here sometime today. It is 6 thirty—Peggy—Nancy—Susie and Tom were here. I got a nice real china place setting some flowers a string of pearls. I gave Tom some typing to do for me. Keeps him busy. Barbara called, said be ready at seven tomorrow, we are going to Sequim. It is 8-15—Eva was in, we had a lively visit. Going to bed early.

May 9, 1971

It is 7 o'clock—The sun is shining, am having coffee—pills—1 slice raisin bread with deviled egg on. Listening to news on chatterbox. Am going on picnic with Buzz & Barbara to Sequim, they will be here within an hour. It is 8 o'clock—I just got home from a wonderful day, we went to the Olympic Peninsula over a draw bridge in Tacoma, over the Hood Canal floating bridge. We spent the day at Johnston's new home at Dungeness Meadows at Sequim WA. Had a wonderful time, a delicious picnic dinner and a nice ride to and from. I am a bit tired but happy. Will watch TV a while and then retire. We saw a terrible wreck on the way home.

May 10, 1971

It is 20 after 8—The sun is shining. I am signing and putting my $5.00 money order in an envelope for the mail carrier to cash. Hope it works, no after thinking it over I won't, if the drug store won't cash it I will just wait until I can get to a post office. It is 10-2-10—little green monster rang, it was Bev. She will be by soon with my Mother's Day gift from Sissy and will take me to the post office to cash my money order. Maybe I can get some material at Pacific Iron and I would like to stop at Value Village. It is 10 after 4—I had a good time with Bev today, we went to White Center, had lunch with Patsy, went to a nursery and bought plants. I have a tomato plant in my bedroom. Went to Pacific Iron and got some outing flannel to finish the baby quilts with. Stopped at Value Village, got 2 bags of scraps. Came home, went to grocery store, got a few things. Went to drug store got napkins and stamps, now relaxing. Got 3 letters to write and have supper, watch TV and as I said relax. It is 10-2-9—Shirley & Dunc were here, brought me a Spider Mum plant—yellow. DD called and reminded me they would be here tomorrow.

May 11, 1971

It is 15-2-7—Yang comes home today and Dee Dee and the kids are coming with her to visit a day or so. That should liven things up. It is 20-2-10—I have been down and had coffee with Viola. It is 11 thirty, I have vacuumed the apartment, got a postcard from Yang, guess I'll go get some chicken and tater chips before the kids get here. It is 7 thirty—Dee Dee—Yang and the boys have been here for supper. I gave them weenies—pizza—hot buns—hot dogs—potato chips—pickles—pink lemonade—coffee. I sure as hell don't like Dee Dee's Ho Ho attitude. Jim & Bev were here, brought me two boxes of groceries, a new late copy of Webster's dictionary and $5.00 bill. How lucky can you get. Guess they are going to sleep at Yang's apartment. Stevie stayed overnight with me. 84 degree's today.

May 12, 1971

It is 8 thirty. Stevie is watching TV, girls haven't been over yet, probably are not up. It is 20 to 3—Gave Yang—DD and the boys fried chicken—mashed potatoes—carrots—mexi-corn—B&M baked beans—raspberry jello with pineapple in for noon day meal. We visited all morning now they have gone to Yang's to swim in pool and I am resting. Looks like rain. Dee Dee discovered a large lump on her left breast. The girls and kids came over for supper, we had oven cooked hamburgers—potato chips—cantaloupe. They all went downstairs and played pool. Snooks—Sissy and Patsy are all planning on coming over tomorrow. Stevie stayed overnight.

May 13, 1971

It is 20-2-9—Had toast and coffee. Stevie had a bad fever so I gave him an aspirin and cranberry juice. He is drawing at the table now, but still looks feverish. I just baked a chocolate cake. The wind is blowing, the sun is playing hide and go seek. First, it shines and then it don't. I told Eva I would not be able to help serve at sewing circle today, on account so much company. 15 minutes 2-9—Snooks and Tinky were here for lunch—Sissy could not come because Billy was sick. Patsy could not come because Holt was sick. Thelma and Pam were here. Thelma is going to take Dee Dee and the kid's home tomorrow. Raining today. Dee Dee has called everywhere trying to find Marvin, she finally tracked him down. I am very very tired tonight, my feet and ankles are swollen. Well that is that I guess. It is 25-2-11—Guess what? Dee Dee & Marvin got together. BAM

May 14, 1971

It is 6 thirty—I am having coffee—gingerbread and pills. What ho dear day have you in store? The sun is shining. It is 10-2-10 at night. Little Marvin almost drown in the pool at El Toro Apts. this morning. His Dad dove in and saved his life. Thelma came at one, we took Kathy and the boys to Monroe and home. Marvin went to drinking whiskey all way, he was getting mean when we left. I really don't know what will happen now. Yang is here, we are having hot scallops and cold tomato juice. Thrasher called tonight.

May 15, 1971

Got up at 3-30—covered my footstool with green upholstery cloth, done some dishes, crocheted on afghan, had breakfast, took a hot bubble bath. It is raining. Wonder how Dee Dee and the kids made out with Marvin. In fact, I wonder if she is still in one piece. Feel mostly sorry for little Stevie. Am mailing my manuscript off to Helicopter Wedding today, wonder how long it will take it to bounce. Yang is spending the day with me. Little green monster only rang once. It was Amelia Thrasher, calling over the welfare letters we got. Rained all day.

May 16, 1971

It is 9 thirty—The wind is blowing, I sure slept good last night. Wonder what will happen today. It is 25 after 11 and raining and I do mean raining. Little green monster is very very quiet. I am sewing and thinking. It is 5 thirty. Sissy and Marvin were here. Bev-Jim & Jim Jr. were here. Yang has not been over. I called Elvina Downs on little green monster, she told me the 4 little Geyman boys were all in Sunday school this morning and they said their Dad was home and all seemed happy. Tommy is going to work for Donnie. Oh yes I get a Noah's Ark through Bev from her neighbor. Nothing more right now. It is 5 after 10—Yang came over and spent the evening. We spent a spell at Viola's, had honey cake and coffee. Pleasant day—Pleasant evening—Adios

May 17, 1971

It is 10-2-9—The sun is shining. It is now 10 thirty at night. I spent the day at Peggy's typing on my book manuscript. Have another order for napkins, went to C Yang at 9 thirty but she wasn't there. Am very tired, think I will just go to bed. Adieu

May 18, 1971

It is 4 thirty I am awake and that is that. 20 after 6—Yang has spent the day with me. She made up an order of napkins and made a storybook of Noah and his Ark. I have been making Snoopy Dogs. Sally called today and is not mad at me, just had a lot of trouble. Cliff came up and got the sewing machine, so Sally could sew. I have to go to clinic tomorrow.

May 6,2011

So this is the end of Novella's Journals. It's funny it should end in the month of May. I have really enjoyed going back into the past. Reading about all our love one's, and all the places that are now gone. Grandma liked mixing it up with her spelling, so the spelling may not be correct. I tried leaving everything the way she wrote it. This is her gift to her children and grandchildren. Robin